Hempology 101

The History and Uses of Cannabis Sativa

4th Edition

Jamie
Smoke 'em if
you got 'em!
Ted

Written by
Ted Smith

Published by
The International
Hempoloy 101 Society

Published by The International Hempology 101 Society
Victoria, British Columbia
www.hempology.ca

Cover Design, Book Design, and Illustrations by Sarita Mielke -
WILD/FREE creative
www.saritamielke.com

Cover Photo by Shayd Johnson - Elephant Room Creative
www.elephantroomcreative.com

Proudly printed and bound in Canada by Friesens
Printed on FSC certified paper with soy-based inks.

All efforts have been made to locate copyright holders of source material wherever possible. Corrections welcome.

ISBN 978-0-9880778-0-5

Library and Archives Canada Cataloguing in Publication

Smith, Ted, 1969-
Hempology 101 : the history and uses of Cannabis sativa / Ted Smith. -- 4th ed.

Includes bibliographical references.
ISBN 978-0-9880778-0-5

1. Cannabis--History. 2. Cannabis--Social aspects.
I. Title.

HV5822.C3S65 2012 362.29'509 C2012-903459-2

MIX
Paper from responsible sources
FSC® C016245

For mom, who taught me to learn, laugh and love

Table of Contents

Introduction

It is hard enough to accomplish anything in this world—let alone in an illegal industry—surrounded by a lot of scattered, distracted, and stoned people (myself included) with little money, but somehow I have come this far.

Cannabis is the most important plant on earth. Cannabis is the Tree of Life. Cannabis has been critical in our development and, though it has been suppressed for a time, it will be critical in our evolution for a very long time.

I would like to thank those who helped or inspired my book and life, though I am sure to forget or omit so many friends who have assisted me, that I will probably regret having tried to make a list in the first place. I would like to thank my beloved parents, Corinne and Warren (1949-2007); grandma Georgina; sisters Susan and (in-law) Sonja; brothers Ken (Buck), Randy and (in-law) Bibber; nieces Kirsten, Hailey, Sara and Faith; nephews Brendan, Ryan and Grant; the rest of my family; my love Gayle Quin; Gavin (1970-94); Louisa; Walbran Steve; Annette; Minneh and Ryan Bushby; Laura and Zoe Casey; Chris Bennett; Sarah and Paul from Sacred Herb; Padra; Daak; Kathleen Cherrington; Jose Janechek; Markham Breitbach; Henry Boston; Logan; Cory; Scott Johnstone; Bob Moore-Stewart; Professors Bob Litke and Leo Groake; all past and present Board members, buyers' club staff and helpers; and last, but not least, Ozzy Ozbourne. Chris Cant deserves special mention for his help re-writing the first chapter. Finally, the team of Whelm King, Andrew Brown, Ryan Fink and Sarita Mielke deserve a great deal of credit for helping me give birth to this epic 17 year long project. These people have inspired and helped me beyond measurement.

Some might criticize me for putting so many quotes in this book. Rather than footnote, I decided to include the words of other activists and thinkers who have made valuable contributions to the cannabis movement. This should both provide a better context for what I write about the herb and help lead readers towards other books that I feel make an important contribution to our understanding of cannabis and its impacts.

I hope that my little book gives you as much pleasure reading as it has me writing. Though nothing is written in stone, I hope that some of my suggestions prove to be truths in your lives, as they are in mine. Peace.

Ted Smith

The International Hempology 101 Society educates the public about the agricultural benefits of growing hemp; the industrial uses of hemp seed, fibre, and hurds; the medical effects of smoking, eating, or topically applying cannabis; the historical uses of cannabis and its influence on religion, economics, and politics; and the negative impacts of prohibition, while experimenting in participatory education in constant, passive, civil disobedience.

Chapter 1 Hemp's Beginnings

Homo sapiens and their direct genetic forebears have roamed the Earth for millennia. Before settling to form the first civilizations, proto-humans were organized into loose tribal groups of nomadic hunter-gatherers. Under these difficult conditions, survival instincts dominated thought processes. There was no development of complex ideas such as a unique sense of self, no concept of linear time, or of associative reasoning. It was from this state, known as the "eternal now," that modern humans began to evolve several million years ago.

As these early hunter-gatherers explored their world in search of new sources of food, warmth, and shelter, they eventually encountered entheogenic plants and fungi. All over the world humans discovered numerous plants that, when consumed, would induce an altered state of consciousness. This altered state of consciousness brought on by the consumption of entheogens has come to be remembered in many cultures as mythical revelation. The Western tradition describes this advent of revelation in the Genesis creation stories as the result of eating from the Tree of Knowledge of Good and Evil.

Knowledge of revelation spread as the first beings to experience it shared their discovery and experiences with the rest of their tribal group. Soon this knowledge permeated an entire culture and played a significant role in human evolutionary development and the foundation of the civilized arts—creative expression, tool use, clothing, and complex language. Religion also developed after revelation. The earliest cults were devoted to worshipping nature gods and goddesses—often with an entheogenic substance at the centre of ritual practice. Under the guidance of tribal shamans, these entheogens functioned as a bridge between the physical and metaphysical worlds, allowing whole tribal groups to commune directly with the gods and goddesses that inhabited their ecosystem.

Well after these first encounters with entheogens, and the awakening of consciousness, another avenue was provided through which the insights of entheogenic plants could be accessed—fire. Fire was brought under human control between 1,000,000 and 500,000 years ago, with the element itself being seen by many cultures as a source of enlightenment, though its practical properties of transmutation are particularly valuable. Fire allowed for the preparation of cooked food, a constant source of heat, the advent of metallurgy, and a controlled method of burning herbs and incense for inhalation. The use of fire was essential to cause some of the chemical reactions necessary to derive a benefit from certain plants, and it was not until this discovery that those secrets would have been available to man. The main psychoactive compound in *Cannabis sativa*, delta-9-tetrahydrocannabinol (THC), requires heat to activate; so, it is not until the discovery of fire that mankind began to utilize cannabis in this fashion. However, due to the extensive use of *Cannabis sativa* as a foraging bush and one of the first agricultural crops, it is certain that the flowering tops of the female plant would have been among the first substances burned for the purposes of intoxication. The psychoactive properties of the plant were most likely discovered by accident after hemp foliage was used for a communal fire.

Hemp seed plant close to maturity

Archaeologists working in sites from China to Western Europe have discovered evidence of prehistoric cannabis being used for agricultural, medicinal, and religious purposes. This evidence, some items dated before 3000 BCE, appears in the form of hemp clothing, hemp fibre used in pottery and construction, stashes of hemp seed used for food, remains of cannabis resin on smoking implements, and even large supplies of dried cannabis flowers. From before the dawn of civilization, human beings have had an intimate relationship with *Cannabis sativa*—the hemp plant.

Cannabis and the Foundation of Civilization

As early hunter-gatherers began to unlock the secrets of civilization, they also began forming symbiotic relationships with the plants that provided the fundamental resources necessary for survival. Primary among these symbiotic plants is *Cannabis sativa*, whose relationship with humankind is hundreds of thousands of years old. The seeds of the hemp plant are especially suited to the human diet, being able to provide the protein, amino acids, and essential fatty acids required to sustain human life. This suggests that hemp was utilized as a primary foraging bush by the varieties of the genus homo who recognized the nutritional value of the plant, and contributed in the millennia-long process of human evolution though a deep natural symbiosis. The cannabis plant is also a likely candidate for humanity's first domestic crop, due to its extreme hardiness and the ease with which it grows. It requires little cultivation aside from sowing of seed.

Dr. Carl Sagan

Dr. Carl Sagan speculates in his book exploring the origins of the human species, *The Dragons of Eden*, that hemp has been cultivated by humans for more than 10,000 years. Sagan cites the example of the Bushmen from the Kalahari region of Southwest Africa—a tribe that claims to have grown and used cannabis since their mythic beginning of time. The Bushmen traditionally utilized the entire cannabis plant. The stalk fibres are used for a variety of functional items from clothing to weapons; the seeds are eaten for food; the roots for their medicinal properties; and the flowering tops for food, medicine, and spiritual enlightenment.

Indigenous to Central and South-central Asia, in the valley regions surrounding the Himalayan Mountains, hemp spread quickly across Asia for several reasons. First, cannabis is an extremely hardy plant that will thrive in almost every environment, and spreads rapidly in nature. Second, interaction with proto-humans aided the dispersion of hemp as tribes in those areas where cannabis was prevalent thrived, expanded, and migrated. Many prehistoric varieties of the genus homo were nomadic, and ranged constantly over a large territory searching for sources of food. Cannabis seed would have been one of the best grains to stockpile for the long winters of the ice ages, as it can be easily dried, consumed raw, and has a short growing season.

As these tribes began to move into new territory, they carried the seeds from their local plants in order to ensure the success of their new communities. Seeds of particular importance belonged to those plants that held an integral role in the agricultural, mythic, and religious traditions of the group. Primary among these was the cannabis plant. The process of human migration helped to spread hemp across the globe from Central Asia to Africa, Europe, and North America.

Wherever the migrations began to settle, the resulting civilizations relied heavily on hemp, along with several other cultivable plants. The incredible nutritional value of the hemp seed provided a stable food supply from which these new settlements could thrive. Hemp has been used for millennia by humans for everything from clothing to building materials, and is still recognized as one of the strongest and most durable natural industrial fibres. Even until the 19th century and the end of the Age of Sail, the great Navies of Europe relied on vast quantities of hemp fibre for sailcloth and rope. Cannabis was particularly prized for its medicinal and psychoactive properties, helping to ensure the continued health and spiritual wellness of the community. Finally, cannabis was a great teacher for early human agriculturalists. Due to its dioecious nature and its status as an early cultivar, *Cannabis sativa* helped teach the basics of farming and breeding that would lead to more advanced farming techniques and specialized varieties of both plants and animals. With so many valuable qualities it is no wonder that so many religions and philosophies, even in modern times, have recognized cannabis as the "Tree of Life."

Cannabis sativa has a complex regionalized history due to geographic, environmental, evolutionary, and cultural factors. In many ways, the evolution of cannabis is very similar to that of mankind. Cannabis is indigenous to Central and South Central Asia, ranging as far north as Siberia and south to India. Over such a vast territory, broken up by the physical barrier of the Himalayan Mountains, varieties of cannabis began to develop independently from one another, as did the cultural traditions that surrounded the plant, until human migration and trade brought them together once again. For millions of years, both proto-humans and hemp struggled with the advancing and retreating ice ages—sometimes so severe that they isolated pockets of flora and fauna for generations before relenting and allowing life to spread and mix again. The ancient Chinese, for example, used industrial hemp for thousands of years before the psychoactive properties were utilized. While in ancient India, on the other hand, cannabis was initially used as an intoxicant. China was introduced to the intoxicating properties of cannabis rather late, around 1800 BCE, through human migration. At the end of the Stone Age, around 12,000 BCE, there were four semi-independent regions surrounding the cradles of civilization where cannabis thrived and formed integral parts of the cultures that developed there—the Hindu Kush region of India and Pakistan, down the Indus River valley; north on the Iranian plateau, across the Russian Steppes from the Black Sea to Siberia and finally into Mongolia; east along the Ganga River, through Nepal and in to China; and west through Mesopotamia, Arabia and Ethiopia to sub-Saharan Africa.

The Indus River Valley: The Cradle of Cannabis

The earliest recorded cultural references to cannabis are found among the civilizations that developed along the Indus and Ganges Rivers, along with their tributaries, flowing from the Hindu Kush and Himalaya Mountain ranges. Mohenjo-Daro, Harappa, and Dholavira—cities which flourished in these regions more than five thousand years ago—were the products of a sophisticated agricultural civilization. Over time, the Indus civilization spread for thousands of miles across South Central Asia carrying with it the seeds and traditions of cannabis worship. The civic centres of the Indus civilization were well planned on a grid system, and highly advanced for their age with supplied well water, basic sanitation, and complex grain distribution systems. The legends of this civilization would become the basis for the Vedic texts of Hinduism and Buddhism, and the Avesta of Persian Zoroastrianism, as well as sharing many traits with ancient Mesopotamian, Iranian, and Indian traditions. Trade routes that carried cannabis incense spanned the Ancient World from the Indus River to the Mediterranean by 2200 BCE.

> The incense our ancient ancestors—the framers of civilization—used to communicate with the gods came from the Hindu Kush region of the Himalayan Mountains. It was gathered from the *Cannabis sativa* plants growing wild in the Pakistan, Afghanistan and Kashmir mountain valleys of the Indus River Waterway. The incense was carried down the Indus on barges and sold to the merchant fleets heading through the Persian Gulf to Mesopotamia or travelling south west along the south Arabian coast and up the Red Sea to Egypt. It was also ferried to the south eastern Arabian coast, from there carried in caravans to Egypt and Phoenicia.
>
> (*Green Gold*, p.20)

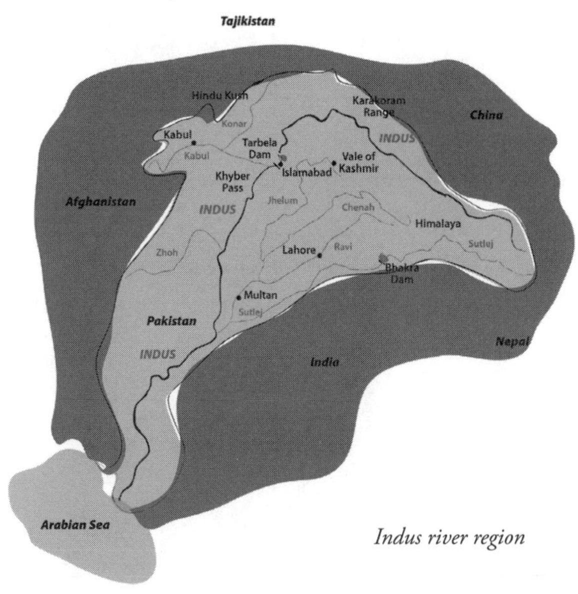

Indus river region

This incense of the Ancient World is what we know in modern times as "Hashish."

Iran and Central Asia

On the Iranian Plateau, to the north-west of the Indus River valley—an area that covers much of modern day Iran, Afghanistan, and Pakistan—another series of cannabis worshipping civilizations developed. An offshoot of the Indo-Iranian peoples who created the Indus River civilizations, the proto-Iranians preserved many of the linguistic and religious traditions of their forebears—including cannabis worship. While the civilizations of the Indus and Mesopotamia were developing advanced settlements, around 6,000 BCE, the proto-Iranians were developing a complex tribal society as a nomadic equestrian culture. These tribal groups would eventually spread across all of Central Asia, roaming the steppes from the Gobi region of China to the Black Sea region of modern day Ukraine. These early Iranian cultures introduced horseback riding to the Mesopotamians during their invasions and conflicts, and are also credited with the construction of the first chariots. These migrations also introduced psychoactive cannabis to China. Hemp had been used for millennia in China as a food and fibre product, but not a medicine until c 2800 BCE when the Gushi nomads brought their cannabis worship through the Gobi desert to Xinjian.

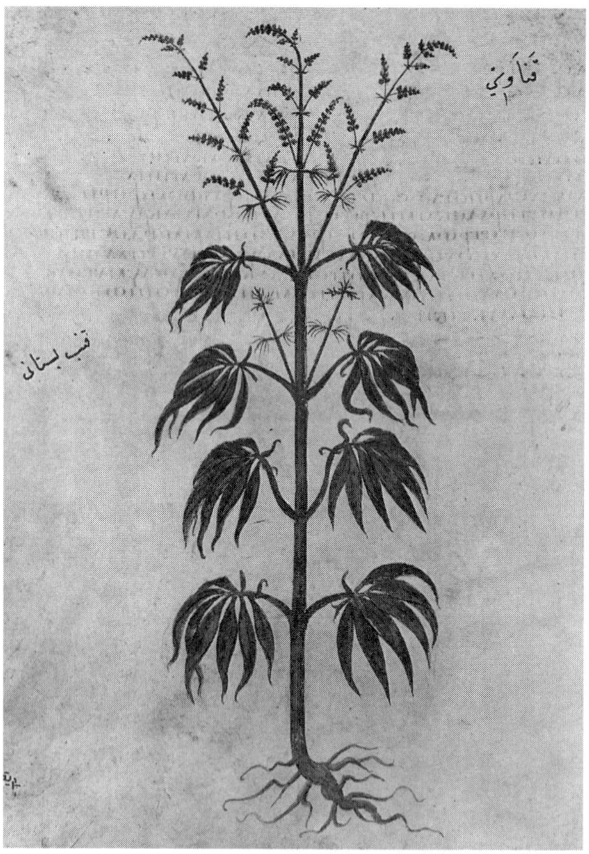

Oldest known drawing of cannabis

The peoples of the steppes were a largely heterogeneous group—made up of more or less nomadic tribes—linked through language, trade, tradition, and family ties. For much of the period between 2000 and 1160 BCE, the Hittites were the dominant culture in the region. They developed one of the first organized monarchies, until their Empire dissolved into minor tribal fiefdoms. By the Eighth century BCE, these tribes had once again been unified, this time under the rule of the Royal Scythes. The entire culture would come to be known as the Scythians, after their rulers, and cannabis played a fundamental part of their daily lives. The Scythians are so influential to the history of hemp that the scientific name for the cannabis plant is taken from the Scythian language.

Herodotus, the Classical Greek historian, famously describes the use of cannabis by the Scythians during a funerary ritual in an account dated 450 BCE.

> [...] After a burial, those involved would have to purify themselves, which they do in this way. First they soap and wash their heads, then to cleanse their bodies they make a little tent, fixing three sticks in the ground, tied tightly together and tightly covered with felt. Inside a dish is placed, with red-hot stones and some hemp seeds.
>
> There is in that country kannabis growing, both wild and cultivated. Fuller and taller than flax, the Thracians use it to make garments very like linen. Unless one was a Master of Hemp, one could not tell which it was- those who have never seen hemp would think it was linen.
>
> The Scythians take kannabis seed, creep in under the felts, and throw it on the red-hot stones. It smolders and sends forth such billows of smoke that no Greek steambath could surpass it. The Scythians howl with pleasure at these baths, which serve them instead of bathing, for they never wash their bodies with water.
>
> (*Green Gold*, p.73)

Herodotus's account of these "hot box" tents was verified in the early 20th century by Russian archaeologists working near Pazyryk, Altai. At each gravesite in the area, researchers uncovered a collection of bronze cauldrons, each with the charred remains of cannabis seeds in the bottom. In addition, smaller vessels for producing cannabis smoke were found, which led archaeologists to conclude that the Scythians used cannabis on a regular, if not daily, basis throughout their entire culture. The Scythians would thrive until 400 BCE in Central Asia, ruling an empire that stretched into India,competing at times with the Romans. These Scythian traditions would, in the following centuries, come to influence much of the interest in cannabis and the deeper mysteries throughout Europe and Anatolia.

Cannabis in the Vedic Tradition

The Vedic Texts, the Sanskrit hymns that are the basis for the Hindu religion, contain the first recorded references to cannabis. Considering that the linguistic origins are nearly 4500 years older than the written text, the continuity of sacred cannabis use is long indeed. Not only is hemp referenced in the Vedas, it is afforded a prominent role.

Cannabis holds an eminent place in the holy Vedas. Bhang (the name for both the hemp plant and cannabis beverage) is the liberator from sin by which one communes with the great Shiva, the facet of the divine trinity embodying spiritual enlightenment. Oaths are sworn upon the bhang leaf. J.M. Campbell reported in an Appendix to the "Indian Hemp Drugs Commission Report of 1893-94," that violation of such an oath is considered more severe than perjuring an oath sworn upon the holy Vedas; the punishment for "one who forswears himself the bhang oath is death."

The early Vedic tale "The Churning of the Ocean" shows particular reverence to hemp, referring to the plant as "ambrosia," "the dew of life," and "the nectar of immortality." In the story, it is hemp that ultimately allowed the Gods to overcome their demonic adversaries, and the name Vijaya (victory) was bestowed upon the cannabis plant in thanks. Tradition dictates that the first bhang plants sprang from the Earth wherever the drops of holy nectar, called amrita, fell from the heavens.

The Hindu god Shiva also has a close relationship with cannabis, as all intoxicating substances were dedicated to him—and tradition holds that bhang was his favourite. In addition to the "Churning of the Ocean" story, several other tales relate Shiva with hemp. Shiva earns his title "the Lord of Bhang" after a hemp plant shelters him from the sun, and a concoction made from its leaves refreshes the god so much that it becomes his favourite food. Shiva is also credited with creating the sacred Ganga River, which tradition says the god carried down from the Himalayas in his hair. The goddess Ganga and the herb which shares its name also share similar qualities, most notably the ability to cleanse sin.

> "Taken in the early morning, such bhang cleanses users from sin, frees him from the punishments of the chores of sin[...]"
> (*Green Gold*, p.34)

Hindu god Shiva

A traditional Sadhu

The Sadhus, a particular branch of Hindu ascetics characterized by their filthy appearance, dust their near naked bodies with ash from the sacred charas, smoked constantly in ritual chillums in praise to Shiva. Sadhus celebrate the birth of the hemp plant with a famous festival known as Kumbha Mela. Four holy sites are visited on a 12 year cycle, with a festival occurring every three years. These holy sites are traditionally regarded as the places where amrita fell from the mythical vessel, or kumbha (hence the name of the festival), and therefore the location of the first cannabis plants. Sadhus and worshippers gather to smoke chillums and praise cannabis with the mantras "Alakh," "Bam Bam Bholanath," and "Bum Shiva!" The largest celebrations of Kumbha Mela attract thousands of holy Sadhus, and tens of millions of other worshippers.

Many Indian festivals, such as Holi, Diwali, and Sripanchami traditionally include bhang preparations, and several other religious sects in India also use cannabis in their rituals. Some examples include the semi-Tantric sects the Nathas, Siddhas and Rasavadas. An Indian wedding devoid of bhang is considered a great insult.

> [...]supplies sent by the family of the bride to the bridegroom's party during their seven day sojourn include a supply of bhang. The name of the father who neglects to send bhang is held in contempt. Again, after the wedding, when the bridegroom and his friends are entertained at the house of the bride, richly spiced bhang is drunk by the guests.... Among the pardeshi or North Indian Hindus of Bombay bhang is not only given at weddings, but the pardeshi who fails to give his visitor bhang is despised by his caste as mean and miserly.
>
> ("Indian Hemp Drugs Commission Report of 1893-94")

The bhang culture of India has endured thousands of years, and the potion itself is still made in the traditional fashion. Cannabis is so ingrained in Indian culture, in fact, that it has traditionally provided the standards against which medical cannabis around the world is measured.

> The resin and resin-bearing parts of hemp are prepared for use in a variety of ways. Three grades of the drug are prepared in India and serve as a kind of standard against which preparations produced in other parts of the world are compared for potency; they are bhang, ganga, and charas. The least potent and cheapest preparation, bhang, is derived from hemp grown in the plains areas. Because bhang can be prepared in a variety of ways, it is exceedingly difficult to determine if a preferred or more common method of producing this poor man's "friend" actually does exist. The intoxicant may consist simply of hemp leaves picked from dooryard plants, dried, and then crushed into a coarse powder. Frequently, however, the leaves are mixed with male and/or female inflorescences and with seeds and small stems. The resulting drug is of inferior quality and may be smoked or made into a decoction. Occasionally bhang is chewed by beggars or fakirs who consider it the giver of long life and a means of communion with the divine spirit. To the wealthier Hindu, bhang is a crude substitute for ganga, somewhat akin to the difference between beer and fine scotch. In the words of W.B. O'Shaughnessy, writing of the medical uses of bhang in India in 1839: "Bhang is cheaper than gunjah and though less powerful, is sold at such a low price, that for one pice enough can be purchased to intoxicate an experienced person." Bhang's special importance to us is that it is, under the name marijuana, the most commonly used hemp product in the United States.
>
> Ganga, the second strongest hemp intoxicant, is prepared from the flowering tops of cultivated female plants. The dried pistillate tops with their exuded resin are generally smoked, sometimes mixed with tobacco leaves. Occasionally the preparation is eaten or made into a drink. Ganja, variously es-

timated as being two or three times as strong as bhang, is consequently more desirable and costlier...

Pure resin of the pistillate flowers is called in India charras or charas. Examined urder the microscope, charas appears as masses of pluricellular hairs stuck together in yellowish clumps, mixed with scraps of inflorescences and leaves. Charas is the most potent hemp intoxicant. While the female hemp tops contain 8 to 12 percent resin, unadulterated charas contains approximately 40%...

Unlike bhang, charas can be obtained only from plants growing at high altitudes. The superior-grade resin is gathered by various exotic methods from uncut plants; the slightly weaker grade is taken from the tops of harvested plants. From the moment that the small unripened flowers begin to exude the resinous drops until the time when the fully mature flowers yield the main crop, harvesters are busy with a variety of methods of collecting charas from the growing plants. Dressed in leather garments, or sometimes naked, labourers run through the hemp fields, brushing against the resin covered plants. The sticky resin clings to the clothes, or, less hygienically, to the sweating bodies, and is later scraped off with a blunted curved knife made especially for this purpose. Occasionally the plant is simply pressed between the palms of the hands, after which the exuded greenish-yellow secretion is removed. In some areas, harvesters pass a leather thong over the resinous parts of the plant and later rub the thong over the edge of a receptacle.

(*Marijuana Reconsidered*)

The survival of this unique bhang culture, uninterrupted to contemporary times, is testament to the human necessity for cannabis as a staple medical, dietary, social, and spiritual product.

China: The Land of Mulberry and Hemp

The Chinese were one of the first civilizations to utilize hemp for purely industrial purposes. Pottery remains from the island of Taiwan, dating c. 10,000 BCE, were found to have strands of hemp fibre pressed into the clay as reinforcement. Along with these pots were tools that resembled the long rods the ancient Chinese would use to decord (separate the fibre from the hurds) hemp. Ancient China was also the largest cultivator of industrial hemp in the Ancient world.

[...]from the time of the earliest primitive societies (about 4000-5000 years ago) to the Qin and Hah dynasties (221 BCE to 220 CE) ancient Chinese techniques of hemp sowing, cultivation and processing developed rapidly and became fairly advanced.

The earliest Neolithic farming communities along the Wei and Yellow rivers cultivated hempalong with millet, wheat, beans and rice. The oldest Chinese agricultural treatise is the Xia Xiao Zhen written circa the 16th century BCE that names hemp as one off the main crops grown in ancient China. The ancient Chinese used the hemp plant for many different purposes. The bast fiber of the male plant was used to spin yarn and weave cloth. From the time of the earliest Chinese societies, until cotton was introduced into China during the Northern Song dynasty (960-1127 CE), hemp textile was the main cloth worn by the ancient Chinese. Many of the accounts of hemp for use in cordage and textiles contained in the ancient Chinese texts have been corroborated by archaeological discoveries.

("The Cultivation and Uses of Hemp in Ancient China")

Curiously, cannabis as a psychoactive substance is not recorded in China until approximately 2800 BCE after being introduced by central Asian nomads. More recent discoveries in the Gobi region of China unearthed evidence of cannabis flowers being used as sacrament by a non-indigenous tribe,the Gushi. Researchers uncovered a stash of dried cannabis, weighing several pounds, in the burial chamber of a Gushi shaman. After this cultural interaction, hemp appears more and more often as a medicine in Chinese tradition until it plays a vital cultural role.

Shen Nung

The mainland Chinese believe that Shen Nung, the father of Chinese medicine, developed the science of healing with plants, and taught his people how to cultivate hemp and other grains, around 2800 BCE. Thanks to the influence of Shen Nung, cannabis would come to play an important role in ancient Chinese healing ceremonies. The healer would either wrap a dead snake around a hemp stalk, or carve an image of a snake into the stalk, to be used in a ritual cleansing. The snake-imbued stalk was used to banish evil spirits from the beds of the sick by beating the ground around the bed. The modern medical symbol of two snakes entwined around a staff finds its roots with these medicine sticks.

Particular aspects of ancient Chinese philosophy were also influenced by cannabis. One of the disciples of the great Taoist master Lao Tsu was also a student of cannabis-aided meditation. *The Secret of the Golden Flower*, recorded during the Han dynasty by Lu-tsu, originated with Master Yin-hsi of the Pss, the monastic companion of Lao Tsu and for whom the *Tao Te Ching* was written. *The Secret of the Golden Flower* helped establish the secretive Taoist cult the Religion of the Golden Elixir of Life, and was written under the influence of THC intoxication: "If there is time in the morning, one may sit during the burning of an incense stick, that is the best. In the afternoon, human affairs interfere and one can therefore easily fall into indolence. It is not necessary, however, to have an incense stick. But one must lay aside all entanglements and sit quite still for a time." Cannabis would be used by Taoists for various meditative purposes in China throughout the following centuries.

Hemp was so important to the ancient Chinese that it held a central role in their burial rituals. The dead were dressed in fine hemp clothing which hashish incense was burned in clay bowls. Some Chinese communities still continue this practice. It is no surprise that China remains one of the world's largest suppliers of hemp to this day.

Cannabis in Africa

Though *Cannabis sativa* is not indigenous to Africa, it arrived there tens of thousands of years ago, and thrived in the sub-Saharan regions of the continent where conditions are perfect for growing cannabis. The Ethiopians are particularly well known for their use of cannabis. In ancient times, it was peoples from the Ethiopian region who first established the Dynasties along the Nile. The Pharaonic dynasties of Egypt that resulted provided one of the largest markets for cannabis in the ancient world. Hashish incense was imported from the Nubian Desert region of the Upper Kingdom and Ethiopia, in addition to being purchased from Asiatic and Mesopotamian caravans. Cannabis worship made its way into Egypt as the territory was conquered from the south. Ancient Egyptian tradition held that a plant from the south was known as the "celestial food" and the "essence of being"— almost certainly a description of cannabis. The new "Rulers of the two Lands" brought cannabis from Ethiopia and other east African territories, and while hemp was never established in Egypt as a staple grain crop, it did see use as a supplemental grain and industrial fibre.

Egyptian society, on the other hand, consumed large amounts of cannabis resin. The Egyptians believed many different oils and incenses had the power to induce altered states of consciousness. Cannabis resin was a popular intoxicant among affluent Egyptians. Surviving papyri show cones of unguents—solidified essential oils—that would melt over the course of an evening and release the oils into the scalp. The oil was held on the head with circlets of brass or gold and elaborate wigs. Imported hashish was a key component of these unguents, and the psychoactive effects of the oil would certainly be felt after being absorbed through the skin. Incense was also burnt for religious purposes in Egypt, often appearing to be carried in small, hand held censors.

Across the rest of Africa, cannabis has been used ubiquitously throughout history. Many of the major African tribes utilized hemp as a sacrament, and the "dagga" cults—as the plant is known there—of Southern Africa have a long history. The Ethiopians are often credited with inventing the first water pipes, although smoking technology, like most of the technologies in Africa, never reached a particularly sophisticated level until Western cultures began to re-explore the continent.

Cannabis in the Hebrew Tradition

Cannabis is referred to often in the Hebrew Tanakh. Hemp is often described in these "Old Testament" stories as incense, honeycomb, honeywood, sweet cane, kineboiin, kaneh bosm, and kanabos—a term derived from the Scythian word "cannabis." In the book of Exodus, Moses is commanded by God to make anointing oil using kaneh bosm as the main ingredient. This sacred oil would be used to liberally anoint the temples, altars, incense burners, ritual objects, and the bodies of the priests, as a means of ritual purification.

> Then the Lord said to Moses, 'take the following fine spices: 500 hekels of liquid myrrh, half as much of fragrant cinnamon, 250 shekels of q'aneh-bosm, 500 shekels of cassia- all according to the sanctuary shekel- and a hind of olive

oil. Make these into a sacred anointing oil, a fragrant blend, the work of a perfumer. It will be the anointing oil.'
(Exodus 30:22-24)

It is clear that this potent psychoactive oil played a vital role in traditions of the ancient Hebrews. Moses himself used a tent full of cannabis fumes in order to commune with He that is called I Am.

This [cannabis] oil was slowly poured over the head and body of initiates of the priesthood. The burning bush that was not consumed from which Moses heard the voice of God was probably a mature cannabis plant covered in has resin shimmering in the mid-day sun. Around 1980, etymologists at Hebrew University in Jerusalem confirmed that cannabis is mentioned in the Bible by name, Kineboisin (also spelled Kannabosm), in a list of measured ingredients for 'an oil of holy ointment, an ointment compound after the art of apothecary' to be smeared on the head. The word was mistranslated in King James version as calamus.
("Crimes of the Ancient Mariners")

The legendary King Solomon, the builder of the first Temple in Jerusalem, certainly allowed his many foreign wives to worship the deities of their homelands—many of which were female cannabis deities—and not only did he allow them to burn incense in their honour, he ordered the creation of 20,000 gold censors and 50,000 smaller incense burners for his own Temple. While Solomon certainly worshipped Yahweh as the creator (using cannabis incense and oils), he also hedged his bets by paying tribute to the other regional deities as he saw fit.

Temple with incense burning

The first records of cannabis prohibition are also found in the Tanakh. In the books of Jeremiah (44:15-23) and Kings II (22:3-23:25) tales are related of how Yahweh, through his chosen people, brings ruin and destruction upon the peoples who worshipped Baal, Asherah, and other "false" gods and goddesses. The acts of King Josiah (612 BCE) are the first recorded legal prohibitions, though most of them would be rolled back following Josiah's death in 609 BCE, with the re-establishment of polytheism and Pagan rituals throughout the Kingdom of Israel.

Mesopotamia

The Mesopotamian culture developed in parallel with the Indus and Egyptian civilizations, and was the midpoint of trade between the two. Mesopotamia was originally a series of linguistically linked city states, known collectively as Sumer, along the Tigris and Euphrates waterways. Some of the more significant of these city states include Eridu, Uruk, and Ur. Eridu was known as the "Mound of Creation" by the ancients, and legend holds that it was there that the Sumerians first ate from the tree of knowledge. Cannabis figured prominently in the mythology and religious traditions of ancient Sumer, so much so that it would directly influence every Empire to ever conquer Mesopotamia.

After millennia of constant warfare, one of the city states began to exert dominance and created the first of the Mesopotamian dynasties. These dynasties lasted in various forms until Sargon the Great united the region under the rule of Akkad and formed the Akkadian Empire c. 2400 BCE. It is from the Akkadian Empire that we receive record of the legend of Atrahasis—one of the first heroes of mankind, and a remnant of an earlier Sumerian tale. According to the legend, Atrahasis used a special incense to hear the wishes of his god, Enki, who could only reveal himself in dreams—which the incense would impart. Likewise, in the myth of Etana—another legendary Sumerian king—the hero seeks the use of incense to aid him in deciphering his dreams. Both of these allusions to incense are certainly referring to a cannabis preparation, possibly in combination with other fragrant combustibles.

Sumerian belief initially assumed that each individual possessed their own god—a personification of luck—who would intercede on his behalf with the major deities. It was recommended that one worship their god daily with an offering of incense and a good chat. This description of daily, semi-religious, use is similar to the way many modern people employ cannabis as a tool for meditation and lifestyle enhancement.

The Akkadian civilization began to decline after 2200 BCE and abruptly disappeared, dissolving into what would emerge as another series of competing city states. Hammurabi of Babylon would unite the region during his rule (c. 1696-1654 BCE), and though the resulting Babylonian empire would not even last two centuries, Hammurabi's Code of Laws and efficient administration made Babylon the jewel of Mesopotamia—a cultural, political and religious hub. From the Akkadians, and the Sumerians before them, the Babylonian empire inescapably incorporated cannabis into its worship practices. Cannabis as incense was used in the Temples of Assyria and Babylon because its aroma was pleasing to the gods.

Assyrian King/God harvesting from the Tree of Life

Following this brief flowering, Mesopotamia was ruled by foreign dynasties for nearly a millennia—the Kassite Dynasty (c. 1594-1155 BCE) in particular—before being swallowed up by the Assyrian Empire. The Assyrians came to power in the region around 900 BCE, and would come to rule the Near East from the Persian Gulf to Egypt. Cannabis featured prominently in the religion of the Assyrians as well—they called it Qunubu—and it is from their culture that we find the oldest complete archaeological evidence of cannabis worship. Assyrian art often depicts flowering cannabis plants as sacred, and images of royalty are generally accompanied by an incense burner. Cannabis is also referred to by name in the Assyrian botanical dictionaries, and in private correspondence of the Assyrian royalty. The Assyrian Empire was eventually overrun by the competing tribes in the region, notably the Medes and the Babylonians. It was Babylon who would succeed in re-establishing regional dominance.

The Neo-Babylonian Empire is notable for a brief, but eventful, history. King Nebuchadnezzar II of Babylon is described in the Bible as being a hashish ("grass") eater. This legendary King plays the villain in the Book of Daniel, as he conquered Jerusalem and sent the Jews into exile, then is punished by god for his arrogance. Nebuchadnezzar also constructed the fabled Hanging Gardens of Babylon—one of the Seven Ancient Wonders of the world. One can only imagine the magnificent specimens of *Cannabis sativa*, the Tree of Life, which would have held a cherished place in these fantastic gardens.

Nabonidus (ruled c. 555-539 BCE), the last King of Babylon, made a special effort to control the hashish trade through the Arabian Desert in order to benefit from the vast wealth being transported through his kingdom. Chris Bennett draws the conclusion that "...Mediterranean demand for genuine incense from the Indus and the Hindu Kush made it profitable for merchants to smuggle incense through the desert wasteland between the governments of Mesopotamia and Egypt." There is little doubt that high quality hashish was a sought after luxury, as it was legendary across the "known world."

The Babylonians under Nabonidus fell to the encroaching Persian Empire, led by Cyrus the Great. Under Cyrus the so-called Achaemenid Empire stretched from Afghanistan to Egypt, and north into Asia Minor. The Persians absorbed many of the cannabis traditions from the Babylonians and the other cultures under their domain, as well as having traditionally used cannabis in their homeland. In particular the Chaldean Magi, the priestly class of Babylonians, were honoured in the Persian traditions that followed. Zarathustra (or Zoroaster) the Persian prophet, who is famed as the father of Western monotheism in worship of Ahura Mazda, is attributed with providing many of the myths and rituals that would be adopted by future monotheistic cults in the region— particularly Christianity and Islam. The Chaldeans impressed Zarathustra so much that Zoroastrian sages would also come to be known as "Magi"—the same branch of Magi were present at the biblical birth of Christ. Zarathustra was supposedly conceived immediately after his parents consumed the sacred soma (hoama) beverage, which contains large amounts of xvarenah—the divine liquid, or spirit—that helped give Zarathustra his wisdom. Though the plant that provided the ancient Persians with soma is still debated, it seems that the soma cult was swallowed up in worship of another psychoactive beverage—bhang. In the *Zend-Avesta*, one of the holy books of Zoroastrianism, bhang is described as Zarathustra's "good narcotic" and one of the heroic figures in their pantheon is enlightened with bhang. Given the cultural similarities between Indian and Iranian (Persian) mythology, and the long tradition of cannabis worship in conquered Mesopotamia, this transition is not surprising. This is clear evidence that cannabis had been worshipped in a continuous line through pre-historic Asiatic and Mesopotamian cultures, right up until the time of Aristotle—known in the Mediterranean as "Classical Antiquity."

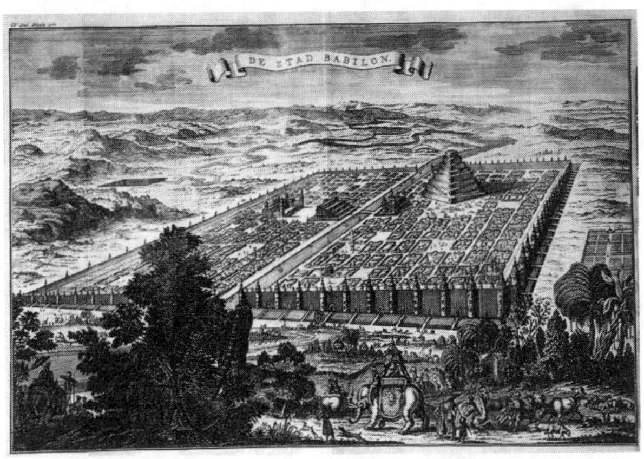

Babylon: City of Gardens

The Hellenistic Period

Darius the Great expanded the Persian Empire to its largest during his reign (522-486 BCE), installed Zoroastrianism as the official religion of his Empire, and led military campaigns against the Scythians and the Greeks, all of which ended in failure. The Empire that Darius created would last until 330 BCE, when a young Macedonian named Alexander brought Hellenistic culture to Mesopotamia for the first time, as he conquered the known world. Alexander the Great took his armies all the way to the Indus River, and brought the known world into a cultural revolution. The resulting Hellenistic period saw a blending of all the traditions that had flourished in the ancient world. This period saw much advancement in the technology, philosophy, and the sciences, and the philo-religious cults that flourished after this meeting of cultures became powerfully influential in the coming Centuries. Two of the more important of these cults were the Gnostics, who developed out of the blending of Zoroastrianism and Hellenistic culture, and the Mythra, a synthesis of Greco-Roman mysticism and Sun god worship.

The Mithra were a continuation of early mystery cults, such as the Greek Eleusinian Mysteries, and as such were extremely secretive. Little written record of their existence remains, save for references in Christian texts, and therefore most of our knowledge about these groups comes from physical remains—the temples, or mithraeum, and the various art and monuments within. The image central to the cult of the Mithraic Mysteries is the tauroctony—a depiction of the Sun god Mithras stabbing the bull of heaven. The blood that spills from the wound is believed to have nourished the Earth and brought about the first spring. In some of the surviving images the stream of blood is depicted as grain, likely hemp or wheat, and, in others, shown pooled into the shape of a cannabis leaf. Many aspects of the Mithraic Mysteries were appropriated by the Roman Catholic Church as the new State Religion of Rome sought to stamp out pagan worship.

> "The worship of Mithras, or of the sun-god, was the most popular of the heathen cults, and the principal antagonist of the truth during the first four centuries of our period." Such is the statement of one who looks at it from the point of view of a Christian ecclesiastic, and indeed the Church Fathers from the time of Justin Martyr onward have declared that the Devil, in the Mysteries of Mithra, had plagiarized their most sacred rites by anticipation."
>
> (*Fragments of a Faith Forgotten*)

Similarly, the various branches of Gnosticism were widely popular, regionalized philo-religious groups who practiced a syncretic theology. This was often a combination of Mesopotamian-Egyptian or Meso-Persian (Zoroastrian) beliefs and the Hellenistic philosophies introduced by Alexander the Great and his successors. The Gnostics preached a deep respect for all living things, and that the human life was a journey in search of truth. They believed that divine revelation was also possible through altering ones consciousness. The Gnostics achieved these altered states through a number of methods, usually used in combination with one or more of the others, by meditating, the use of cannabis incense, sleep deprivation, repetitive exercise or chant, breathing routines, sexual activity, music and dance, or intoxication. These activities were intended to open the energy channels between the seven chakras of the human body, which are located up the spine from the groin to the pineal gland, or "third-eye," in the middle of the forehead.

Three distinctly identifiable varieties of Gnosticism existed in the pre-Christian period—the Zoroastrian (Magiian), Hermetic, and Christian Gnostics. It is from the Gnostic beliefs that the idea of a Christ gained so much power. All the branches of Gnosticism taught of "Christ" as a state of being, a conscious awareness that, once attained, revealed the god-like qualities of the human spirit. While the Magiian and Hermetic Gnostics believed that Christ was a state of being attainable by any individual, the Christian Gnostics were obsessed with the apocalyptic promise of a physical manifestation of Christ as a "saviour" in the material world.

By the time of Christ, the Ancient world was blanketed by a heterogeneous body of similar syncretic monotheistic beliefs, with small pockets of ethnic monotheists (the Kingdom of Jerusalem, for example) aggressively defending their orthodoxy against the encroachment of other cultures—often by harshly prohibiting various actions or substances. When Jesus of Nazareth was born, expectations for a messiah ran high among both the Gnostics and the ancient Hebrews, as per their ancient prophesies. While Jesus may have been an ordained Rabbi of the Hebrew faith, it is certain that he was at least an initiate of the intermediate Gnostic and Mythraic mysteries. According to G.R.S. Mead, "The Gnosis was pre-Christian; the Christ illumined its tradition, and by His public teaching practically threw open to all what had been previously kept 'secret from the creation of the world'- to speak more accurately, the intermediate grades of the Mysteries." Jesus's involvement in the mystic cults is also recognized by his contemporaries, of which T.W. Doana writes, "In the Clementine Recognitions, the charge is brought against Jesus that he did not perform his miracles as a Jewish prophet, but as a magician, an initiate of the heathen temples[...]"

Jesus's impressive philosophy of peace, love, and forgiveness was very similar to that practiced by the Gnostics, and unlike the one practised by the Hebrew priesthood of the period. Once Jesus had passed through both his rabbinic training and the initiation of the Gnostics, he proclaimed that all people should have equal access to the divine power and knowledge. Armed with an intimate understanding of the various messianic prophecies, Jesus preached that this knowledge led to a direct relationship with the divine—an experience available without the guidance of spiritual specialists. In order to spread his message openly to the world, Jesus sought the aid of his fellow initiates, who would become his apostles. By manipulating the Christ prophecies, up to and including the falsification of death and resurrection on the cross, Jesus attempted to rouse the population to follow his example—undermining authority by making authority irrelevant. Jesus empowered the masses by spreading his knowledge of healing, communication, and meditation that had been jealously guarded by the priesthoods and secret societies— making him probably the most famous activist of all time.

Jesus, in revealing the Mysteries of the Gnostics and proclaiming the anointing oil of the Hebrews, among other things, to be common knowledge, enraged the various groups so thoroughly that they threatened revolt if the Roman prefect did not deal with the problem. Cannabis "anointing oil" was one of the most potent cures in the ancient world, particularly for the skin conditions the Bible refer to as "leprosy."

Jesus being anointed at Bethany

> What we call leprosy is caused by Mycobacterium leprae, a bacillus discovered in 1868[...] That disease was, in fact, known in New Testament times but was then called elephas or elephantiasis. Ancient sara'at of lepra, on the other hand, covered several diseases, all of which involved a rather repulsive scaly or flaking skin condition- for example, psoriasis, eczema or any fungus infection of the skin.
>
> (*Jesus: A Revolutionary Biography*)

In biblical times, the gift of a simple cannabis and olive oil salve would have had profound impact on communities that could not afford to approach the established religions for healing. With their monopoly upon helping the sick and threatened, the professional healers—either of the priesthoods or the cults—condemned Jesus:

> This revealing of what had been hidden so long likely contributed tremendously to Jesus's crucifixion. The open teaching of ancient "mysteries" not only upset the elite of Judaism. The Gnostics, who had revealed their secrets to Jesus, may have come to see their prize pupil as the desecrator of their holy secrets, by revealing openly to the unworthy that which had been "hidden since the creation of the world."
> (*Sex, Drugs, Violence and the Bible*)

Pontius Pilate, the Roman prefect of Judea, though loathe to act openly against the popular mystic washed his hands of the incident. Pilate sentenced Jesus to death, bowing to the pressure of the powerful Gnostic and Hebrew establishments. Jesus, his life in peril, utilized the impending crucifixion to his advantage and, faking his death, completed the messianic myth of death and resurrection:

> "In the Fourth Gospel Jesus, hanging on the cross, declares that he thirsts. In reply to this complaint he is proffered a sponge allegedly soaked in vinegar- an incident that also occurs in the other Gospels. This sponge is generally interpreted as an act of sadistic derision. But was it really? Vinegar—or soured wine—is a temporary stimulant, with effects not unlike smelling salts. It was often used at the time to resuscitate flagging slaves on galleys. For a wounded and exhausted man, a sniff or taste of vinegar would induce a restorative effect, a momentary surge of energy. And yet in Jesus' case the effect is just the contrary. No sooner does he inhale or taste the sponge then he pronounces his final words and 'gives up the ghost.' Such a reaction to vinegar is physiologically inexplicable. On the other hand such a reaction would be perfectly compatible with a sponge soaked not in vinegar, but in some type of soporific drug—a compound of opium or belladonna, for instance, commonly employed in the Middle East at the time. But why proffer a soporific drug? Unless the act of doing so, along with all the other components of the Crucifixion, were elements of a complex and ingenious strategem—a stratagem designed to produce a semblance of death when the victim, in fact, was still alive. Such a stratagem would not only have saved Jesus' life, but also have realized the Old Testament prophecies of a Messiah."
> (*The Holy Blood and The Holy Grail*)

Cannabis is a likely candidate for the soporific proffered to Jesus for several reasons. Both of the groups that Jesus studied from—the Hebrew priests and the Gnostics—used cannabis preparations in many of their rituals, including executions. Additionally, certain meditative techniques from India, Persia, and Mesopotamia, techniques which Jesus certainly would have been familiar with through study of Gnosticism and Zarathustra, required the adept to consume the Soma beverage in a death and rebirth ritual.

Jesus being passed sponge of 'vinegar'

> How did Jesus come (apparently) to die immediately after he had taken the bitter drink? Was it really vinegar that he was given? [...]A passage in the Talmud states, "The one on his way to execution was given a piece of incense in a cup of wine, to help him fall asleep." (Sanh. 43a) [...]Perhaps the supposed drink of vinegar instead contained the active ingredients of the sacred drink of the Indians and Persians, Soma and Hoama (respectively) [...] Soma, the sacred drink of India, enabled an adept to enter a deathlike state for several days, and to awaken afterwards in an elated state that

> lasted for a few days more. In this state of ecstasy, a "higher consciousness" spoke through the adept, and he had visionary powers. In addition to Asclepias acida, the Soma might also have contained Indian hemp (cannabis indica)—tradition has it that it featured in the drink of Zarathustra[...]
>
> (*Jesus Lived in India*)

Given that "incense" in the context of the Hebrews meant hashish, and the intimate connections between Zarathustra, the Gnostics, and Soma rituals, the evidence suggests that cannabis played a significant role in the resurrection myth. Jesus thus abandoned his public life, leaving his teachings in the hands of his many disciples.

Over the next several centuries, the disciples of Jesus found converts and formed communities throughout the Mediterranean region. These early "Christian" communities existed right alongside the Gnostics, Mithra, Hebrews, and various other belief structures throughout the Mediterranean, and adopted many of the local traditions for their own use—early Christians practiced an extremely syncretic philosophy:

> It is in the ancient religion of Persia- the religion of Mithra, the Mediator, the Redeemer and the Saviour- that we find the nearest resemblance to the sacrament of the Christians, and from which it was evidently borrowed.
>
> M. Renan, Speaking of Mithraicism says: It had its mysterious meetings: its chapels, which bore a strong resemblance to little churches. It forged a very lasting bond of brotherhood between its initiates: it had a Eucharist, a Supper so like the Christian mysteries, that good Justin Martyr, the apologist, can find only one such explanation of the apparent identity, namely, that Satan, in order to deceive the human race, determined to imitate the Christian ceremonies and stole them.
>
> (*Bible Myths and Their Parallels in Other Religions*)

The Roman Empire stretched from England to Palestine at the time of Christ, but it was soon on the decline. As the various Emperors tried to enforce control over an increasingly unruly variety of cultures under their rule, the resources of Rome were stretched far past their limits, and decline came quickly. The Emperor Constantine I (272-337 BCE), in order to appease a diverse and persecuted populace, repealed the draconic persecutions of Christians installed by his predecessor Diocletian, and initiated a climate of religious tolerance with the Edict of Milan. Catholicism was made the official State Religion of Rome in 380 BCE by Emperor Theodosius I, thus completing the transformation of the Catholic Church as a political entity.

The Roman rulers found the Catholic Church a perfect vehicle through which to maintain their Empire. The Church collected tithes and encouraged its members to pay Roman taxes. The new State Religion also functioned as a propaganda machine, using the Christian doctrines to ensure compliance to Catholic rule. In the process of Catholicization, the remainder of Roman paganism and the mystery cults were swept away or driven underground. A few of these pagan rituals remained, having been absorbed into Catholic dogma as the groups were dismantled, but many of the ancient mysteries were lost to the world.

Cannabis in the Islamic Tradition

Cannabis use declined sharply after the Roman Empire converted to Christianity, as the cults that worshipped hemp as the Tree of Life were eliminated. The influence of Rome was sufficient to stamp out much of the ritual use of cannabis in the near east, and when the prophet Mohammed founded Islamic culture c. 610 BCE, the same prohibitions existed for Moslems. The Islamic faith splintered after the death of Mohammed, and the various sects adopted competing versions of Islam. As the new faith spread it was heavily influenced by the cultures who converted, peaceably or otherwise, to Islam. The long traditions of hashish use amongst the Persians, Egyptians, and Levantine cultures were rapidly embraced and eventually spread hashish across North Africa into Spain.

The Islamic Abbasid Empire played an important role in absorbing this culture after they founded the city of Baghdad in 762, and made it their seat of government. Islamic intellectual culture flourished in Mesopotamia, the ancient homeland of the Assyrians, and the secrets of alchemy, mathematics, and medicine were revealed to Moslem scholars.

> An apocryphal Sufi tale has it that Sheik Haydar (1155), the Persian founder of a Sufi sect, was the discoverer of hashish. Haydar spent ten years in a remote monastery. There he received no visitors, except his closest disciples. In the heat of the Arabian summer Haydar fell into a deep depression and for the first time in a decade decided to venture outside the confines of the monastery. While wandering through the sweltering heat over still countryside Haydar came across a plant that seemed to sway of its own accord, unlike the vegetation around it. Stricken by the plants movement Haydar picked a few of its leaves, and in curiosity ate them.

> On his return, Haydar's disciples found him ecstatic and full of joy. Alarmed to find their sober teacher in this unusual happy state, his worried pupils questioned him. Haydar calmed their fears, and told them about the miraculous plant he had found making them swear an oath that they would not reveal its secrets to anyone except their fellow Sufis.
>
> It is said Haydar told his followers: "God has granted you the privilege of knowing the secrets of the leaves. Thus when you eat it, your dense worries may disappear and your exalted minds may become polished."
>
> (*Green Gold*, p.20)

The mysterious Sufi sects share traits with the Mithra and Gnostic traditions, in particular the seven grade initiation process and secretive nature. The Sufis also drank bhang in honour of the mysterious Moslem prophet Al-Khidr—the "Green" or "Verdant One." Al-Khidr (Al-Khizr) is identified as a teacher of the prophet Moses, or Musa as recorded in the Qu'ran, as well as being the companion of Alexander the Great as he sought the Fountain of Life. According to the mythology, Al-Khidr succeeded in the quest, where Alexander failed. "When Alexander sought he did not find what Khizr found unsought." (Sikandar Nâma LXIX.75) The "water of life" described in the story is most certainly bhang, as Al-Khidr is the Islamic patron Saint of Cannabis. Though this fact is disputed by the Islamic majority, it is obvious that the hemp plant has deeper roots in Islam than it does the Christian tradition.

The Hashishin

The Hashishin, or Assassins, were another secretive group that lived in the mountains of the Iranian plateau, which is now Afghanistan and Iran. The term "assassin" is derived from one Persian name for the group, a reference to their ritual use of hashish, both smoked and in a bhang beverage. The Hashishins also perfected the art of "hot-boxing," using small, portable, tents that would cover a brazier upon which hashish was heaped, enclosing the smoke along with the occupant. The Hashishin thrived from approximately 970 CE into the 13th Century, protected in their mountain strongholds, and subtly manipulated the politics of the Eurasian world through the method that would bear their name. The Hashishin trained young men to infiltrate the courts of various rulers and, if the ruler did not bend to their wishes, they would trigger these assassins to kill the vital political figures of that government—often in a suicide attack, with the men having been promised a life in paradise for successfully completing their mission.

Young Assassins were first trained in the language and customs of the culture they were to infiltrate. Following this period of training the Hashishin performed a ritual

Francois Rabelais

indoctrination on their recruits—a preparation of bhang was created and given to the youth, which would render them unconscious. Upon waking, they would find themselves in a garden full of young women ready to pleasure them—a glimpse of paradise to come—until they were given another bhang drink and brought back to "reality," thus reinforcing the promise of eternal bliss.

The practice of assassination was introduced by the first leader of the Hashishin, Hassan-i-Sabbah, who founded the capital of his empire at Alamut. Hassan found himself surrounded by much larger powers and used assassination as a way to maintain independence with relatively little manpower or loss of life. The stronghold of Alamut, protected by the faithful Hashishins, thrived and became a centre of learning—particularly of alchemy and philosophy. The Hashishin referred to themselves as "the faithful ones" and claimed to have knowledge about the structure and nature of the universe unavailable to the rest of the world.

> Works on science nowadays considered occult, such as alchemy, formed an important part of the Neoplatonic school which provided so many ideas germane to the creation of Isma'ilis doctrine. Studies in alchemy had been translated from

> Greek to Coptic texts as early as the eigth century under the Umayyads at Baghdad. Sufis such as al'Husayn b Mansur, "the wool carder," admired by many Isma'ilis and Sufi poets such as Attar, were spoken of as 'conjurers' and 'alchemists.'
>
> Hashish has an ancient and accepted importance in the history of Persian mysticism, where it has been used traditionally not as a stimulant but as a spiritual soporific, producing a quiescence of the soul which is known as keyf or kaif, which translates as intoxication, carouse or placid enjoyment. The plant from which the drug is derived is correctly called hemp, *Cannabis sativa*. In his study of the Egyptians written in 1860, Edward William Lane describes popular story-tellers recounting of Ez-Zahir, which was based on the life of Sultan Baybars. In this story fedayeen were always described as using beng, or hemp, and henbane, mixed with hashish. Lane records that even at that time it was common practice. Other writers confirm this use of a mixture of hashish and other drugs, and one author on oriental spiritualism explains this use for the effect of "raising the imagination until it attained to a beautiful realization of the joys of the future world[...]"
>
> (*The Assassins*)

The Hashishin were viewed as such a threat by the surrounding empires that foreign rulers, particularly the Sunni Moslems, went to great lengths to eliminate them. The Hashishins were finally defeated in 1256 by Hulagu Khan, the great grandson of Jenghiz Khan, who sought out their mountain strongholds so that his fate would not be sealed by an Assassin's knife. Hulagu besieged and destroyed the city of Alamut, destroying the great library that housed many ancient texts from the Zoroastrian, Egyptian, Greek, Jewish, and Gnostic doctrines. Hulagu would also sack and burn the library in Baghdad several years later, further contributing to the deterioration of knowledge in Central Asia. The remaining Hashishins, and other mystics, dispersed throughout the Sufi sects or went into hiding, taking with them what knowledge they could.

Cannabis in the Middle Ages

Shortly after the dispersion of the Hashishin, Europeans began to take a determined interest in the Far East. This is largely thanks to the travels of Marco Polo and the arrival of Eastern culture and trade goods, notably hashish and opium. The knowledge of the ancients slowly trickled back into European society in the form of alchemy and magic—a discipline taught at several medieval universities.

Francois Rabelais, a Benedictine monk with a Bachelor of Medicine, was one of the first and most successful cannabis activists in the Middle Ages. Rabelais lived from 1494 until 1553 and published a series of books, Guargantua and Pantagruel, of the adventures of two giants, Gargantua and his son Pantagruel. The stories related by Rabelais are parables that ridicule his contemporaries—church, state, and society—while at the same time transmitting secret or forbidden knowledge about cannabis and other occult subjects. The book *Pantagruel* contains the most references to cannabis using parables to describe the properties and uses of hemp fibre, as well as details concerning initiation rites into secret societies that used cannabis. Rabelais occasionally referred to cannabis as a "bean" or "magic bean," similar to the later parables of Jack and the Beanstalk—a story developed by later alchemists to further transmit secret knowledge. The good herb Pantagruel spoke of is identified as hemp in the fifth book, confirming Rabelais parables. Rabelais was forced into hiding more than once, and *Gargantua* and *Pantagruel* were condemned by the Church and the scholarly establishment. In spite of his conflicts with contemporary scholars, Rabelais became extremely influential as one of the early Humanists and the impact of his writing has been felt for centuries.

Many historians have underestimated the importance of hemp in Europe, but new evidence is now coming to light about the role of hemp in the military and economic history of that continent.

> These new research methods are changing opinions on the history of hemp cultivation in Finland. According to current opinion, hemp cultivation reached Finland from Russia (through Karelia, an area bordering modern Finland and Russia) approximately in the 14th century. There is, however, very little recorded information concerning hemp in Finland, even from the 16th century. However, the lack of written source material does not mean that hemp would not have been cultivated in Finland before this time. Paleoecological and macrofossil research, which have become more common during the last few years, have begun to establish earlier cultivation dates and broader geographic distributions of hemp cultivation in Finland. The oldest site of hemp cultivation in Finland is on Ahvenanmaa (a large island between Finland and Sweden). In macro-fossil studies, hemp seeds were found in a habitation and burial complex near the present castle of Kastelholma. They were dated from the Viking age (800-1050 CE). Hemp seeds

have been found in several southwestern excavations in Finland, dating from a long continuous period from 1100-1500 CE. Hemp was a commercial commodity during that time. Usually it was traded as fibre and not as seed. Thus, the seed discoveries indicate that in this area, hemp was cultivated and not imported. An interesting discovery was made in Suojoki (country of Keuruu in Central Finland). In the beginning of 1990, excavations were made in a boggy meadow bordering a lake where a large quantity of boat parts were found (e.g, main boat parts, planks, oars, etc.). The cracks between the planks had been caulked with tarred hemp. Hemp serves this purpose well, since it does not rot as quickly as flax. The discoveries in Keuruu have been dated to be from the 13th century.

(*History of Hemp in Finland*)

This evidence makes it clear that cannabis existed on the fringes of Catholic society and thrived in the more wild parts of Europe, in spite of the efforts of the Holy Roman Emperors and Popes directed at ending pagan worship. The mystical experiences induced by psychoactive substances remained alive in the kitchens of the alchemists, while the teachers of Zoroastrian mysticism and Hermetic Gnosticism continued their work in secret. The Christian High Priests, who had lost contact with the divine flux, perceived alchemy to be nothing more than the vain attempt to create gold from lead, rock, or other base metals. It was through these alchemists and "witches" of the dark ages that faith in the Mother Goddess remained alive through the early Christian purges. So much knowledge was destroyed in the early period of Christianity that much of the information from the dark ages has been lost to us. Before the alchemical texts of the late Middle Ages, much of the information regarding cannabis use and Mother Goddess worship can only be found in the records of purges. Even after the beginnings of the Renaissance any association with cannabis could fetch an author or scholar an immediate death sentence, thus alchemists resorted to using code and esoteric symbolism to mask their activities.

The salamander is a curious symbol in alchemy illustrated in many famous alchemical texts including the *Book of Lambspring*. The key that unlocked one aspect of its esoteric symbolism was found in a fourteenth century painting from an alchemical text showing a man intoxicated on Amanita muscaria mushrooms. He clutches one mushroom in his hand as he dances about holding his other hand on his forehead as if the revelation is too intense. Behind him a tree grows with a spotted mushroom for a top. A salamander or

Farmers bailing hemp in Finland

> lizard floats upward parallel to the Amanita tree. Next to it another salamander roasts upon the fire in much the same way as the philosopher in the *Book of Lambspring* roasts a salamander on a fork in the fire[...]
>
> In fact, the description of the Salamander in the *Book of Lambspring* has similarities to the sacred drink of the Mithraic Mysteries, and the details of its production allude to the alchemical laboratory operations that produce a sublimate oil by carefully maintaining heat necessary to vaporize the psychoactive resin produced on cannabis leaves and flowers. Just before the dried vegetable matter carbonized in the retort a viscous red oil would appear in the neck of the glass receiver. This oily sublimate they called the eagle, salamander or red lion.
>
> (*Green Gold*, p. 240)

Later alchemists were bolder, some almost blatant in there reverence of cannabis.

> One of the most famous engravings from European alchemy is a woodcut esoteric mandala by alchemical adept and doctor of medicine, Hienrich Khunrath, for his masterful treatise *Amphitheater of Eternal Wisdom* published in 1604. The alchemical mandala engraving titled "The First Stage of the Great Work" is a circle that contains the alchemists workshop where all the elements in it are drawn in perspective toward an offset center which is an open door above which is written in Latin "While sleeping, watch!" On the left side the alchemist kneels in supplication near the opening of a Scythian-like tent. In the left foreground before the tent is a large censor with smoke billowing forth from it. In the smoke is written in Latin, "ascending smoke, sacrificial speech acceptable to God."
>
> To the right of the center is laboratory equipment and high above everything else alone near the ceiling beams is a curious seven-leafed chandelier that is out of perspective compared to the converging lines on the beams. The chandelier looks more like a seven-fingered marijuana leaf with a flame at the tip of every finger. The only other flame in the engravings is in the tent itself. The plaque below the flame in the tent says "Happy is the one who follows the advice of God." On the cross beam above the seven-fingered marijuana-leaf chandelier is written "Without the breath of inspiration from God, no one finds the great way."
>
> (*Green Gold*, p. 233)

The First Stage of the Great Work by Hienrich Khunrath

Though the Church, and later the secular governments of Europe and North America, effectively suppressed knowledge about mushrooms and cannabis from reaching the mainstream, the alchemists managed to pass the sacred knowledge forward. Even the modern crackdown on entheogenic plants and their derivatives has failed to prevent these substances from surfacing in societies across the globe.

> European cannabis use remained quite secretive until the advent of the mid nineteenth century group, the elite "Le Club Des Hacshicshins," a name inspired by the nickname given to the hashish using Isma'ilis. The club members would gather together once a month costumed with turbans and daggers. "The prince of the Assassins" would go from member to member offering a spoonful of hashish with the statement "This will be taken from your share of paradise." This elite group included some of the most famous and creative artists of that time (Dumas, Hugo, Gautier, Baudelaire, De Nerval, Balzac, etc.) and was founded by Dr. J. Moreau, an expert on the effects of hashish.
>
> (*Green Gold*, p. 244)

The influence of hashish is powerful indeed. Under the influence of cannabis, the raw energy produced by the creative personalities in the room overcame a serving woman who dropped her tray and had to leave. Le Club Des Haschischins also inspired Aleister Crowley, the British mountaineer, magician, and cabalist. His book,

The Psychology of Hashish, is a wonderful testament to the mind-expanding capacities of drugs, and *On the Most Holy Grass of the Arabs* is a delightful account of humanity's spiritual journey. He introduced H.G. Wells to the experience of hashish, and also joined Aldous Huxley on a peyote journey in Berlin while Huxley was still a young man. While Crowley's influence on history has been controversial, many modern intellectuals trace the roots of their interest in psychedelics to Crowley and his influence on society has not yet been fully understood.

The Future...

Cannabis, along with many other entheogens, has played an integral role in our evolution for millions of years. This fact alone should warrant a deep and deliberate interest in these sacred plants and fungi. As humankind has matured, these ancient secrets have slowly been crossing borders, cultures, and languages; even in spite of the huge efforts of world governments and religions to fight the "War on Drugs" by prohibiting the cultures that revere these magic plants and worship the Mother Goddess. Humanity has come a long way from the Dark Ages, but there is still much work to be done. The continued prohibition of cannabis and other entheogens, particularly in the "free" world, is further evidence that the authoritarianism responsible for centuries of persecution of peaceful, loving, people is not yet gone.

Chapter 2 Hemp in the Field

Fibre Wars

> And God said, "Behold, I have given you every herb bearing seed, which is upon the face of all the earth, and every tree, in the which is the fruit of a tree yielding seed; to you it shall be for meat.
> (Genesis 1:29)

For thousands of years there was such an abundant supply of cannabis growing in the wild that it was unnecessary to actually plant seeds. As villages grew larger and travelling distance increased to wild patches of cannabis and other food sources, it became apparent that a domesticated crop must be grown. The earliest civilizations could depend upon hemp seeds as a food supply; hemp fibre as clothing, rope, basket and net making material; and the flowers as a medical and spiritual necessity. In essence, this one plant could provide all of their basic needs. Cannabis became the first and most important crop that humanity has ever grown.

> Some of the earliest evidence of hemp in North America is associated with the ancient Mound Builders of the Great Lakes and Mississippi valley. Hundreds of clay pipes, some containing cannabis residue and wrapped in hemp cloth, were found in the so-called Death Mask Mound of the Hopewell Mound Builders, who lived about 400 BCE in modern Ohio. In his 1891 study, Prehistoric Textile Art of Eastern United States, Smithsonian Institute ethnologist W.H. Holmes describes the recovery of large pieces of hemp fabric at one site in Morgan County, Tennessee: the "friends of the dead deposited with the body not only the fabrics worn during life but a number of skeins of fibre from which the fabrics were probably made. This fibre has been identified as that of the *Cannabis sativa*, or wild hemp."
> (*The Great Book of Hemp*, p. 124)

Of course, there were many other food and medical plants that were grown in these earlier times, but none were as diversified and hardy as cannabis. It could grow in places many other food crops could not, withstanding severe weather changes and storms. It had a short growing season. It did not have to be pampered once planted, as it actually killed the weeds around it because it grows faster and taller. To top it all off, if proper dew retting was done, which will be explained later, the remaining leaves and flowers actually put most of the nutrients that it used back into the ground. This allowed early farmers to grow more than one season of hemp in the same field for about 10 years in a row before there was a noticeable decrease in output as the nutrients were used up.

Hemp Harvest in Kentucky

> Cannabis hemp was widely grown across Britain in the Middle Ages, from at least 800 to 1800 AD, though the amount grown varied widely through the centuries. It was mainly grown for fibre which was used to make sails, ropes, fishing nets and clothes. Old clothes were recycled into paper. Oil was produced from the seeds and was burned in lamps. It may also have been used as a folk medicine and for food, but it's a mystery whether or not it was taken as a drug. In this section we'll first explain what types of evidence of hemp cultivation there are, then summarise where and when hemp was grown in Britain.

Hemp "peasant's clothing"

The evidence that hemp was grown in Britain comes in several different forms. First there is some written evidence in parish records and government reports. There aren't that many references to hemp, because agricultural practices were not widely written about. Secondly there are many places in Britain today with names such as Hemphill or Hempriggs, and many more places are marked on old maps such as Hemp-buttis, Hempisfield and Hempriggis. Thirdly there is evidence from pollen analysis of lake sediments, although again not much for two reasons. Firstly the sites chosen for pollen studies, tended to avoid agriculturally favourable areas. Secondly, until 1987 it was difficult to identify hemp's pollen.
(http://www.ukcia.org/culture/history/hmpukhis.html)

The cannabis grown throughout central and northern Europe could not produce as much THC as plants grown closer to the equator, and hence was not as psychoactive. Most large civilizations around the world grew cannabis for fibre and seed for thousands of years until the prohibitions of the past hundred years. As societies grew, so did their need of hemp for rope, canvas, paper, cooking oil and food.

Although Rabelais claimed the glories of hemp for France, the Moors had founded Europe's first paper factory in 1130, utilizing hemp cultivated around the city of Xativa (as in sativa) in Alicante province, Spain. Additional Moorish hemp-milling operations were established in Toledo and Valencia. The other countries of Europe soon followed suit, producing hempen rag paper in the same manner as had the Chinese a millennium earlier. Printers began publishing the Bible on hemp paper as soon as Gutenburg invented movable type in the fifteenth century.
(*The Great Book of Hemp*, p. 118)

When Europeans conquered America they immediately began using slaves to clear land and farm. The soil in North and South America is much better than in Europe where farming and war have slowly deteriorated the land over thousands and thousands of years. Hemp became so important to the new international economy that it could be used as money in the colonies from 1631 to the early 1800s.

Colonies promptly made the production of hemp compulsory. The Virginia General Assembly in 1619 officially did "require and enjoine all householders of this Colony that have any of those seeds to make tryal thereof in the nexte season." This was reiterated several times. Hemp farming was introduced into New England when Puritan settlements were established. It was grown on Manhattan Island by 1626 and in Massachusetts by 1630. Thomas Morton wrote in 1632 that hemp grew "twice as high" in his superior American soil as in old England. In 1640, Connecticut ordered every family to plant hemp.
(*Hemp:Lifeline to the Future*, p. 24)

Tariffs protecting hemp were passed in the U.S. in 1789, 1816, and 1861, and were successful until 1872 when a duty on imported jute (a.k.a. burlap) was taken away to allow the cheaper raw material into the marketplace. Manila hemp, a relative of the banana and not actually hemp, took over the markets for rope and sail cloth, as it didn't need tarring, floated and was cheaper, even though hemp was better in cold temperatures.

The "Golden Age" of the Netherlands was the 16th and 17th centuries. Much of her prosperity came from the shipping that was passed through her ports, sustained by a strong hemp, or hennep, industry. One region boasted at least 28 hennipkloppers, or windmills, used to process the hemp crop. The power of the wind was captured by sails drawn over the wooden frames of the mill's four blades. They used a fabric known as canefas, derived from the Latin cannabis and leading to the English canvas. Other wind and water mills were used to press oil from the seeds, and so on. Such mills were also common in Germany to process hanf (hemp).

(*Hemp:Lifeline to the Future*, p. 9)

In 1806, a Declaration was passed in London, England, signed by the king, stating that all Canadian farmers must grow hemp or face serious repercussions. The mid-1800s saw history's peak production of hemp. The growing British Navy's demand for hemp rose drastically. Napoleon burned all of the hemp fields in Russia to limit the British supply of rope and sail.

By the 1700s and 1800s, Russia's largest agricultural export was hemp, which supplied sails and rigging for American, Canadian and European ships. Meanwhile, Britain's arch-rival, France, had more than eight hundred thousand acres of hemp under cultivation. During wartime, hemp supplies were often cut off to punish enemy nations, so each country endeavoured to maintain its own source of supply.

(*Hemp Horizons*, p. 30)

In the later half of the 1800s, the United States and Canada began exporting hemp to Europe as fast as possible. It was difficult competing with Russian hemp in particular because the labour was cheap in that country and the fibre was better quality. Many measures were taken to encourage hemp production in America, as the limited amount of tilled soil and the labour-intensive hemp harvesting practices did not make it easy for the industry to develop.

USS Constitution

> The Federal Government in 1841 authorized a bounty, which allowed for the payment of not more than $280 per ton for American water-retted hemp, provided it was suitable for naval cordage. Many of the planters prepared large pools and water-retted the hemp they produced. But the work was so hard on Negroes that the practice was abandoned. Many Negroes died of pneumonia contracted from working in the hemp-pools in the winter, and the mortality became so great among hemp hands that the increase in value of hemp did not equal the loss in Negroes.
> (*History of Agriculture in the Northern United States*, p. 16)

You could pay your taxes with hemp for quite a while in the United States and the American Constitution was printed on hemp paper. The strain 'Kentucky Hemp' became one of the best species of hemp for fibre and hurd production yet found in the world.

Many people have argued that the cotton industry was the most important factor in the development of the United States through the 17th and 18th centuries. Cotton replaced flax as the highest valued fabric during these times, as the invention of the fly-shuttle, spinning jenny and cotton gin revolutionized the production of cotton. The production of cotton in the southern U.S. increased exponentially shipping 10 bales to England in 1784 to one third of a million bales by 1820 to 2.5 million by 1860. Thousands of rich, white settlers made millions of dollars upon land stolen from Native Americans using the forced labour of millions of black slaves from Africa.

The first president of the United States, George Washington, grew hemp and proclaimed farmers should, "Sow it everywhere." It has also been reported that he grew cannabis in his garden for smoking, using strains quite different from those grown in the field for fibre.

During the Civil War, hemp bales were used as portable shields to protect Confederate forces as they drove out 3,500 Union soldiers who were protected in trenches. The battlefield is now a historic site, where Civil War re-enactors show visitors how the 1863 "Battle of the Hemp Bales" was won, though they are unable to use real hemp bales.

> Hemp farming was hard work; hemp had to be cut by hand and gathered into shocks to dry before being spread on the field for retting (soaking). After retting, the stems were gathered up and broken using a hemp brake. Next the hemp was hackled by flaying it on a pincushion of long needles to further separate the fiber from the inner woody core of the plant, called the "hurd". Hemp farming, especially the separation of the fibers in the harvested stalks, was so labour intensive that the feudal estates of Russia, Prussia, and Poland, with their millions of serfs, undercut the tenant farms and wage labour of Western Europe. The collapse of the serf system in the 1860's in Eastern Europe forced the hemp business to find other sources of cheap labour, and the plantations of southeast Asia expanded to meet the demand.
> (*Hemp Culture*, p. 13)

After a while, other fibre crops began to replace established cannabis markets and products. Although hemp was always used for rope and sailing cloth, with over sixty tons on the U.S.S. Constitution and most other similar warships of the 1800s, slowly but surely, different products like manila, kanef and mass produced cotton chipped away at hemp's fibre crown. A variety of nutritional foods became available as cities grew larger, creating a diversity of foods and spices never seen before. The hemp seed staple was replaced by more exotic and expensive foods. After the invention of the cotton gin, hemp use in domestic homes decreased dramatically. Flax remained alive through the 1800s as a cottage industry, used in threads, towels and linens, until it was discovered that its fatty acid composition was an excellent chemical compound for producing paints, varnishes, linseed oil and linoleum. These were traditional uses of hemp seed oil.

> Because Kentucky stayed loyal to the Union, the Lincoln government looked for ways to help its hemp farmers. The government helped set up cloth mills to supply cloth for the war effort and paid top prices for Kentucky hemp for the now less-finicky Navy. After the war, however, the industry fell into a steep decline. The parts of the state that grew hemp became backwaters, relying on the cheap labour of former slaves who worked the winter months breaking hemp. The ready availability of this labour force, and its dependence on hemp processing for subsistence, became one reason Kentucky's hemp industry's transition to mechanization in the early 20th century was delayed. Post-Civil War freer trade with countries that exported cheap tropical fibres killed off even more hemp operations, jute and iron bands replaced hemp for cotton bales, and Kentucky farmers sought other valuable crops.
> (*Hemp Culture*, p. 23)

Hemp For Victory!

Hemp was still used for ropes and sails through the turn of the century, but the only people who wore hemp clothing and ate hemp seeds were the poor who couldn't afford cotton clothes or imported food. For many reasons, especially in the 1920s, hemp was looked down upon by the upper class as being peasant food and clothing. A new age of synthetic materials was embraced by the middle-class.

Machinery in the Making

The main problem with hemp was that there was no machine that could break the hurds out of the tough, fibre stock quickly and inexpensively. By 1896, about 300 patents had been issued in the U.S. for that very purpose, most of which were complete failures and none doing the proper job. Otherwise, the opportunity for hemp to return as a premier fibre crop had returned. The Southern plantations were destroyed during the Civil War, and in 1865 slavery was abolished in the USA, which dramatically affected cotton profits. Since flax was hard on the soil, farmers and businessmen turned to hemp to replace the thousands of tons of imported fibres that had taken over the markets.

Years	Imports (T)	U.S Prdctn. (T)	Total (T)
1876-80	459	7 396	7 855
1881-85	5 393	5 421	10 814
1886-90	10 427	8 270	18 697
1891-95	4 962	5 631	10 593
1896-1900	4 985	5 177	10 162
1901-05	4 577	6 175	10 752
1906-10	6 375	5 150	11 525
1911-13	5 982	5 100	11 082

Average annual imports and estimates of average annual production of hemp fibre in 5-year periods from 1876 to 1910, inclusive, and from 1911 to 1913, inclusive

The 1880s saw a resurgent interest in hemp. It was eventually grown, with active federal assistance, in Illinois, Iowa, Texas, New York, Ohio, Wisconsin, Minnesota, Kentucky, Nebraska, California, and briefly in the South, where it met too much local resistance from cotton farmers to create an industry. Although hemp was not used on boats anywhere near the scale it was before, new markets for twine and clothing were opening up. The demand for good equipment was heard around the country, and people from all walks of life, including Thomas Jefferson, tried their best to invent it.

> Production increase during wartime due to the increased demand by the Navy and reduction in foreign sources, but tended to decline in peacetime, when imported sisal, jute and abaca cut into hemp's traditional markets. In 1901, it was observed that "No horticultural varieties are recognized in this country. Nearly all of the hemp grown here in recent years is of Chinese origin." In fact, it was known that introduced foreign strains had to be grown "for at least three generations (three successive years) in the country where it is to be grown for fiber" to achieve satisfactory adaptation to the local growing environment. In an effort to support the industry in the face of foreign competition, the USDA ran an aggressive hemp breeding program under the direction of Lyster Dewey. Germ plasm was collected from around the world, and breeding selection was initiated in 1912.
> (*Fiber Wars*, p. 17)

The hemp industry expanded quickly, as farmers were in awe of its rapid growth, the condition it left the field in and the low maintenance it required. As machines were invented to replace the different manual chores in reaping and manufacturing hemp, organizations began to build bigger and better mills. In 1918, Andrew

Wright, a researcher for the Wisconsin Agriculture Experiment Station, took over promotion and organization of the hemp industry in that state. He was so successful that the hemp acreage in Wisconsin, and the U.S. for that matter, did not slow down, even though every other hemp producing country in the world was cutting back at that time.

> Hemp was still used more extensively than any other soft fiber, except jute, in 1913. The Agriculture Department decided to encourage the industry anew. Fiber specialist Lyster Dewey reported that the drop in domestic production was primarily due to an increasing difficulty in securing sufficient labor to care for the crop; secondly, to the lack of labor-saving machinery; and thirdly, to the increase in livestock, tobacco and corn production. Meanwhile jute, "inferior in strength and durability and with only the element of cheapness in its favour, is usurping the legitimate place of hemp." He noted that the new machinery for harvesting hemp and preparing the fiber, "together with the higher prices paid for hemp during the past three years," had aroused new interest in the industry. New uses for hemp pulp, known as hurds, were being developed for paper, plastics, explosives and so on. In 1916 the Department proposed making paper from the waste pulp instead of using timber from the forests. Bulletin 404 proved the value of hurd, which was very important for industry, because "without a doubt, hemp will continue to be one of the staple agricultural crops of the United States." Better yet, hemp produces four times as much pulp per acre as does forest land.
> (*Hemp:Lifeline to the Future*, p. 35)

It was discovered in 1916 that the hurds, which until that time were nothing more than a by-product of hemp burned in the mill's furnace or used in stables as animal bedding, could be used for paper production. Hemp fibre had been used for centuries to make paper, as it was stronger, lighter, more durable, and did not turn yellow or brittle like wood paper did over time. This was a huge discovery, giving even more value to a crop that showed huge potential in other areas. It was also superior to wood, as it was easier to break down, with no bark or knots in it, it uses less caustic soda and does not need sulphite—the worst by-product of wood paper making. With the addition of modern harvesting equipment, hemp was ready to become America's most important crop again. When George Schlichten began publicly displaying the results of his work creating an efficient harvesting machine, it sent ripples through the competing pulp industry.

> In 1916, Schlichten took his first production of hemp sliver to the New York market. It sold for a record price, $100 a ton more than any other fiber had previously brought. The experts pronounced it better than the finest of Italian hemps. A spinning mill owned by J.D. Rockefeller purchased Schlichten's entire crop and paid him to supervise the unfamiliar fibers into yarn. The mill was so impressed that they tried to buy exclusive rights to the invention. They offered Schlichten a considerable sum- half again as much as he really wanted- but Schlichten was not ready to sell out, especially to Rockefeller.
> ("The Schlichten Papers")

One of the first machines made to process hemp in field

In August of 1917, George W. Schlichten finally finished what he had spent the last 20 years and $400,000 to create—the decorticator. His machine could quickly and easily separate the tough fibres from the hurds, after taking off all of the flowers and leaves right in the field. This process left a significant amount of plant material behind in the field that could be tilled into the soil, which made fertilizing the crop less expensive. Without having to leave the plant cut down in the fields to ret, or using some other process to separate the fibres from the hurds, the time and energy needed to prepare hemp for processing was dramatically reduced. Retting left the hurds useless, except as a fuel, and weakened the strength of the fibres. Now with this revolutionary equipment, a better product could be produced.

Schlichten was well aware of the potential consequences that would result from this technological breakthrough. He knew it was a crime to cut down trees for paper when there was a cheaper, cleaner, and more economical way to do it. He knew also that one day the trees would run out and that we would need this machine in the future. After someone suggested that he'd be hung because of his German name, he replied:

> "Oh well gentlemen, if you think I deserve to be hanged, you don't need to force me to do it. I am perfectly willing to be hanged. But my deeds cannot be hanged; what I am doing for the country and for the world in general, that cannot be destroyed."
>
> Schlichten explained the advantage of his machine was that it worked with dried rather than retted hemp. Previously, hemp had to ret- that is, rot or ferment in the field or in stagnant ponds- for several weeks to weaken the pulp enough that the rot-resistant fibers could be separated. Retting the stalks destroyed most of the properties of the hurds, leaving them scattered in the field and so full of dirt that they were uneconomical to use. Retting also weakened and discoloured the useful fibers.
>
> Decorticated hurds were clean and easy to cook into paper. They preserved the natural glues that made paper stick together. When mechanically baled, they would transport efficiently and load easily in a paper digester. They made a superior paper, using far fewer chemicals, at less cost than tree pulp. The long fibers were stronger and cleaner than anything that could be produced by retting.
> ("The Schlichten Papers")

Literally hundreds of other inventors had failed before him. The labour costs of harvesting and processing hemp were cut by a factor of one hundred with this new machine, and put all other attempts at making a decorticator to shame. George was ecstatic about the potential for his machine to rejuvenate the hemp industry.

Harry Timken, President of the Timken Roller Bearing Company, heard about the decorticator and went to see Schlichten. He called it, "The greatest invention of the world" and set up a meeting with Edward W. Scripps, his partner Milton McRae, and Edward Chase, his right hand man. Edward Scripps was the owner of Scripps Newspaper Company, based in San Diego, which had just bought the timber rights to large tracts of land in the Pacific Northwest.

Exactly how it happened, no one is quite sure, but why the decorticator was never introduced to the agricultural community is obvious. Some stories have suggested that George eventually sold the patent but was convinced that problems mass-producing the decorticator did not allow for its introduction into the marketplace before his death in 1923.

When Rudolf Diesel invented the diesel engine in 1892, he anticipated using fuel from a variety of sources, including vegetable and seed oils. Henry Ford saw the potential for hemp to supply our fuel needs, as well as the potential for plastics made from hemp and other agricultural products. The Rockefeller and Rothschild families, which owned Standard Oil and Shell, did everything they could to eliminate these fuels as competition, including keeping prices so low that other energy sources could not compete.

Henry Ford

The decorticator and hemp plant threatened many powerful industries. The media and paper companies quickly joined forces with the Southern cotton farmers. The cotton farmers had three reasons to come down on hemp. First, it was a direct threat to the cotton industry; secondly, some had allowed their black slaves to grow cannabis on the plantations, and were looking for every opportunity to enslave, degrade or condemn them; and finally, the chemical companies that sold pesticides and fertilizers to cotton farmers, and supplied fabric producers with bleaches, inks, and other chemicals, were keen on eliminating the use of hemp in other products like plastics, paints, varnishes, and fuels. Slowly but surely, these people convinced the public that the new synthetic drugs, plastics, and clothing were superior to hemp and other natural products.

> There is no clear evidence to prove beyond a doubt that the tax act was intentionally concocted to destroy the nonnarcotic hemp industry, or to create a climate that would favour the timber and petrochemical industries, although these outcomes indeed happened. On the other hand, from historical records, we are able to trace how government actions severely hampered the development of the hemp-fiber and seed-oil industries.
> (*Hemp Horizons*, p. 52)

Certain economic circles heard about the decorticator and figured out the cotton industry, the wood pulp paper industry, and the synthetic chemical industry, would all be put in serious jeopardy if hemp were to be used on a large scale. In the early 1920s, the Hearst newspapers began running stories about coloured people and Hispanics who were going aroud raping, robbing, and killing while under the influence of a new drug called "marijuana." The "reefer madness'" campaign struck to the very hearts of most Americans and Canadians. These crazed addicts were accused of destroying families, ruining their healthy bodies and minds, thereby making them unfit to enter into the Kingdom of Heaven. Many forms of civil disobedience, sexual perversion, and social disruption were blamed upon those addicted to the demon weed—marijuana.

Reefer Madness Takes Hold

Cannabis was made illegal in Canada, with the Narcotic Act of 1923, to possess, distribute or cultivate without a license. The newspapers lead the media smear campaign against cannabis. In 1922, a series of articles that appeared in MacLean's Magazine written by Mrs. Emily Murphy—AKA Janey Canuck—were published in a book called The Black Candle. It contained accusations that were bluntly false and unfounded, but Canadians ate it up. Mrs. Murphy was a leader of the Irish Orange Order, a religious sect demanding a pure white Canada. Racism was very alive in Canada then, and her plea was heard and answered. When Mackenzie King passed the law through government he probably never intended to use it on a white man, he just wanted to control the minorities for the good of the people. We will look into these issues later in chapter 5.

> Charles A Jones, the Chief of police for that city (L.A.), said in a recent letter that hashish, or Indian hemp, grows wild in Mexico but to raise this shrub in California constitutes a violation of the State Narcotic law. He says, "Persons using this narcotic, smoke the dried leaves of the plant, which has the effect of driving them completely insane. The addict loses all sense of moral responsibility. Addicts to this drug, while under the influence, are immune to pain, and could be severely injured without having any realization of their condition. While in this condition they become raving maniacs and are liable to kill or indulge in any form of violence to other persons, using the most savage methods of cruelty without, as said before, any sense of moral responsibility.
>
> When coming from under the influence of this narcotic, these victims present the most horrible condition imaginable. They are dispossessed of their natural and normal willpower, and their mentality is that of idiots. If the drug is indulged in to any great extent, it ends in the untimely death of its addict".
> (*The Black Candle*, p. 332)

Emily Murphy aka Janey Canuck

There were numerous special interest groups that were behind the conspiracy to eliminate cannabis from the marketplace, including the Hearst Newspaper Company, timber companies, DuPont Chemicals, Southern cotton farmers, oil companies, pharmaceutical businesses, and racist fanatics. It is impossible to point the finger at one person, or to one particular event. These individuals, companies, and industries collectively organized to eliminate cannabis from the marketplace. The group stopped any large sales of hemp for use in production of other products, pressuring the government and other companies into buying raw materials other than hemp, stopping all investment in hemp related products or production, stopping private and government research on the growth or production of hemp products, and suppressing information about the use and history of cannabis. They believed that eliminating cannabis was the best way to ensure the health of the economy and their children.

When the laws were enacted, the only groups opposed to the 1937 Marijuana Tax Act were poultry farmers and the medical community. While the doctors were completely ignored, farmers were able to import hemp seed, but only after it was sterilized at a temperature high enough to guarantee the seed could not sprout. The following comes from a speech made to the House Ways and Means Committee by Ralph Loziers, general counsel for the National Oil Seed Institute:

> "Respectable authorities tell us that in the Orient, at least 200 million use this drug; and when we take into consideration that for hundreds, yes, thousands of years, practically that number of people have been using this drug. It is significant that in Asia and elsewhere in the Orient, where poverty stalks abroad on every hand and where they draw on all the plant resources which a bountiful nature has given that domain- it is significant that none of those 200 million people has ever, since the dawn of civilization, been found using the seed of this plant or using the oil as a drug."
>
> "Now, if there were any deleterious properties or principles in the seed or oil, it is reasonable to suppose that these Orientals, who have been reaching out in their poverty for something that would satisfy their morbid appetite, would have discovered it[...]"
>
> "If the committee please, the hempseed, or the seed of the *Cannabis sativa* l., is used in all the Oriental nations and also in a part of Russia as food. It is grown in their fields and used as oatmeal. Millions of people every day are using hempseed in the Orient as food. They have been doing that for many generations, especially in periods of famine[...]The point I make is this- that this bill is too all inclusive. This bill is a world encircling measure. This bill brings the activities- the crushing of this great industry under the supervision of a bureau- which may mean its suppression. Last year, there was imported into the U.S. 62,813,000 pounds of hempseed. In 1935 there was imported 116 million pounds[...]"
>
> (*The Emperor Wears no Clothes*, p. 32)

In Nov. 1937, the Marijuana Tax Act had been passed in the U.S. with almost no debate. Cannabis was once again going to be ploughed under public eye, to be replaced by synthetic materials, pills, and processed food. Most people in the hemp business were not aware of the impending doom facing the plant, and continued to produce new products and improve harvesting techniques. In the mid-1930s, several versions of decorticators appeared on the market that were almost as efficient as Schlichten's invention.

Though many in the farming community continued to promote hemp production in the late 1930s, they were not able to stop the influence of money hungry industrialists from slowly eliminating hemp from the marketplace. Popular Mechanics even printed an article titled, "New Billion Dollar Crop," which was the first time a figure that high had ever been used for an agricultural commodity. The new laws placed further barriers to growing hemp that forced farmers into other crops. Except for a brief revival during the Second World War,

Chapter Three

FEBRUARY 1938: POPULAR MECHANICS MAGAZINE:

"NEW BILLION-DOLLAR CROP"

FEBRUARY 1938: MECHANICAL ENGINEERING MAGAZINE:

"THE MOST PROFITABLE & DESIRABLE CROP THAT CAN BE GROWN"

Modern technology was about to be applied to hemp production, making it the number-one agricultural resource in America. Two of the most respected and influential journals in the nation, Popular Mechanics and Mechanical Engineering, forecast a bright future for American hemp. Thousands of new products creating millions of new jobs would herald the end of the Great Depression. Instead hemp was persecuted, outlawed and forgotten at the bidding of W. R. Hearst, who branded hemp the "Mexican killer weed, marihuana."

As early as 1901 and continuing to 1937, the U.S. Department of Agriculture repeatedly predicted that, once machinery capable of harvesting, stripping and separating the fiber from the pulp was invented or engineered, hemp would again be America's number-one farm crop. The introduction of G. W. Schlichten's decorticator in 1917 nearly fulfilled this prophesy. (See pages 13-15 and Appendix.)

The prediction was reaffirmed in the popular press when *Popular Mechanics* published its February 1938 article "Billion-Dollar Crop." The first reproduction of this article in over 50 years was in the original edition of this book. The article is reproduced here exactly as it was printed in 1938.

Because of the printing schedule and deadline, *Popular Mechanics* prepared this article in spring of 1937 when cannabis hemp for fiber, paper, dynamite and oil, was still legal to grow and was, in fact, an incredibly fast-growing industry.

Also reprinted in this chapter is an excerpt from the *Mechanical Engineering* article about hemp, published the same month. It originated as a paper presented a year earlier at the Feb. 26, 1937 Agricultural Processing Meeting of the American Society of Mechanical Engineers, New Brunswick, New Jersey.

Reports from the USDA during the 1930s, and Congressional testimony in 1937, showed that cultivated hemp acreage had been doubling in size in America almost every year from the time it hit its bottom acreage, 1930-when 1,000 acres were planted in the U.S.—to 1937-when 14,000 acres were cultivated with plans to continue to *double* that acreage annually in the foreseeable future.

As you will see in these articles, the newly mechanized cannabis hemp industry was in its infancy, but well on its way to making cannabis America's largest agricultural crop. And, in light of subsequent developments (e.g., biomass energy technology, building materials, etc.), we now know that hemp is the world's most important ecological resource and therefore, potentially our planet's single largest industry.

The *Popular Mechanics* article was the very first time in American history that the term "billion-dollar"* was ever applied to any U.S. agricultural crop!

*Equivalent to $40-$80 billion now.

Experts today conservatively estimate that, once fully restored in America, hemp industries will generate $500 billion to a trillion dollars per year, and will save the planet and civilization from fossil fuels and their derivatives—and from deforestation and the Greenhous Effect!

If Harry Anslinger, DuPont, Hearst and their paid-for (know it or not, then as now) politicians had not outlawed hemp—under the pretext of marijuana (see Chapter 4, "Last Days of Legal Cannabis")—and suppressed hemp knowledge from our schools, researchers and even scientists; the glowing predictions in these articles would already have come true by now—and more benefits than anyone could then envision—as new technologies and uses continue to develop.

As one colleague so aptly put it: "These articles were the last honest word spoken on hemp's behalf for over 50 years...."

KENTUCKY HEMP FIELDS

For a fascinating delineation of hemp's role during the period 1782-1900, read "The Reign of Law: A Tale of the Kentucky Hemp Fields", James Lane Allen, published by McMillan & Co., 1900.*

*You'll find a reproduction of the first chapter of this book in our Appendix.

You can download a free e-book here http://www.gutenberg.org/etext/3791

Jack Herer re-printed this from Popular Mechanics, 1938
source: The Emperor Wears No Clothes, 1985

in a 1942 campaign titled "Hemp For Victory," hemp was slowly choked out of public existence in the U.S., with the last crop grown in Kentucky in 1958.

> In 1942, patriotic farmers at the government's request planted 36,000 acres of seed hemp, an increase of several thousand percent[...]Thus hemp, *Cannabis sativa*, the old standby cordage fiber, is staging a strong comeback. [...]The power breaker makes quick work of it[...]
>
> The old Kentucky river mill at Frankfort[...]has been making cordage for more than a century. All such plants will presently be turning out products spun from American-grown hemp: twine of various kinds for tying, winding armatures and upholsterer's work; rope for marine rigging and towing; for hay forks, derricks and heavy duty tackle; light duty firehose, thread for shoes for millions of American soldiers; and parachute webbing for our paratroopers. As for the U.S. Navy, every battleship requires 34,000 feet of rope, and other crafts accordingly.
>
> (*Hemp for Victory*)

Why Not Use Hemp to Reverse the Greenhouse Effect & Save the World?

In early 1989, Jack Herer and Maria Farrow put this question to Steve Rawlings, the highest ranking officer in the U.S. Department of Agriculture (who was in charge of reversing the Greenhouse Effect), at the USDA world research facility in Beltsville, Maryland.

First, we introduced ourselves and told him we were writing for Green political party newspapers. Then we asked Rawlings, "If you could have any choice, what would be the ideal way to stop or reverse the Greenhouse Effect?"

He said, "Stop cutting down trees and stop using fossil fuels."

"Well, why don't we?"

"There's no viable substitute for wood for paper, or for fossil fuels."

"Why don't we use an annual plant for paper and for biomass to make fuel?"

"Well, that would be ideal," he agreed. "Unfortunately there is nothing you can use that could produce enough materials."

"Well, what would you say if there *was* such a plant that could substitute for all wood pulp paper, all fossil fuels, would make most of our fibers naturally, make everything from dynamite to plastic, grows in all 50 states and that one acre of it would replace 4.1 acres of trees, and that if you used about 6% of the U.S. land to raise it as an energy crop—even on our marginal lands, this plant would produce all 75 quadrillion billion BTUs needed to run America each year? Would that help save the planet?"

"That would be ideal. But there is no such plant."

"We think there is."

"Yeah? What is it?"

"Hemp."

"Hemp!" he mused for a moment. "I never would have thought of it.... You know, I think you're right. Hemp could be the plant that could do it. Wow! That's a great idea!"

We were excited as we outlined this information and delineated the potential of hemp for paper, fiber, fuel, food, paint, etc., and how it could be applied to balance the world's ecosystems and restore the atmosphere's oxygen balance with almost no disruption of the standard of living to which most Americans have become accustomed.

In essence, Rawlings agreed that our information was probably correct and could very well work.

He said, "It's a wonderful idea, and I think it might work. But, of course, you can't use it."

"You're kidding!" we responded. "Why not?"

"Well, Mr. Herer, did you know that hemp is also marijuana?"

"Yes, of course I know, I've been writing about it for about 40 hours a week for the past 17 years."

"Well, you know marijuana's illegal, don't you? You can't use it."

"Not even to save the world?"

"No. It's illegal", he sternly informed me. "You cannot use something illegal."

"Not even to save the world?" we asked, stunned.

"No, not even to save the world. It's illegal. You can't use it. Period."

"Don't get me wrong. It's a great idea," he went on, "But they'll never let you do it."

"Why don't you go ahead and tell the Secretary of Agriculture that a crazy man from California gave you documentation that showed hemp might be able to save the planet and that your first reaction is that he might be right and it needs some serious study. What would he say?"

"Well, I don't think I'd be here very long after I did that. After all, I'm an officer of the government."

"Well, why not call up the information on your computer at your own USDA library. That's where we got the information in the first place."

He said, "I can't sign out that information."

"Well, why not? We did."

"Mr. Herer, you're a citizen. You can sign out for anything you want. But *I* am an officer of the Department of Agriculture. Someone's going to want to know why I want all this information. And then I'll be gone."

Finally, we agreed to send him all the information we got from the USDA library, if he would just look at it.

He said he would, but when we called back a month later, he said that he still had not opened the box that we sent him and that he would be sending it back to us unopened because he did not want to be responsible for the information, now that the Bush Administration was replacing him with its own man.

We asked him if he would pass on the information to his successor, and he replied, "Absolutely not."

In May 1989, we had virtually the same conversation and result with his cohort, Dr. Gary Evans of the U.S. Department of Agriculture and Science, the man in charge of stopping the global warming trend.

In the end, he said, "If you really want to save the planet with hemp, then you [hemp/marijuana activists] would find a way to grow it without the narcotic (sic) top—and then you can use it."

This is the kind of frightened (and frightening) irresponsibility we're up against in our government.

Top: Jack Herer re-printed this from Popular Mechanics, 1938
Bottom: Poster used to gain support of farmers to grow hemp

It is a sad fact that the greed and prejudice that has prohibited this wonderful plant has contributed to the degradation of our forests, air, water, children, families, and spirits. Unfortunately, we have also lost all of the species of hemp that had grown accustomed to North America. But efforts to rejuvenate the hemp industry are starting to roll all over the world. Many countries never stopped growing hemp, including Russia, India, China and France. They continue to make cigarette papers, notably Zig-Zag, out of hemp fibres in France, although marijuana use is still frowned upon there. In 1992, world production was 124,000 tons of fibre, a mere one percent of world production of vegetable fibre, and much less than the 1940 peak of 832,000 tons.

Hemp in the Field

Hemp grows best in the 14-27 °C, although it can survive colder or warmer temperatures. It can grow well between 32° and 60° Northern latitude—a much wider range than most other crops. Hemp prefers humid weather, loving lots of rain during the first six weeks of the season. Once the roots have penetrated into the ground deep enough, hemp can withstand fairly dry conditions, although with little water hemp matures slower, grows less, and reduces yield. Seedlings can withstand as low as -8 °C for a night or two, while older plants can withstand a frost of minus 5 or 6 °C. They can also survive severe storms, as Joe Strobel of Ontario found out in 1994, saying, "After a particularly strong storm, all the hemp plants were lying flat. Would you believe that they all came back and stood straight up. That's one strong plant."

> Hemp needs remarkably little: some soil, water, sunlight and air. The crop needs little attention. It is even self-seeding, self-weeding and self-fertilizing. Like people, hemp successfully adapts to its circum-

stances. Different types have distinct characteristics. Some strains do better in a wet climate, while others flourish in a drier one. Almost any soil or climate condition can support hemp growth, from equatorial tropics right to the edge of the arctic circle. Of course, like any crop, hemp performs better in ideal conditions. It prefers great soil and weather; but a quality yield has also been realized in even the most harsh conditions. The soil can be worn, the water undependable, the sunlight patchy and the air dirty. For this reason, people often refer to cannabis as a "weed". In fact, hemp is an important domesticated crop that is suited for almost anyplace; and people have planted it almost everywhere.

Hemp has been grown as a windbreak or to protect and isolate certain crops for selective breeding, since a thick stand of hemp provides a pollen barrier. It can also be grown to rebuild and aerate the soil structure and to neutralize the pH level of acid soil. Hemp is sown on dung heaps to compost the manure and grown on hillsides to anchor soil and prevent erosion. Special environmental uses include growing hemp as an oxygen crop, for erosion control,manure digestion, reforestation and soil improvement through its deep tap-root system.

(*Hemp: Lifeline to the Future*, p. 165)

Gentleman standing between rows of hemp

Although hemp plants are very resistant to diseases, the following ailments can afflict them: Cuscuta Europaea, "gemeine Seide"; Orobanche ramosa L. branched broom rape; Phytium de Baryanum Hesse, damping off, which will cause "Wurzelbrand"—brown soft lesions on young stems; Peziza Kaufmanniana Tisch., Bacillus cubonianus Macch. will cause many longish, somewhat protruding white-gray spots with a fissured surface, up to 10 cm long; Peronospora cannabina Otth., false mildew, causes yellow spots on the upper side of the leaf and a black-gray mold on the other side; Phyllosticta cannabis Speg., a leaf spot disease; Septoria Peck, a leaf spot disease; Pseudomonus cannabina, stripe disease; Botrytis cinerea Fr., gray mold; Sclerotina sclerotiorum Mass., hemp canker; Macrosporium cannabrium, brown leaf spot; and Fusarium sp., wilt. With proper care and maintenance, all of these diseases can be avoided or eliminated. Most are caused by seed and soil born fungi, or because the soil was wet for too long.

The hemp plant can be attacked by the hemp flea beetle, Psyloides attenuata, the European corn borer, Prausta nubilalis, Grapholita delineata, and Ostrina nubilalis. Most of these pests can be eliminated by using, the environmentally safe, Bacillus thuringenesis and/or proper crop rotation.

Weeds are generally not a problem if the crop is planted early enough in the season, as the canopy of leaves smother all opposition. If planted for seeds. some weeds may creep in because the plants are not always close together. This weedless environment leaves the field in excellent condition.

"WINTER'S ALL-TIGHTENING FROSTS."

Harvested Hemp Waiting For Processing

Hemp can be grown continually in the same field, although it is very hard on the soil. Hemp is a heavy feeder, requiring nitrogen, phosphoric acid, and potassium every year for an optimum yield. If the flowers and leaves are returned to the soil, either by dew retting or composting after stripping the leaves, up to 70% of the nutrients absorbed by the plant during growth are returned to the soil at the end of the season. The roots make up 10% of the dried weight, the stems about 60%, and the leaves about 30%, so 70% of the plant's nutrients are returned to the ground with 40% of the plant's weight. Hemp grows best in a four year rotation of cereals, clover for green manure (compost), corn, and hemp, though a three year rotation without clover is also used. Beans can be substituted into this rotation and other crops are being tried around the world according to each area's climate.

The roots leave the soil in excellent condition because they tap deep into the earth, and if the soil is loose enough to allow it, they bring nutrients closer to the top for other plants to use. This also helps break up the soil and allows for deeper root penetration in the next year. That process, combined with the fact that hemp leaves the field virtually free of weeds, proves that hemp is one of the best crops to grow in an organic vegetable garden and other holistic farms.

Hemp grows best on rich and fertile, neutral or slightly alkaline, well-drained clay-loam or silt-loam soils. Hemp grows best with a pH level under five and will not grow well in still, impervious clay soils or light sandy, gravel-type soils. New strains may be developed which can grow in any climate. A fair amount of water must be available in the subsoil or the crop may need irrigation. Hence, hemp needs the very best of our available farmland, so as to yield maximum results.

Crop Yields	Nitrogen	Phosphoric Acid	Potassium
Hemp (1 000 lbs of clean fiber)	62.7	33.2	101.3
Corn (50 bushels and 1.5 T. of stover)	74.0	11.5	35.5
Wheat (25 bushels of grain, 1.25 T. of straw)	48.0	8.0	24.0
Oats (50 bushels of grain, 1.25 T. of straw)	48.5	8.0	34.0
Sugar Beet (20 T. of roots)	100.00	18.0	157.0
Cotton (400 lbs of lint)	29.2	22.5	35.3

Crop yield with different plants

As the above chart shows, except for sugar beets, hemp usually uses more nutrients than the other crops, although one must keep in mind that all of these other crops are completely taken away from the field, except for sugar beet tops. So only about 30% of the nutrients that are needed to grow hemp are actually taken if the tops and flowers are returned. Therefore, being relatively easy on the soil, hemp can be grown successively without experiencing the dramatic decrease in yield other crops do. However, 10 consecutive years of growing hemp, without heavy fertilizer, will exhaust the nutrient supply within good soil.

Barn yard manure is an excellent source of the nutrients hemp needs, and should be tilled into the soil before the proceeding crop, or in the fall. Spreading manure just before sowing is likely to cause more harm than good. The most commonly used commercial fertilizer mix is about 6% phosphoric acid, 12% potash, and 4% nitrogen (in the form of nitrate of soda or sulphate of ammonia), although different soils, different stains, and different climate conditions may call for different properties of nutrients. The fertilizer can be applied at rates between 75 to 200 Kg of N/ha, 80 to 120 Kg of P2O5/ha, and 160 to 200 Kg of K2O/ha, with varying results. The fibre content in the stem decreases once a certain limit in the amount of Nitrogen is used. Ploughing a field of clover under the soil the year before hemp is planted is an excellent, economical way of fertilizing a crop. If, because of dry weather or poor soil conditions, a crop of hemp grows stunted, it may be best to plough it under or burn it to regenerate the land.

Hemp proponents often claim that hemp could be grown on marginal land and would not affect the production of other crops. This is simply not true. Hemp needs a rich, fertile loam and high

Hemp bale waiting for pick-up

nutrient levels for high productivity. This limits its production to areas which are already being farmed. The Midwestern corn and wheat belts would be ideal sites for large cannabis plantations.

If hemp were grown on marginal land, it would cost more to produce. The farmer would use the same inputs, seed, labour, machinery, fertilizer. The marginal land would produce less and the cost per unit would be higher.

In order to introduce farmers to grow hemp, it must appear more profitable or beneficial than growing any other crop. No matter what the government energy policy, farmers must be willing to grow it for personal gain.

("Hemp as Biomass?")

Hemp can also be used to revitalize poor soil, although the yield is directly affected. Much of the land that is turning into desert, either naturally or manually, can be recovered with the right irrigation, fertilizer, correct crop rotation, and love. This could work in places like Costa Rica where the land has been almost completely destroyed, first by clear-cutting rain forest and then by farming the land without proper fertilization or tilling. Hemp is an excellent plant to till back into poor soil because it produces so much biomass in a short time, while pulling up nutrients from deep in the ground with its roots.

Hemp seed plants are seeded at rates of between one to 24 kg/ha resulting in five to 120 plants per square meter. The average hemp crop grown for seed yields between 20 to 30 bushels, or 900-1300 lbs, per acre. If the seeds are pressed for oil, usually it is about 25% of the seed's weight, 14-21 gallons of oil per acre would be extracted. The left over mash from this process is very high in protein and could be used as human or animal food. When hemp is grown for seed, the fibre quality is much poorer than when grown specifically for fibre, although it can still be used for many products, including paper. The seeds have traditionally been used as birdseed for hundreds of years, with doves, quails, and poultry, all devouring the seeds as quickly as possible. In fact, one of the few complaints of farmers is that birds are always in the fields eating the seeds.

When hemp seed is sown thickly for fiber production, the plants usually grow from 5 to 8 feet tall. However, when the plants are thinly spaced in rows for seed production, they may, under favourable conditions, reach a height of 12 to 16 feet. If the plants are not crowded, they become much branched and are bushy. Uniform stems approximately 3/8 inch in diameter and 5 to 8 feet long are especially desired for fiber production, because they can be handled well by the harvesting and processing machinery available in this country.

Hemp is a dioecious plant, that is, the staminate (male) and pistillate (female) flowers are borne on separate plants, rather than both on one plant. The flowers of the two types of plants are different, but the male plant is easily distinguished from the female, as the anthers are about the size of a wheat kernel. The male plants die soon after discharging their pollen; this is usually about 3 to 5 weeks before the female plants mature seed and die.

The fiber of commerce ranges from 4 to 8 feet in length and has the appearance of a flat, fine ribbon. It lies very close to the epidermis or skin of the plant. Spinners desire the fiber ribbon 1/16 inch or less in width. The long strands of fiber are called "line" fiber to distinguish them from "tow" fiber, which consists of shorter, broken, tangled pieces.

(Farmer's Bulletin No. 1935)

Common hemp seed

Some impressive steps toward the development of a THC free strain of cannabis have been made, although once grown in the field for two consecutive seasons the THC content rises to normal hemp levels of 0.3 %. There is really no need to develop a THC-free strain of hemp since it takes about one acre of hemp to grow enough flowers to produce one joint. Some speculate that the THC and other cannabinoids act as part of the plant's immune system.

Most of the research done in hemp genetics is directed towards creating the highest quality and quantity of fibre yield possible, resistance to weeds, insects and disease, and a low THC content. Once the hysteria over marijuana has disappeared, and the crops have adapted to their environment,there is potential for the development of new strains that far out-produce the fibre we make today. Some research done by the Agricultural Research Department in the Netherlands with 92 different populations of hemp gives us an excellent example of the range of yields in hemp. Total bark content in drug strains and wild plants is about 12%, while modern strains of hemp produce up to 28%. As the bark content increases, the hurds decrease in total weight from 74% to 52%, while the primary fibres goes from 10% to 23%, and secondary fibres from 1% to 10%. It was found that attempting to grow strains with a fibre content over 28% resulted in too huge of an increase in secondary fibres, which negatively effects quality and costs.

Primary bark fibres are longer than secondary fibres, making the plants yielding the highest amount of primary fibre the most valuable. Both are longer than the fibres in the woody core. Fibres are comprised of a link of chains of cellulose molecules—the building blocks of trees and many other plants. This rigid structure is what gives strength and flexibility to the tissue by gluing together the cells with lignin and pectin. While the bast fibres produce the best quality paper, the hurds can be used to produce paper for most of our needs, thereby maximizing the production of each plant by utilizing each component part with the most economically feasible product possible.

It is imperative that we develop hemp production around the world because of the environmental catastrophes that are looming over our heads. Consider also, that if our federal governments break down, if welfare and unemployment cheques stop coming, and Western society quickly falls into ruin, the only plant that we can grow, locally and globally, which will keep us alive, is *Cannabis sativa*.

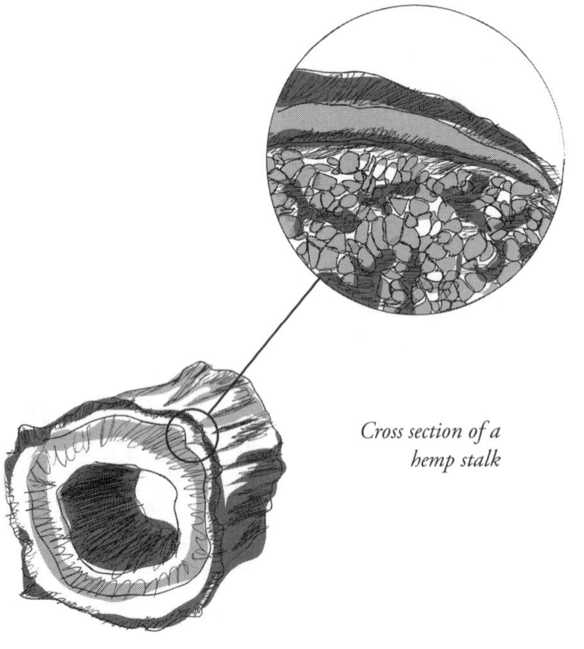

Cross section of a hemp stalk

Hemp Around the Globe

Hemp is being legally grown in Austria, Australia, Canada, Chile, China, Croatia, Czech Republic, Denmark, England, Finland, France, Germany, Holland, Hungary, Ireland, Italy, Democratic People's Republic of Korea, Republic of Korea, the Netherlands, New Zealand, Nicaragua, Poland, Portugal, Romania, Russian Federation, Slovenia, South Africa, Spain, Switzerland, and the Ukraine. German, Austrian, and Swiss farmers do not even have to apply for a license to grow hemp. Global production levels have fallen since the 1960s when about 300,000 tons were grown per year, to 1997 when approximately 55,500 tons were grown around the world. In 1998, there were 23 mills around the world that used hemp to make paper, most in India and China.

In 1931, the Soviet Union created the Institute of Bast Crops at Glukov, in the Ukrainian Republic, and for the last 60 years have experimented with the breeding, agronomy, mechanization, and economy of hemp fibre. Between the 1950s and 1980s, Russia was producing more hemp than any other country. They have an enormous backlog of information about hemp. They have experienced, along with the rest of the world, a decline in hemp production. In 1930 for example, 140,000 ha of hemp grew in the Ukraine while 500,000 ha grew in Russia, but in 1993 only 8,000 ha were left in the Ukraine and 35,000 to 40,000 ha in Russia. After a few years of decline, many in Russia are making an attempt to bring hemp back into the market. The Vavilov Institute in Russia currently has about 400 varieties of hemp, down from the previous high of 1,400 strains. One of the researchers from the Vavilov Institute is Dr. Sergey Grigoryev.

> Our current priorities are to proceed with studying the current state of the collection and to add the resulting data to those obtained during the past years of research. That means, first of all, to use the results of field experiments in identifying distinctive features, individual uniqueness, typical biological properties and traits valuable for breeding in certain soil and climate environments. This would provide grounds for a conclusion on phenotypic similarity and difference of accessions within each ecogeographic hemp group. Thus it would become possi-

> ble to identify the existence of valuable commercial characters in different accessions, such as: early-maturing, cold-resistance, high seed productivity, high oil content in seed, fibre percentage, resistance to afflicting pests etc., i.e. to identify Sources of Valuable Properties available in the hemp collection.
> ("The History of Hemp in Russia")

China grows over 50% of the world's hemp right now, where it has been used locally for thousands of years. In 2006, the Chinese planted 797,000 ha of hemp producing about 600,000 tons of fibre. Much of this hemp is made into clothes which are exported around the world. With no forests to cut down, China has been dependent upon fibre crops for a very long time.

In Australia, the hemp plant is seen as a possible saviour for their agricultural communities, since much land has been lost to improper irrigation and tree farming. Australia began giving out licenses to grow hemp in 1998. A crop grown at the University of Tasmania at Hoburt in 1992-93, in cooperation with the Tasmanian Hemp Company, produced stem yields of 8.0, 8.4, and 6.1 tons per hectare, in fields grown at different times of year. After a few improvements, yields of 10 to 12 ton/ha are expected.

> Enthusiasm for an industrial hemp industry has grown in Australia in recent years. Legislative frameworks developed by some State Governments have given the industry the opportunity for broad-scale commercial production and/or for the development of research programs. Although there has been small-scale experimental production of industrial hemp under a permit system in most States in the last several years, no nation-wide policy has been developed for the crop. This lack of a coordinated national approach has led to a large number of ad hoc trials being conducted for a range of purposes, including variety assessment, machinery development, and the determination of better agronomic practices. One exception was a comparative trial in 2001/02 that was run concurrently at five sites (extending from Rockhampton to Hobart) to test the effects of latitude on six selected varieties.
> (Queensland Government, http://www2.dpi.qld.gov.au/hemp/16241.html)

In England, hemp was first grown as an experiment in 1993, and has been legal since 1998. The cost of obtaining a license and the lack of production facilities has hampered the development of the industry. Most hemp products sold in Britain come from Russia and China, though a few entrepreneurs are trying to establish a local hemp industry.

In 1994, 100,000 tons of hemp were grown in France for cigarette paper and cloth. There are three French organizations that direct the hemp movement, the Federation National des Producteur de Chanvre (F.N.P.C.), the Commite Economique Agricole de la Production du Chanvre (C.E.A.P.C.), and the Cooperative Centrale des Producteur de Semence de Chanvre (C.C.P.S.C.). Mr. Jean-Paul Mathieu has been the director of all three organizations for almost two decades, and is very optimistic about the economic potential hemp shows in his country. These three groups work as such: the F.N.P.C. researches the breeding of new strains, as well as the agronomy and processing of hemp; the C.E.A.P.C. organizes the relationship between growers, buyers and the marketplace; and the C.C.P.S.C. organizes the growth and distribution of hemp seeds.

It is somewhat surprising how small the hemp industry is in France and how under-developed their harvesting and production techniques are, when you consider that in 1965, a collection of 100 fibre, hemp accessions were evaluated for quality, productivity, and feasibility, with the intention to create the best possible fibre crop that could be grown in France.

In Holland, the future prospects of hemp are promising. They are already a country devoted to high value crops and have a much more liberal policy towards marijuana, eliminating many constraints put on hemp by misinformed and disillusioned people. In 1989, Holland began a four year, ten million dollar project on hemp research and development. The program was initially started to deal with a problem the potato industry was having with microscopic nematodes. It was correctly believed that by using hemp in the crop rotation this problem would be eliminated.

Hungary is a traditional hemp growing country. In the last twenty years, the dissolution of the Soviet Union and its economy has lead to a decline in production. In 1991, there were 6,000 ha grown. In 1993 only 300 ha were grown, which was less than half of England's new crop. Since they have had hemp harvesting and manufacturing machinery for years, it has been a favourite touring ground for American, European, and Canadian hemp activists and enthusiasts. Although this machinery is outdated and in need of modern refinement, it works. The established research organizations in Hungary have developed many excellent strains of hemp. The seeds from Hungary have been grown all over the world these last few years.

Romania has maintained a hemp industry for decades and is a major exporter to the U.S. and the rest of Europe. In 1993, Romanian farmers planted 40,000 acres of hemp.

In 1994, the Hempstead was the first American company to grow hemp. The site was the old Timpkin ranch, where Schlichten created the original decorticator. They only grew half an acre. The United States Dept. of Agriculture's Desert Research Facility co-ordinated the project, and DEA agents regularly checked the fields. The crop went off without a hitch with the hemp sold to interested entrepreneurs before it was ever grown. More hemp was going to be grown in 1995. However, because some states have passed laws allowing the medical use of cannabis, a back-lash towards these people and hemp farmers has slowed down any potential growth in the hemp field. Though people such as actor Woody Harrelson have been challenging the laws that forbid hemp from being grown, the U.S. federal government continues to resist any introduction of hemp into the marketplace.

There have even been serious problems getting some hemp products into the U.S. In particular, in 2001 the DEA decided foods with even a trace of THC were illegal, seizing a bunch of Canadian hemp seed products at the border. In response the Hemp Industries Association filed a suit and the rule was stayed by the United States Court of Appeals for the Ninth Circuit in a unanimous decision. It was in the fall of 2004 that hemp food products were finally allowed back across the U.S. border.

Many people in the U.S. have tried to convince their government to allow hemp production. However, since the federal government has not been easily swayed from prohibitionist policies, farmers are turning to state governments to open the door. A total of 11 states have passed laws that allow for the cultivation of hemp, though the federal government has not acknowledged any of these as legitimate and the DEA continues to stop any plants from being grown. The U.S. states that have attempted to legalize hemp production include California, North Dakota, Hawaii, Idaho, Minnesota, New Hampshire, New Mexico, Oregon, South Carolina, Vermont, and Wisconsin. While more hemp products are imported into the U.S. every year, there does not seem to be much hope that the current U.S. administration will change their position any time soon.

In Canada, Joe Strobel and Geof Kime grew 10 acres of hemp on Joe's farm in Tillsonberg, Ont. In 1993, The RCMP came by three times to check the THC level. The crop was harvested with an old hay machine and sold to an American company to process since there was no equipment in Canada then. In 1994, seven different farmers obtained 11 licenses, including Joe and Goeff; Gordon Schiefele; and Claude Pinsonneault in Ridgeton, Ont.; Dr. J. Moses in Manitoba; another farmer in Manitoba who was unwilling to release his name due to the prohibition scare; Dr. Slinkard in Saskatchewan; Fiona Briody in Barrhead, Alberta; and one more Albertan farmer frightened of exposure.

In British Columbia in 1996, Brian Taylor tried to get a license in Grand Forks but it was not given to him after he was "lied to, mislead, and set up" by officials from the Ministry of Health. After growing an illegal crop of hemp, spelling the word "HEMP" in big letters with hemp plants in a field on the side of a mountain, Brian was arrested. He then became the mayor of Grand Forks, after the election in Nov. 1996, leading the hemp movement by example. Efforts like this finally lead to changes in law, though the government remains paranoid of THC content.

> As a result of their proven low THC content, Health Canada has approved 27 cultivars or varieties of industrial hemp for the 2006 growing season (1). Cultivated plants usually consist of a single main stalk and a growth of leaves, with the potential to grow to up to 7 metres (21 ft) in height. However, hemp plants usually reach heights between 2 and 4.5 metres (6-15 ft), with a period of seeding to harvest ranging from 70 to 140 days, depending on the purpose, variety, and climatic conditions. One hectare of hemp can yield an average of 800 kg of grain which in turn can be pressed into 200 litres of oil and 600 kg of meal. The same hectare will also produce an average of 6 tonnes of straw which can be transformed into approximately 1.5 tonnes of fibre.
> (Canada's Industrial Hemp Industry)

In 1998, the Canadian Government, via the Ministry of Health, issued hemp licenses across the nation. We owe this change in policy to people who have continually and constantly approached the government with information about hemp, raising the consciousness of the community. There was a drop in production after the crop of 1999 because the U.S. market was cut off by the DEA, and there were few production or distribution networks established in Canada. However, as a result of the border temporarily closing to the U.S., many products have been developed and sold in Canada over the past few years that we might not have otherwise seen. There are currently 27 different strains of hemp available from Health Canada. Approximately 1/3 of the hemp grown in Canada is organic. Now that the border is open the industry is exploding, as we will discuss further in the next chapter.

Since hemp can grow in so many climates and has so many uses, the future of the plant seems secure. As

Left
The uses of hemp

Bottom
Total number of hectares licensed for hemp cultivation from 1998 to 2006 for Canada and selected provinces

Year	*Canada*	*BC*	*AB*	*SK*	*MB*	*ON*	*QC*	*NB*	*NS*
1998	2 400	72	38	263	606	1 164	24	214	19
1999	14 202	225	754	3 093	8 887	1 023	86	4	126
2000	5 487	291	306	1 426	2 906	217	239	0	102
2001	1 316	96	113	392	472	209	30	0	0
2002	1 530.35	200.25	123	449.40	596.70	142	19	0	0
2003	2 732.97	7.20	153.30	672.45	1 467.78	397.18	12.93	4.05	18
2004	3 530.79	18	638.58	1 003.91	1 655.28	182.51	10.46	4.05	18
2005	9 725.20	0	916	3 428.80	5 018.40	251.20	73.80	19	18
2006	20 552	111	2 103	6 154	11 726	346	88	8	18

the environment deteriorates, in part, from the use of chemical pesticides, herbicides, and fertilizers, more farmers and consumers are turning to earth-friendly agricultural practices. Hemp could be an important part of crop rotation for organic farms around the world, if the regulations restricting its cultivation continue to ease. As the benefits of hemp become public knowledge, markets for hemp foods and other products will continue to grow in North America and around the world. Hemp is making a comeback.

Many argue that growing a large volume of hemp to supply most of our needs would be a disastrous plan since it would use a lot of premium farmland. It seems that currently the price of corn is increasing in part because it is being grown for bio-fuel. As the price of oil continues to go up, more land will be devoted to bio-fuels and the prices of other agricultural commodities, like wheat, will also increase due to scarcity and increased production costs. Since we have to grow lots of hemp on prime farmland, we would grow less corn, wheat, and other crops.

There are several reasons why hemp may help solve some of the current problems faced by the agricultural community instead of aggravating an already strained situation. First, since hemp is at least four times more valuable than all other crops, farmers and their communities will finally be earning more money, reviving agricultural life in all areas. The other crops will become more valuable because they will be scarce, something that would also benefit agricultural industries. Second, if we were to stop eating meat there would be more land and resources available to grow hemp and other foods. Third, if farmers gained the capacity to produce their own fuels, then food prices would stabilize while farmers would reduce the environmental impact of their operations. Finally, the local production of hemp products will stimulate the economy of mid-sized cities and towns throughout the world, undermining the control of global food production by multi-national companies, benifiting of small family businesses.

Chapter 3 Industrial Hemp

Methods of Fibre Production

It is estimated that *Cannabis sativa* has over 30,000 uses. When one considers its intangible benefits it is obvious that the trade value of this plant cannot be measured in dollars. Every part of cannabis has considerable potential for human benefit. In the future it is possible that we may be living in a world where almost everything contains cannabis. This will be discussed in the final chapters. This chapter looks at the history of hemp production, the machinery which has been developed to harvest and process hemp, the different products which can be made from hemp, and in what areas we need to further develop industrial procedures so as to efficiently supply the growing demand for hemp products.

This particular area in the resurrection of hemp is one of the fastest growing branches of cannabis today. While some argue that hemp will eventually supply everything from our food and clothes to our building materials and fuels, others argue that there are other sources which are just as environmentally safe, and which may in fact be more appropriate to use. It is undeniably true that hemp has the capacity to provide us with most of our material necessities, as it once did so very long ago. Although such a possibility may seem distant, it will not remain so for very long. This is because for the first time in many years, money is being generated by those in the hemp industry and these funds are being directed towards educating and informing both farmers and consumers as to hemp's true nature. Once this ignorance is overcome, hemp's revival will progress much faster.

The methods used to process hemp determine the quality of the fibre and products made from it. First, the fibres and hurds need to be separated. Hemp was traditionally cut down and let to "ret" in the field before being broken apart by hand. There is a fine line between retting and rotting. If the fibres become too waterlogged, they are no longer useful for textiles, cordage or many other products, although the biomass is still useful for other purposes. Historically, continuous periods of rain have occasionally prevented harvest or otherwise ruined a crop, but adequate equipment should overcome this old problem. After the pectin has dissolved, the stalks are dried out. This process of leaving the stalks in the field to break apart naturally is called dew retting, and the fibres produced by this method are light brown and coarse, perfect for rope, twine and fine paper.

Water retting is a process where bundles of hemp are submerged in clean water laced with calcium and chlorides. These chemicals break down the pectin, a process which takes seven to 10 days. The stalks are then rinsed, washed, sun-dried and stored. The fibre is of finer quality than is made with dew retting, though it is more expensive. Warm water retting is a very similar process, except after soaking for 24 hours, the temperature of the water is heated to varying degrees for two to three days. This gives you a very uniform, clean fibre.

Green retting refers to all processes whereby the fibre and hurds are separated by machinery right after harvest. The decorticator, as invented by George W. Schlichten, is such a machine. This yields an excellent fibre and leaves the hurds in excellent shape too.

Chemical retting refers to all processes in which the stalks are submerged in a heated tank with chemicals designed to break down the pectin. When the hemp has dried, the fibre and hurds are still held together and must be decorticated, scrunched, hacked and combed.

Different retting processes developed over literally thousands of years as more uses for hemp were discovered, new technology invented and demand for high quality products increased. One problem faced by fibre manufacturers in northern countries is the storage of hemp over the winter after the harvest, given the sheer mass of plant material needed to maintain a factory for an entire year. Farmers in countries that do not get cold and wet can leave the dead stock standing in the field for a fairly long time, though they must pay close attention to the crop so it does not break down too much. All by-products containing fibre may be used in the production of paper. Right now this process is more expensive than wood pulp. The cost of producing non-wood paper is artificially high in North America because the equipment for non-wood paper production is obsolete, and governments, until recently, have denied any help to those attempting to set up the proper processing plants.

> Although there are thousands of non-wood paper mills in the world, only a few of them use hemp as a fiber source. At present 23 paper mills use hemp fiber, at an estimated world production volume of 120,000 tons per annum. Most of the mills are located in China and India, and produce moderate quality printing and writing paper. Typically, these mills do not really have a fixed source of fiber, but they simply use whatever can be found in the region. About 10 of the mills are located in the western world (U.S., U.K., France, Spain, eastern Europe, Turkey), and these mills produce so-called specialty papers such as:
> -cigarette paper: even popular American cigarette brands have a 50% hemp cigarette paper and filter. Some countries still have legislation prescribing the use of hemp in cigarette papers because other fibers (like spruce) generate hazardous fumes when incinerated (!).
> -filter paper (for technical and scientific uses)
> -coffee filters, tea bags
> -specialty non wovens
> -insulating paper (for electrical condensators)
> -greaseproof papers
> -security papers
> -various specialty art papers
>
> These papers can generally only be produced from special fibers like hemp, flax, cotton and other non-wood fiber sources. The average hemp pulp and paper mill produces around 5,000 tons per annum. This should be compared to a "normal" pulp mill for wood fiber, which is never smaller than 250,000 tons per annum. The only reason the remaining mills can still produce at this extremely small size is that there is a very special use for the pulp. This partly explains the high price for hemp pulp: about U.S. $2,500 per ton versus about U.S. $400 for a typical bleached wood pulp.
> ("Hemp Pulp and Paper Production")

Making paper is primarily the rearranging of elementary fibres from any source, be it a tree, hemp stalk, an old pair of jeans or even a scoop of algae, into a flat, thin sheet. While wood pulp paper can only be recycled 4 or 5 times, hemp paper, since the fibres are so strong, can be recycled up to 20 times.

Hand-made hemp paper

The steps taken for processing hemp into paper are as follows:

1) Cleaning- the fibres need to be washed clean of all dirt, rocks and other contaminants.

2) Fibreing- separating the fibre from the hurds by either chemical process or mechanically ripping them apart. This is now pulp.

3) Cutting- some long fibres need to be cut to size.

4) Classification- fibres are sorted by length (Centrifugel and gravitational) and size (various seizing processes).

5) Bleaching- if paper or board needs to be bleached, and the whiter the paper the better contrast with the ink, hemp pulp can be bleached with relatively harmless hydrogen peroxide.

6) Refining- the fibre surfaces are roughened so that the fibres adhere better to each other, strengthening the paper.

7) Dilution- the pulp is diluted to lay the fibres in a homogeneous sheet.

8) Formation- the fibre/water is poured through a fine wire mesh that catches the fibres.

9) Drying- sheet is dried by pressing and steam boiling.

10) Sheeting- the formed sheet is cut to size.

This process is basically the same for both manual and mechanical production of paper, dating back thousands of years. Different sizes and lengths of fibres determine the quality of the paper produced. One problem that does not seem likely to go away when hemp hurds are used in wide-scale production of paper is that the fibre must be stored outside for long periods of time without serious harm being done to them. If the bales of hemp are left in dampness it could cause excessive dilution of the caustic liquor or pectin, and the stalks will deteriorate quickly. Hence, this expense must be factored in when one considers the cost of conversion to non-wood sources of pulp. On the other hand, the process of breaking the logs down to fibres small enough to make paper is much more expensive, energy consuming and labour-intensive than it is for hemp. Hemp needs less caustic soda in the fibreizing process.

Every tract of 10,000 acres of hemp, raised year after year in rotation, is equivalent to a sustaining pulp-producing capacity of 40,500 acres of old growth clear-cutting, on average. This is including the fact that the weight of a cubic foot of hurds is about 5.4 lbs as compared to a cubic foot of poplar chips that weigh about 8.93 lbs.

The first jeans made by Levi Strauss were made from hemp. Hemp has been used for various types of cloth, ranging from rough canvas for sailing to fine silk underwear. Some reports suggest hemp fibre is 4 times stronger than cotton. Currently hemp fibre products range from shower curtains and yoga mats to skateboards and shoes.

> You may be wearing more hemp than you know. Designer Ralph Lauren recently revealed that he has been secretly using hemp fiber in his clothing lines since 1984. In a June 1995 article titled "World's Oldest Fabric Is Now Its Newest," the New York Times "outed" Lauren and interviewed Calvin Klein, who said, "I believe that hemp is going to be the fiber of choice in both home furnishings and fashion industries." Hemp linen was featured in duvet covers, decorative pillows, and pillow shams in the fall 1995 C.K. Home Collection. Klein hinted that hemp would soon make an appearance in his clothing lines as well.
> (*The Great Book of Hemp*, p. 7)

Unfortunately, there is no hemp fibre processing facility in North America that can make any type of fabric. Until a hemp clothing factory is built in North America, the largest market in the world will continue to import hemp clothing from China and Eastern Europe.

Adidas shoe made from hemp

Hurds Hit the Market

When the decorticator was created, the paper industry felt threatened along with the companies who obtained contracts to deforest the West Coast. These people effectively threw a blanket over George's decorticator and continued to rape the land of trees, knowing full well that eventually the timber would run out. As the potential for hemp products grew in the early 1900's, so did the economic interests competing against it. With every new discovery, more industries saw hemp as a threat.

> Thousands of tons of hemp hurds are used every year by one large power company for the manufacture of dynamite and TNT. A large paper company, which has been paying more than a million dollars a year in duties on foreign-made cigarette papers, now is manufacturing these papers from American hemp grown in Minnesota. A new factory in Illinois is producing fine bond papers from hemp. The natural materials in hemp make it an economical source of pulp for any grade of paper manufactured, and the high percentage of alpha-cellulose promises an unlimited supply of raw material for the thousands of cellulose products our chemists have developed.
>
> It is generally believed that all linen is produced from flax. Actually, the majority comes from hemp- authorities estimate that more than half of our imported linen fabrics are manufactured from hemp fiber. Another misconception is that burlap is made from hemp. Actually, its source is usually jute[...]
>
> All of these products, now imported, can be produced from home-grown hemp. Fish nets, bow strings, canvas, strong rope, overalls, damask tablecloths, fine linen garments, towels, bed linen, and thousands pf other everyday items can be grown on American farms. Our imports of foreign fabrics and fibers average about $200,000,000 per year; in raw fibers alone we imported over $50,000,000 in the first six months of 1937. All this income can be made available for Americans.
> ("New Billion Dollar Crop")

Except for as paper and fibre board production, hurds are used as barnyard litter and stable bedding, a substitute for sawdust in packing ice and, in rare cases, for fuel. Until the idea of producing paper from hurds came into the picture in 1916, they were considered to be useless by-products. Now there is movement towards the full production of hurd-based paper.

It has been suggested that garbage dumps may be able to supply us with most of the cellulose fibres we need for paper and cardboard production. Combined with as little as a 15% hemp fibre content, recycled fibre could construct a hard, useful paper product. The introduction of recycled fibre/hemp fibre paper would not necessarily curb hurd paper production, because the hurds are much less expensive than the fibres, and an excessive supply of hurds has historically been more of a problem than a resource possibility. As for the actual cost of producing hemp paper on a large scale, it is very hard to predict. As modern equipment and technology continues to develop, we may find processes that will drastically reduce the costs of hemp paper. The economic and environmental cost of wood pulp paper production will likely soar through the roof in the future. Certainly, recycling fibre materials of all sorts will become a priority as time goes on.

> Whatever the precise details of the very beginnings of the hemp building system, without a doubt the first people to successfully develop and promote the idea were France Perrier and Francis Aujames.

Hemp hurds courtesy of Building with Hemp

> Their imagination helped shape the basic ways in which hemp and lime might be incorporated in a variety of building systems and form a new system on its own, with its trade name of Isochanvre. An early example of a 'hemp house' was built near Tours, in France, and the product won many prestigious awards in the late 80s and early 90s.
>
> However, their claims of having patented an almost magic process to treat the hemp in some way, to somehow mineralize the hemp hurds, before they were mixed with lime, were doubted as being necessary. Although their loose fill insulation product using hurds treated with silicates of sodium and potassium was used with some success in a housing estate in Brittany. They were also unable to validate their claims of archeological evidence of bast fibers mixed with lime having been found in the structure of a Merovingian bridge when I contacted them some years ago. They have now ceased trading.
>
> (*Building With Hemp*, p. 34)

Isochanvre, a French company created by France Perrier, developed several patents from which two types of products were created. Isochanvre Isolation (insulation) is poured or blown in roof trussings, floors, partition walls and backing. Isochanvre insulation fibres were mixed with pure cement without additives, to be used for flagstones, walls, floor levelling, insulative coating, insulating for mortar for stone walls, etc.

> In ancient times, people added handfuls of hemp fiber to their clay to strengthen the brick they used for building. A problem still facing much of the world today is the availability of decent, affordable housing. With the shortage of quality wood and the rising price of tree-dependent materials like wood molds used to cast concrete, hemp deserves serious consideration.
>
> Fabricated boards and panels are superior to wood in many ways for construction of homes, offices and other buildings. The simplest way to make hemp into boards is to chop up or grind the stalk into chip, then bond it together using natural resins or glues and clamp it into molds under high pressure. To make it even stronger, just add heat. Compressed agricultural fiberboard (CAF) was invented in Sweden in 1935, using a combination of high pressure and temperature. Hundreds of millions of square feet have been installed in Europe, the United Kingdom, Canada and Australia. A new generation of hemp construction boards will soon be available in Oregon.
>
> (*Hemp: Lifeline to the Future*, p. 96)

This could work for any biomass material—hemp and lime work well together—for a variety of reasons. Hemp building products are usually 100% environmentally friendly. No toxic gases are released during its growth or production, no noise pollution or polluted water are exhibited in its manufacturing process, and to top it all off it is entirely recyclable. So, if the fibres are no longer good for paper or fibreboard production, they can be used to build homes. Homes made with hemp should be more flexible than those made with concrete or brick, and should be better at withstanding earthquakes, tornadoes, and hurricanes.

To mix hempcrete for casting in any of the positions it might be used, a particular blend of limes and binders needs to be mixed with the hemp. The exact mixture of materials will depend to a certain extent on the climate where they are to be used and method of application. In dry climates and if the hempcrete is to be applied by hand between shuttering boards, then fast acting binders such as cement or fast acting hydraulic limes should be avoided as large amounts of hempcrete will not be able to be mixed in advance. In damp, cool climates the quality of water should be reduced so as to speed up the drying time…

> To mix hemp with lime based binder in order to use it as a plaster it is preferable, if applying the substance by hand, to use a hemp chip that has been sieved so that only the smaller particles (ie. 1-5 mm in length) remain. … When using hemp plaster in hot dry climates, ground limestone can be added to the mixture to retain moisture for longer.

Anyone seriously interested in building with hemp should buy the book *Building With Hemp* by Steve Allin. Full of pictures and illustrations, this book provides a step-by-step guide to refurnishing old buildings and creating new structures using simple, environmentally friendly products. You can build an entire house, except for the electrical wiring and windows, using hemp. Over 150 homes made out of hemp are standing in France. Because of its very high thermal inertia hemp is an excellent insulator and keeps rooms cool in the summer and significantly reduces the heating costs in the winter. A conventional wall of 20 cm, plus a screen wall, insulation barrier, vapour barrier, and plaster, is equivalent in strength and effectiveness as a 20cm wall of hempcrete. The two-step process of installing a hempcrete wall, and thinly coating it with a natural lime to allow the wall to breath, is much faster and inexpensive than standard wood/concrete construction. One cultivated hectare of hemp, six to eight tons, or 60 cubic meters of hempcrete, is enough to build an

Hemp insulation courtesy of Building with Hemp

Type of Mix	*Ingredients*	*Measurement*
Lime/Binder Mix	Hydrated Lime	7 parts
	Hydraulic Lime	1.5 parts
	Cement	1.5 parts
Lightweight Mix	Hemp	10 parts
	Lime Mixture	1 parts
	Water	3 parts
Wall Mixture	Hemp	10 parts
	Lime Mixture	2.5 parts
	Water	4 parts
Floor Mixture	48.5	10 parts
	Lime Mixture	3 parts
	Water	4 parts
Hemp Plaster	Hydrated Lime	8.5 parts
	Lime/Binder Mix	1.5 parts
Plaster Mix (manual)	Hemp	10 parts
	Lime Mixture	9 parts
	Water	5-6 parts
Plaster Mix (sprayed)	Hemp	10 parts
	Lime Mixture	7 parts
	Ground Limestone	2 parts
	Sand	2 parts
	Water	5 parts

Rotary drum mixture: All quantities of materials are given in parts per volume courtesy of Building with Hemp

entire hemp house of 135 square meters. All of these factors combined give a strong indication that hemp will eventually supply most of the biomass we need to build our homes, schools, and workplaces.

The Suffolk Housing Society in Britain is conducting an experiment where they have built two houses using hemp for all possible component parts, except for the timber, and two identical houses using traditional building materials. They are trying to determine if there is a difference in heating costs, comfort, and durability. The first results published in 2003 indicate that the hemp houses provide better insulation in the winter, and keep the house cool in the summer.

Top and Bottom: Hempcrete interiors courtesy of Building with Hemp

> If the hemp homes fare better than the traditional building method it could have a significant impact on the future of the building industry.
>
> The society has developed links with a French housing association, Hennebont OPC, which has also embarked on a hemp building project. The project was prompted by the enthusiasm for hemp construction by local architect Ralph Carpenter who persuaded St Edmundsbury Borough Council and Suffolk Housing to undertake the project which is also being supported by the Housing Corporation. It has already received attention from the Hawaiian state congress, who sent its assistant floor leader to Suffolk on a fact finding visit.
>
> The project is being funded by the society and with grants from the Housing Corporation and St Edmundsbury Council.
>
> (http://www.suffolkhousing.org/pages/hempage.html)

Other companies have developed plywood by pressing hemp fibres together and adding glue. A similar process could make 2x4s, 4x4s, and other dimensional sizes. As the world's natural resources become scarce, using agricultural crops to make building materials will be the most economical and environmentally friendly option.

Another important use of hemp hurd that provides a multitude of potential purposes is plastics. This will be critical as fossil fuels become scarce.

> Hemp can be used to manufacture a variety of plastic products. The hurds (short core fibers) may be processed into cellophane packing material, which was common until the 1930's, or they may be manufactured into a low-cost, compostable replacement for Styrofoam.
>
> Henry Ford used hemp-and-sisal cellulose plastic to build car doors and fenders. Several German firms are now developing 100% hemp cellulose plastic composites for the manufacture of snowboards and skateboards. An Austrian firm, Zellform, has created a hemp-plastic resin called Hempstone for use in musical instruments, loudspeakers, and furniture. Plant-based plastics made from hemp can

> be completely biodegradable, and have the potential to reduce oil consumption and the processing of petrochemicals. Hemp plastic packaging (for use inside cereal boxes, for example) and hemp-foam disposable plates and cups could be composted at home, lowering the high cost of landfilling or recycling petroleum-based plastics.
> (*Hemp Horizons*, p.120)

Though the cost is still prohibitive, the possibility of living in a house built from and furnished in hemp is very real today. Most of the packaging used today could be made, at least in part, from hemp. Indeed, there are very few household products that could not be made with hemp. Now we will turn our attention to providing energy from hemp to sustain our activities.

Fuels of the Future

There are real possibilities that in the future, biomass could produce a great deal of the energy that we need. Several biomass conversion techniques are being developed which produce liquid petroleum fuels and petroleum-based products such as plastics, cellophane, polyvinyl chloride (PVC), etc. These are the methods being developed now:

1) Ethanol can be produced from food crops with high sugar or starch content. This fuel is compatible with spark plug-type internal combustion engines, but cannot be used in diesel engines. This well established technology is already operating on a commercial scale. The most efficient crops to produce this type of ethanol using this method are sugarcane, sugar beets, maize, cassava, pineapple, sweet sorghum, and potatoes.

2) Ethanol is produced by fermenting and distilling lignocellulose material from trees, grasses, and agricultural crops. This process involves the hydrolysis of cellulose into fermentable sugars and then into ethanol, in a very similar method to the previous one. However, not only can grasses, shrubs, fast growing trees and some hardwood trees supply biomass, but fast growing water plants such as water hyacinth, sea kelp, and even alga can do so at a much faster rate than most agricultural plants could ever attain.

3) Methanol, wood alcohol, is produced from wood, crops, and grasses. Currently, methanol is commercially synthesized from natural gas. When accomplished directly, the lignocellulosic material is converted into a synthetic gas in a high temperature thermochemical process, then the gas is cleaned to the proper hydrogen ratio, liquefied, and catalytically converted into methanol. Both methanol and ethanol burn at a lower temperature, and are less volatile than gasoline, reducing the risk of explosions and fires.

4) Bio-fuel is a fuel very similar to diesel fuel that can be obtained from vegetable crops by pressing their seeds and refining the oil. The waste product is excellent livestock food. The possible crops include oil palm, coconuts, soybeans, corn, sunflowers, cotton, rape (a plant of the cabbage family), groundnuts, and of course hemp. This fuel is almost interchangeable as a food oil.

5) Pyrolysis, or fractional distillation, is the process used by petrochemical companies to convert ancient fossilized biomass into fossil fuels. Georgia Tech and Tech-Air developed the technology in 1972 to create charcoal, oil, and combustible gas from forestry waste. The system can vary the distribution of energy among the products by controlling the operating conditions, the air-to-feed ratio, the size of the reactor, etc. This method produced approximately 100 gallons of methanol per oven dried ton of biomass. This process is the most effective form of biomass conversion, as the other methods are criticized for not having the potential of supplying our present, phenomenally huge, consumption of energy.

The "U.S. National Fuel Commission's 1980 Final Report" concluded that the process of converting biomass into energy, as compared to the use of coal for electrical production, was more feasible for a number of reasons. Biomass is renewable and available locally; it is easier to burn and turn into gas; it is at least 10 times lower in sulfur content, so no abatement procedures are necessary for sulfur or nitrogen; and biomass waste can be used as a fertilizer, whereas coal ash has no value. Coal conversion mobilizes trace metals and coal tars are very highly carcinogenic, coal mining is destructive, and coal production increases CO2 in the atmosphere. The cost of transportation for biomass is much less than that for coal. Also, the actual conversion process of turning biomass into energy is easier and faster than coal.

Hempcar has traveled USA on hemp seed

> The efficiency with which certain plants are able to capture light energy and use it to assimilate carbon dioxide into carbohydrates is the most important factor in selecting plants with the greatest biomass production potential. Many tropical grasses such as sugarcane, sorghum, and maize (corn) have a pathway for photosynthesis commonly known as C4 photosynthesis which is more efficient than the pathway common to most other plants, especially dicots like hemp. As Alexander (1985) states in his book The Energy Cane Alternative, "together with certain of its tropical grasses relatives, sugarcane is the finest living collector of sunlight known to man." Given that these plant species share with hemp the potential for multiple product use and that some of these are widely adapted, especially sorghum, many believe that biomass production will rely heavily upon plant species which utilize the C4 photosynthetic carbon fixation.
>
> *("Can Hemp Save Our Planet?")*

Pyrolitic conversion could supply the United States with 75 Quadrillion BTU (75 Quads) of energy, roughly their annual consumption, by simply converting six percent of continental U.S. acreage. If concentration is placed upon growing high yielding biomass crops, then 5 billion dry tons of biomass could produce 75 Quads, each dry ton making about 15 million BTU. It is obvious to many that much more research is needed into all these technologies so that we may discover which methods work best with which crops in particular areas of the world. One thing is certain, however. One day fossil fuel will run out. Period. Whether or not hemp is the best source for producing biomass for energy is a question that is still up for debate.

Here is the auto Henry Ford "grew from the soil." Its plastic panels, with impact strength 10 times greater than steel, were made from flax, wheat, hemp, spruce pulp

Top: Cars made with hemp fiberglass bodies
Bottom: Car from 1941 with plastic panels

No one can question the fact that hemp is one of the fastest biomass producers available to farmers around the world. For example, hemp has eight times the methanol potential of corn. As opposed to coal and oil, which contribute greatly to acid rain, biomass fuels burn clean, producing no ash or sulphur during combustion. Growing and burning biomass fuels contributes less carbon dioxide and water vapours than fossil fuels, and therefore contribute less to climate change.

Many food processes produce a waste product, such as nut shells or tomato vines that could be used for fuel. Many weeds and shrubs which are cut down beside highways could be collected for biomass. Water hyacinth is a noxious weed that can yield up to 16 tons/acre and is harvested to prevent clogging in lakes and waterways. Farm animal and human waste can produce methanol. Yard waste has a high cellulose content and makes for excellent biomass. Algae and other water plants may also be better energy producers than hemp. Other sources of energy, such as solar or wind power and possibly the use of water as biomass, must also be further looked into as we approach the inevitable shortage of fossil fuels. When hemp is grown en mass, it is likely to be used for purposes other than energy, even though it is possible. Since sugarcane and other plants that produce more biomass than hemp are grown in tropical or sub-tropical climates, it may only be in the northern hemisphere that hemp is a good option for fuel.

When Diesel died in 1913, there was much public debate about which sources of energy should be used in the development of corporate America. Before alcohol was prohibited in 1919, many farmers were learning to make their own fuels from various biomass sources by using simple distillation processes. When the prohibition of alcohol was repealed, the restrictions placed upon making biofuel on the farm made it cheaper and easier to continue using fossil fuels.

> "Here in America there's [...] a revolution in materials that will affect every home," reported Popular Mechanics in 1941, citing Henry Ford's

prediction that he would some day "grow automobiles from the soil." After 12 years of research, Ford Motor Company had completed an experimental car with a plastic body. Its tough panels were moulded from a mixture of 70% cellulose fibers from hemp, wheat straw and sisal, plus 30% resin binder, under hydraulic pressure of 1500 pounds per square inch. The plastic withstood blows 10 times as great as steel could without denting. While the streamlined car looked like its steel counterpart, its design took advantage of the properties of plastics. The total weight of his vehicle was about two-thirds that of a regular car. This meant better gas mileage. Ford also planned to fuel his fleet of vehicles with plant power, but was thwarted first by alcohol prohibition, then by hemp prohibition, and forced to use petroleum.

(*Hemp: Lifeline to the Future*, p. 99)

There are many possible sources of seed oil other than hemp. A Russian variety of hemp, Olerifera, reportedly contains 40% oil, while 30% is the most quoted figure. The high protein cake which makes up the remaining weight is an excellent raw food source. A good seed crop can yield up to 1200 lbs /acre and the potential for larger yields is very good. In comparison, flax seeds contain 36% oil, and sunflower seeds about 40-50% oil. A soybean crop yields 2400 lbs/acre, groundnut 1160 lbs/acre, rapeseed 900 lbs/acre, and sesame 715 lbs/acre. The oil extracted from all of these seeds can be used as a liquid fuel for diesel engines, precision motor oil and aircraft motors, as well as the human body. This process is 100% environmentally friendly, right from the harvesting and production, to the waste products from production and burning, to the conversion of the biomass into energy. Since hemp oil and most other seed-based oils, burn at a lower temperature than fossil fuels, it is much easier on the engine, carburetor, and exhaust systems.

Hemp oil has many other uses in addition to being a fuel. Soothing rubs can be made from the oil, and even from the roots, too. Hemp oil is very effective at protecting the skin from sunburns, relieving the pain of a burn and preventing peeling. Another traditional use of hemp seeds is for house paints, stains, and inks. Several representatives from different hemp industries made a presentation to the House of Representatives to protest the new law and try to ensure that hemp was not to be included in the prohibition of marijuana. Representing the Department of the Treasury in defence of the 1937 Marijuana Tax Act, Clinton Hester acknowledged many of the businesses that used hemp products.

They raise the seeds for use in the manufacture of birdseed. They make oil out of it. Most of the seed, however, that is used in the manufacture of oil is imported from Manchuria, but it may develop in this country.

Then after the seed is used for making of oil, they take that seed and crush it, and make meal and meal cake, and that is sold to cattle raisers.

The oil is used in the manufacture of varnish and paint and soap and linoleum, and then in the case of the mature stalk they use that for making fiber and fiber products. Of course, they are entirely outside the bill.

(Clinton Hester Testifying To The Committee On Ways And Means, House Of Representatives, 75Th Congress, 1937)

Most of today's paints and varnishes are made from a flax (linseed) oil which only forms a thin layer over the wood, encouraging rot and easily peeling off over time. If hemp oil is boiled before being used, the drying time decreases. Hemp was the original base for printing inks, but it has been replaced by flax because it dries faster. The new, non-toxic soy-based inks that are appearing on the market are not as good as hemp ink, and are harder to process because hemp contains 57% LA and 19% LNA as compared to soy oil at 50% LA and 9% LNA.

We will discuss the specific nutritional details concerning hemp seeds in the next chapter on medical cannabis, but we should mention here that hemp seeds have been used as a food source for millennium. Many cultures continue to use hemp seeds in their traditional and daily recipes.

Hempcrete blocks, hemp seed stain, hemp insulation and hemp fiber board

Hemp-Based Economies

It is really quite impossible to correctly determine the exact economic effect the mass production of hemp would create. Countries that develop hemp farming and production facilities will be able to take advantage of increasing consumer concern about the environmental and social impacts of the products and services they are purchasing. Though the initial cost of developing these industries is substantial, the potential long-term revenue opportunities are great once an economy of scale has been reached. That is, when larger production facilities are built, and efficient and inexpensive harvesting equipment is available, the cost of hemp products will be less than the cost of similar products available on the marketplace.

> If we used more farmed products and fewer synthetics, we would go back to a more sustainable life. There would be more farmers and more industry to use the farm products. There would be fewer toxics and un-recyclable wastes. This is exactly the story that the hemp people talk about.
>
> Hemp is a healthy crop which helps the soil, smothers weeds and needs no insecticides. It could make the difference between the survival of the family farm and its extinction. It is much more valuable per acre than corn or other grains and has many markets because it can be used as a wood substitute and for food, feed for animals, clothing and industrial raw material.
>
> Farmers all over the world are taking advantage of the surging market. Yet here in North America, where hemp has thrived since colonial times, farmers are not allowed to grow it. In effect, the government is subsidizing farmers all over the world while penalizing American farmers.
>
> (Introduction, *Hemp Today*, 1994, p. xi, xii)

Willie Nelson

We must also consider the fact that many companies and entire industries will collapse and possibly disappear forever when communities have the ability, technology, and raw materials to supply most of their necessities locally with hemp. The loss of certain industries will be offset by the introduction of new products, the revival of agricultural communities, improved health in the population, and savings incurred from more efficient uses of energy. There is more than enough evidence to show that if we reconsider our spending habits, we can drastically cut our rates of consumption and waste without hurting our lifestyles or economy and healing the planet. A non-violent, organic, holistic, open-minded, and friendly atmosphere often surrounds people who smoke cannabis and/or purchase eco-friendly products. This attitude is slowly but surely growing, behind the scenes and in the hemp stores, as well as coffeshops, farms, and street corners around the world.

> The economic benefits of hemp agriculture have become obvious to many politicians, especially those with large farming constituencies. Farmers across the continent have been mauled by low commodity prices, which, in real terms, are the lowest they've been in modern history. At the same time, they've had to pay more for fertilizers, pesticides, and seeds. Farmers also have to compete with colleagues who have succumbed to the pressure to use genetically modified seeds to try to raise yields and break even.
>
> Many American farmers are ready to grow hemp, once the government relents. They've joined organizations like Hemp Industries Association (HIA), a farmers and hemp-manufacturers group started in 1992, which lobbies for fair and equal treatment of industrial hemp and pushes for a level playing field to compete with other natural resources and synthetics.
>
> (*Hemp Culture*, p. 66)

Many industries will be born in this agricultural, economic, and environmental revolution. Small businesses that produce locally grown hemp products sold in neighbourhood stores will begin to appear and expand all over the globe. No one can accurately predict the effects that the on-coming technological evolution will have upon the human race, but there is no doubt that we must become a more compassionate and thoughtful community if we truly wish to help the planet out of its current environmental downward spiral, using the newest available technology to the best of our ability. We need to embrace hemp to build a foundation upon this transformation of our collective production, consumption, and waste, before our planet falls into ruin.

Chapter 4 Healing Nature

Cannabis and Our Diet

There are many different organisms that have developed efficient biological functions to accomplish specific healing or nutritional purposes. Plants, fungi, animals, and simple life forms have developed the capacity to internally generate complex chemicals using water, air, sunlight, food, nutrients from the soil, and other sources of materials. Some chemical structures are created by host life forms for the benefit of other life forms. The interdependent, interconnected natural structure of life is a delicate, evolving, complex pattern. All conscious life observes Mother Nature for secrets that reveal food, medicine, and shelter. Passing new knowledge or advantageous genetic mutations on to future generations is critical for specie survival and evolution. Humans have a great capacity to learn, share, or keep secrets.

> For much of history the herbal lore of women has been secret. As pointed out in John Riddle's book, *Eve's Herbs*, (Riddle, 1997), botanical agents for control of reproduction have been known for millennia, but have often been forgotten over time or lost utterly, as in the case of the Greek contraceptive, sylphion. The same is true for other agents instrumental in women's health, frequently lost due to religious constraints. One botanical agent that exemplifies this lost knowledge is cannabis. As will be discussed, its role as an herbal remedy in obstetric and gynaecological conditions is ancient, but will surprise most with its breadth and prevalence. Cannabis appears in this role across many cultures, Old World and New, classical and modern, among young and old, in a sort of herbal vanishing act.
>
> (*Cannabis Treatments in Obstetrics and Gynecology*, p. 6)

Cannabis has evolved along with humankind for millions of years. This was confirmed with the discovery of receptors in the brain that are perfectly designed to accept cannabinoids. This was followed by the discovery of endo-cannabinoids, which are naturally produced chemicals that help regulate most of the body's systems. Cannabis has the capacity to produce nutritious food, clothing, paper, fuel, building materials, and plastics. Cannabis can reduce stress, relieve symptoms of medical problems and strengthen the immune system, while also inducing mystical experiences and heightened states of awareness. It is no wonder that the history of humankind is so wrapped up in tales involving cannabis, and no wonder why hemp and marijuana are so important to the future of our species.

One of the most ironic circumstances surrounding prohibition right now is the dominant attitude among North Americans that marijuana is physically harmful, mentally disturbing, and socially disruptive. In reality, marijuana has more medical applications than any other plant or substance known to humanity. The ingestion of cannabis has been proven over and over again, in scientific tests and at home, to help most people with mental problems feel better when in the proper set and setting. The social climate that surrounds the cannabis culture is peaceful, loving, and creative. Most negative side effects from smoking the herb are a result of prohibition. Contrary to what the prohibitionists have stated, cannabis may be the safest and most reliable medical and recreational drug known to humankind.

The complex chemical relationship between cannabis and the human body leaves little doubt that our ancestors were eating cannabis seed and leaf long before written history. Hemp seeds provide the best combination of proteins, essential fatty acids, and essential amino acids of any known food source. While this by itself does not confirm a long relationship with cannabis, the existence of the body's endo-cannabinoid system does strongly point to the possibility that cannabis has been very important in the development of our species. Before we discuss endo-cannabinoids, though, a general discussion of the plant's chemical make-up is useful.

Future vision of a cannabis dispensary illustrated by Sean Newton

Cannabis was originally assigned to the Urticaceae (nettle) family. However, more recent botanical findings indicate that it belongs to the Cannabaceae (hemp-like) family (Cannabinaceae, also: Cannabiaceae, and Cannabidaceae), a subdivision of the Moraceae (mulberry) family. Cannabis's closest relative is hops, Humulus lupulus L., which also belongs to the Cannabaceae family. No other relatives have been described to date (Schultes et al. 1975*).

The chemical compostion of the resin is now very well understood. The pure resin, known as hasish, contains four primary components: the cannabinoid <> tetrahdrocannabinol (THC) with three variants. Two of these variants, cannabinoil (CBD) and cannabinol (CBN), result as an artifact only when the resin is stored. These substances are responsible for the psychoactive effects (Murphy and Bartke 1992). The structures of some sixty additional cannabinoids with mild or no psychoactive effects have also been determined (Brenneisen 1996; Clarke 1981*; Hollister 1986*; Mechoulam 1970*; Schmidt 1992*). The resin also contains a number of essential oils (caryophyllene, humulene, farnesene, selinene, phellandrene, limonene), various sugars, flavonoids, alkaloids (choline, trigonelline, piperidine, betaine, praline, neurone, hordenine, cannabisativine), and chlorophyll, none of which are involved in the psychoactive effects of the drugs (Binder 1981*: Brenneisen 1996; Hai 1981, 13*).

Cannabis pollen has been shown to contain <>THC as well as THCA, an alkaloid-like substance, flavone, and phenolic substances (Paris et al. 1975).

The leaves of *Cannabis sativa* contain choline, trigonelline, muscarine, an unidentified betaine, the cannabamines A-D and, surprisingly, the phenethylamine hordenine, an alkaloid found in many cacti (El-Feraly and Turner 1975), In additional, water soluable glycoprotiens, serine-O-galactoside, and hydroxyproline have bee found in the leaves from Thai and African populations (Hillestad and Wolod 1977; Hillestad et al. 1997).

The roots of *Cannabis sativa* have yielded friedelin, epifriedelinol, N-(p-hydroxyl-B-phenethyl)-p-hydroxy-trans-cimmamamide, choline, and neurone as well as the steroids stigmast-5-en-3B-ol-7-on (or 7-keto-B-sitoserol), campest-5-en-3B-ol-7-on, and stigmast-5, 22-dien-3B-ol-7-on (Slatkin et al. 1975).

The characteristically scented essential oil, which lends, so to speak, hemp its bouquet, contains among other things eugenol, guaiacol, sesquiterpene, caryophyllene, humulene, farnesene, selinene, phellandrene, and limonene.

The essential oil also contains caryophyllene oxide, a sesquiterpene. This odoriferous substance has been used to train police dogs to detect drugs (Martin et al. 1961; Nigam et al. 1965). Caryophyllene oxide is also present in the essential oils of other plants, such as mugwort (Artemisia vulgaris L.) and spice clove (Syzgium aromaticum [L.] MERR. Et PERRY). Hemp's essential oil is usually free of or contains only trace amounts of THC.

(*Marijuana Medicine*, p. 4)

There are about 420 different compounds in cannabis, with 60 to 70 of the chemical molecules generating a psychoactive or psychotropic effect to one degree or another. The main psychoactive ingredient in cannabis is delta-9-tetrahydrocannabinol, or THC, which is the chemical tested for when attempting to calculate the potency of the plant. The THC content for most marijuana is between 6-27%, with some reports claiming as much as 35% THC. Psychoactive and/or pharmacologically active chemicals contained in cannabis include cannabavarin (THCU), cannabitriol (CBT), cannabinol (CBN), cannabicycol (CBL), delta-8-THC, cannabidiol (CBD), cannabichromene (CBC), and cannabigerol (CBG).

Of the almost 70 cannabinoids present in cannabis, tetrahydrocannabinol, or THC, is by far the most studied as it is responsible for most of the euphoric effects from consuming the plant. THC forms in beautiful crystals called trichomes on the leaves and buds, forming a shape that looks like a glass mushroom. THC is formed as cannabinoids add molecules and grow into more complex chemicals. There are many different chemical pathways to the formation of THC. As seen in this diagram, Cannabigerol (CBG) is the first component of one possible pathway. It undergoes chemical change to form either cannabichromene (CBC), or cannabidiol (CBD). Delta 9-tetrahydrocannabinol (THC) is then derived from CBD. Another cannabinoid, cannabinol (CBN), is formed from THC when it loses a molecule. In hemp plants there is a high concentration of CBD and CBC but little THC, making it good for many medical problems but not psychoactive.

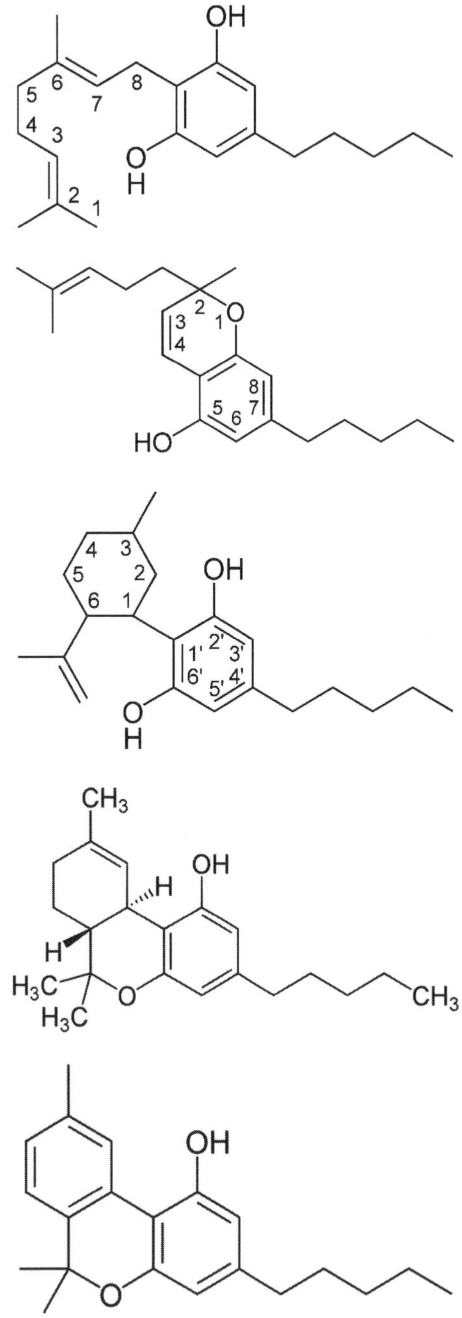

From top to bottom: CBG, CBC, CBD, THC, CBN

In the fall of 1988, a group of St. Louis University Medical School researchers announced their discovery of a receptor site on the membrane of mouse nerve cells. THC, considered the most powerful compound in cannabis resin, was found to attach to the brain at these points. Two years after this cannabinoid-specific protein receptor was reported, a group at the National Institute of Mental Health pinpointed the DNA that encodes the same receptor in rats. It is now known that people have the receptor, too. In the human brain, these cannabinoid-receptors are clustered in several areas. The cerebral cortex, the primary area, is also the home of higher thinking, perception, emotions, and cognition. Other clusters appear in the hippocampus, the section of the brain associated with memory; the cerebellum and striatum, which are associated with movement; and the basal ganglia, an area involved in movement control and coordination.

This produces the psychoactive effect of cannabis, as well as its amazing broad effect on neuralgic and musculoskeletal functions throughout the body. Research at the National Institute of Mental Health suggests that the arrangement of these receptor sites indicates that THC analogs and antagonists might eventually serve to ease symptoms of movement disorders like the tremors of Parkinson's disease and Huntington's chorea. Cannabinoids could also possibly affect the transfer of data between the three memory centers: immediate, short-term and long-term. The limbic system of the brain surrounds the upper stem and includes the hippocampus. Long-term memory is thought to reside in the mid-brain and cerebral cortex, Short-term memory is associated with the upper brain stem. Immediate memory is a function of the cortex. The possibility of using cannabis to treat memory disorders like Alzheimer's has yet to be adequately explored.

Once the human brain's receptors were identified, researchers extrapolated that there must be a natural, internal chemical that connected to the cannabinoid-receptor and sent biochemical signals cascading through the nerve cell to produce its effect.

In 1992 William Devane and Raphael Mechoulam of Hebrew University identified the natural brain molecule that binds to the cannabinoid receptor. Mechoulam, famous for his discovery of delta-9-THC in the 1960s, pursued a strategy of investigating other chemicals that, like THC, are fat soluble. By separating these substances from those that are water soluble, his group extracted from pig brain an oily, hairpin-shaped chemical substance that attached to the cannabinoid receptor. They called it anandamine, from the Sanskrit word ananda, for "eternal bliss." A small sample was sent to Roger Pertwee, a pharmacologist at Aberdeen University, who had devised a sensitive test for cannabinoids that monitored a substance's ability to stop muscle-twitching in mouse tissue, when dropped on certain nerves. Pertwee ran his tests on Mechoulam's experimental substance. "We didn't know what it was- just that it was a greasy substance." But the anandamine depressed the twitch just like THC, and that December the results were published in the journal SCIENCE. The results of the follow-up studies showed that anandamine acted like a very precise key that would lock only onto cells containing the receptor. Once anandamine attached to the cells, it triggered biochemical changes similar to those of THC and related chemicals. Not only did the substance fit the same lock as THC. It also seemed to open similar neurological doors.

(*Hemp For Health*, p.65)

The interaction of these cannabinoids and the body generates a broad range of medical impacts that cannot be duplicated easily by synthetic drugs which usually only contain one or two different chemicals, not six to 12. Each plant only contains six to 12 different cannabinoids, some in very small amounts, which is why each strain has a different mental and physical effect. Even on the same plant there will be different amounts of these cannabinoids in different places. For example, there is less THC in the larger fan leaves than there is in the buds. The other chemicals, especially the essential oils and flavonoids, help the body absorb and use the cannabinoids, as well as possibly having their own medical benefits. These are some of the factors that make cannabis almost impossible to accurately synthesize. Only a handful of the 70 cannabinoids have been studied, leaving much to discover.

The neurotransmitter receptor sites that the body creates for endo-cannabinoids are not finished forming until around the age of 16. There is some evidence that using cannabis before these receptors are fully developed could inhibit learning functions and possibly cause other mental health symptoms.

> *Cannabis sativa* L. produces more than 60 terpeno-phenols that have not been detected in any other plant. One of these constituents, 9-tetrahydrocannabinol (THC) has been the object of thousands of publications, as it is by far the major psychoactive principle in marijuana and hashish. Cannabidiol (CBD), a nonpsychoactive component, has also been widely investigated due to its anti-inflammatory, antischizophrenic and antiepileptic properties. Surprisingly, the other plant cannabinoids have been mostly neglected. Cannabinoid acids, which are precursors of the neutral cannabinoids, such as THC and CBD, were shown to be antibiotic and were actually used for some time in veterinary medicine in Czechoslovakia about 50 years ago. Most of the other plant cannabinoids were assayed for possible psychoactivity. When none was found, interest in them waned.
>
> The discovery of the endocannabinoid system and the plethora of activities of the endocannabinoids raise the possibility that some of the plant cannabinoids may cause related effects. The best-known endocannabinoids, anandamide and 2-arachidonoyl glycerol, have been found to play a role not only in the central nervous system but also in most physiological systems that have been investigated—the immune, the cardiovascular, the reproductive, the respiratory, the skeletal systems, to name a few. Some of the activities are CB1/CB2 cannabinoid receptor-dependent, but many are not. Numerous additional receptors have been proposed. Is it possible that some of the plant cannabinoids, which are not psychoactive (and presumably do not bind to the CB1 receptor), are also active in these systems?
>
> *("Plant Cannabinoids: A Neglected Pharmacological Treasure Trove")*

Studies show that THC has mild anti-biotic, anti-inflammatory, anti-spasmodic, anti-carcinogenic, antiseptic, anti-fungal, anti-oxidant, euphoric, stimulant, muscle-relaxing, anti-epileptic, anti-emetic, appetite stimulating, bronchodilating, anti-depressant, hypotensive, and analgesic effects. Cannabidiol (CBD) has sedative, muscle-relaxing and analgesic effects. Cannabichromene (CBC) promotes the analgesic effects of THC and is sedative. Cannabigerol (CBG) is sedative and has anti-microbial properties, as well as lowering intraocular pressure—something critical to glaucoma patients. Cannabinol (CBN) is mildly psychoactive, lowers intraocular pressure and is anti-epileptic. Cannabis also contains terpenes and flavonoids that also have physical impacts that have not been extensively studied.

> This article examines harm reduction from a novel perspective. Its central thesis is that harm reduction is not only a social concept, but also a biological one. More specifically, evolution does not make moral distinctions in the selection process, but utilizes a cannabis-based approach to harm reduction in order to promote survival of the fittest. Evidence will be provided from peer-reviewed scientific literature that supports the hypothesis that humans, and all animals, make and use internally produced cannabis-like products (endocannabinoids) as part of the evolutionary harm reduction program. More specifically, endocannabinoids homeostatically regulate all body systems (cardiovascular, digestive, endocrine, excretory, immune, nervous, musculo-skeletal, reproductive). Therefore, the health of each individual is dependant on this system working appropriately...
>
> Evolution has selected the endocannabinoids to homeostatically regulate numerous biological phenomena that can be found in every organized system in the body, and to counteract biochemical imbalances that are characteristic of numerous damaged or diseased states, in particular those associated with aging. Starting from birth, cannabinoids are present in mother's milk, where they initiate the eating process. If the activity of endocannabinoids in the mouse milk is inhibited with a cannabinoid antagonist, the newborn mice die of starvation. As life proceeds, endocannabinoids continuously regulate appetite, body temperature, reproductive activity, and learning capacity. When a body is physically damaged, the endocannabinoids are called on to reduce inflammation, protect neurons, regulate cardiac rhythms and protect the heart from oxygen deprivation. In humans suffering from colorectal cancer, endocannabinoid levels are elevated in an effort to control the cancer. They help relieve emotional suffering by reducing pain and facilitating movement beyond the fears of unpleasant memories.
>
> *("Harm Reduction: The Cannabis Paradox")*

The relief of pain, relaxing of the stomach muscles, and stimulation of appetite are very important benefits for people suffering from cancer, AIDS, Hepatitis C, or from side-effects from prescription drugs. Cannabis also helps those suffering from arthritis, spinal cord injuries, head injuries, migraines, chronic pain in joints or from serious injuries, fibromyalgia, Alzheimer's disease, Parkinson's disease, insomnia, ulcers, diabetes, Crone's disease, Irritable Bowel Syndrome (IBS), Amyotrophic Lateral Sclerosis (ALS or Lou Gehrig's Disease), Multiple Sclerosis, epilepsy, glaucoma, anckolysis spondylitis, lupus, dystonia, tendonitis, pruritis, asthma, drug/alcohol addiction, and many mental health issues. Women have historically used cannabis for the treatment of menstrual irregularity, menorrhagia, dysmenorrhea, threatened abortion, Hyperemesis gravidarum, childbirth, postpartum hemorrhage, toxemia, seizures, dysuria, urinary frequency, urinary retention, gonorrhoea, menopausal symptoms, decreased libido, and as a possible abortifacients. Many rare medical problems have symptoms that can sometimes be helped with cannabis. As with any plant or drug, everyone has a different reaction to each variety of cannabis depending upon a person's weight, diet, metabolism, drug tolerance, mental state and other environmental, physical and psychological factors.

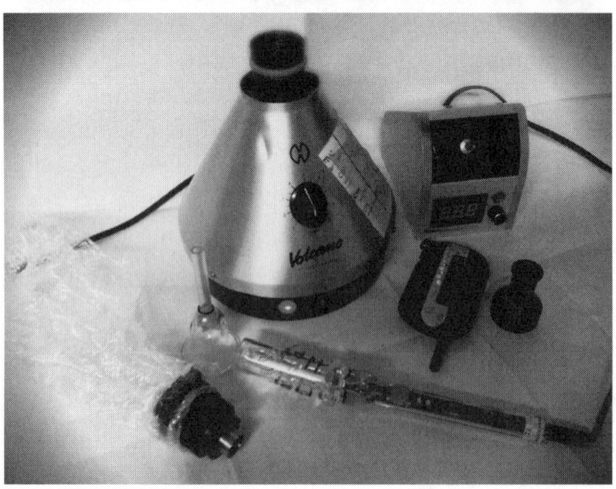

Top: Dried cannabis buds
Bottom: Various vapourizers used to eliminate smoke

Eating cannabis does not break down the cannabinoids as quickly as smoking, leaving the cannabinoids in your body from eight to 72 hours, depending upon the quality and quantity eaten and the individual's metabolism. It is good for most people suffering from a medical problem to eat small doses about 12 hours apart to maintain a constant level of cannabinoids in the bloodstream. This usually allows people to smoke less while achieving the same symptom relief, if not better. In Chapter seven, there are recipes for making edible and skin cannabis products.

When directly applied to an open cut, cannabis stops the bleeding. When infused into a vegetable oil or salve, cannabis helps the skin with second degree burns, skin problems caused by prescription drugs, rashes, bug bites, and skin infections of various types. When applied to the skin, cannabis is an anti-inflammatory, a muscle relaxant, and painkiller that flushes the body of toxins.

There are many potential negative and positive health impacts from using cannabis that vary depending upon the individual, the quality of cannabis and the method of ingestion. Some people are allergic to the smell of cannabis, or have bad reactions to eating or smoking it. Smoking or eating cannabis with pesticide residue, mold, or that have been grown with too much fertilizer can cause serious lung or stomach problems. Using metal, wood, or stone pipes exposes users to nasty chemicals that off-gas when the material is heated, leaving glass and ceramic pipes as the healthier alternatives. Proper scientific studies on smoking cannabis are lacking, but evidence suggests that smoking one joint may cause as much damage as a cigarette, though it could be four cigarettes. However, cannabis does not cause lung cancer, and may in fact help prevent the disease in people who smoke both. Smoking cannabis can trigger schizophrenic episodes in people with a predisposition towards mental health issues, though it does not seem to actually cause these types of problems. Cannabis makes linear thinking more difficult while improving non-linear mental functions such as word association, writing, and the production of music. No death due to cannabis consumption has ever been recorded in history.

Smoking causes the chemicals to be absorbed quickly, which creates a fast delivery system, but breaks down the cannabinoids enough that they start to disappear after 20 minutes. Since the carcinogens in THC are toxic to the hair-like cells that keep the lungs free of mucus, and the tars could cause chronic bronchitis, it is necessary for some to consider alternative methods of ingesting cannabinoids. Vapourizers, water pipes, and other similar smoking devices, could prove perfect for asthma sufferers or people with other respiratory problems.

In America today there are more than 20 million regular marijuana smokers. Many of these regular smokers have used the drug since the late-1960s or early-1970s. Yet there is no epidemiological evidence of immune system damage from marijuana use. As Dr. Hollister notes:

"Clinically, one might assume that sustained impairment of cell-mediated immunity (from marijuana smoking) might lead to an increased prevalence of opportunistic infections, or an increased prevalence of malignancy, as seen in the current epidemic of acquired immune deficiency syndrome (AIDS). No such clinical evidence has been discovered nor has any direct epidemiological data incriminated marijuana use with the acquisition of human immunodeficiency virus infection or the clinical development of AIDS."

("Health Aspects of Cannabis")

Smoking any material is not good for the lungs, though in moderation some substances like cannabis cause relatively few problems. Heavy, long-term pot smoking can cause chronic bronchitis. The practice of inhaling as deep, and for as long as possible, substantially increases the negative impact of smoking upon the lungs and does little to increase the absorption of THC. The heat of the smoke causes damage to the throat and lungs, which is partly why some use a bong or vaporizer and why others will only inhale lightly, commonly referred to as "Grandma tokes." Some of the harmful chemicals contained in the cannabis plant include hydrogen cyanide, carbon monoxide, nitrogen oxides, phenols and volatile aldehydes, as well as the solid tars. While these chemicals have been shown to cause cancer, the anti-cancer properties of cannabis may somehow over-ride the potential cancer causing effects of these materials, which would explain why so relatively few pot smokers get mouth, throat, or lung cancer and even these cases may be the result of impure cannabis or tobacco smoking. There is also evidence suggesting that smoked cannabis is an expectorant which cleans the lungs of tars, phlegm, and other unwanted materials.

A federally-funded study by Vera Rubin and Lambros Comitas in the early-1970s looked at the long-term effects of "ganga" or marijuana smoking on the Jamaican population- a culture where marijuana use has long been tolerated and encouraged. It was an ambitious project involving two governments, 60 subjects, and more than 45 professionals. Jamaica was chosen because of widespread marijuana use in the working class. The goal of the study was to gauge the general biological effects of chronic or long-term marijuana smoking.

While not concentrating specifically on immunological effects, Dr. Rubin and Comitas carefully examined the health of their subjects. They reported:

"No serious disease was detected, except for one case of hypertension, and there were no evident signs of nutritional deficiencies. Hemoglobin levels were adequate and serum protein values (albumin and globulin) fell within normal limits. Intestinal parasites, when present, resulted in only light infections. These examinations indicate that ganga smoking does not affect general physical health[...]"

(*Ganga in Jamaica*, p. 78)

Bob Marley

The effects of smoking cannabis on heart rate and blood pressure can vary dramatically. Initially, smoking causes the heart rate to increase, about as much as jogging. Frequent users develop a tolerance to this effect. This is only a potentially minor problem for people with heart problems, hypertension, cerebrovascular disease, and coronary atherosclerosis. The effect of smoking cannabis on blood pressure can even depend on whether a person is standing (decrease) or lying down (increase). A "head rush" which is experienced by many smokers could partly be the feeling of a decrease in blood pressure, with the momentary dizziness being subdued simply by lying flat. After a short amount of time, cannabis use generally lowers blood pressure, which leads to less stress of the body's systems. Marijuana's ability to help many people physically and mentally when dealing with stress could actually lessen a person's chances of having a heart attack.

> Despite the work of Rubin and Comitas, U.S. officials continued to insist that marijuana "harmed" the immune system. These claims were based on studies conducted with extremely high doses of synthetic delta-9-tetrahydrocannabinol (THC)- marijuana's psychoactive ingredient- and were conducted using laboratory animals or test tubes. Several small studies involving long-term marijuana smokers were conducted in the mid-1970s. These studies found no difference in the immune system of marijuana smokers. In 1988, the federal government authorized a team of experts from several federal agencies to study the effects of smoked marijuana on the immune system. Seventeen subjects were entered in the double-blind, randomized study. After a two week abstinence from marijuana, the subjects received oral THC or placebo. Several of the subjects also received marijuana cigarettes. The researchers were unable to detect any difference in baseline values of lymphocyte functions, plasma prolactin, adrenocorticotropic hormone (ACTH), cortisol, luteinizing hormones or testosterone.
>
> The results of the study were published in 1989. Despite the expenditure of federal funds, the use of federal employees in conducting the study, and the authorization of federal authorities to proceed with the study, the results of these experiments have not been aggressively dispensed to other federal agencies. As late as June 1991, federal officials were still claiming marijuana could harm the immune system.
>
> (*Marijuana and AIDS*, p. 82)

Up until the last century, most medical practitioners depended upon alchemists and herbalists for their prescriptions. Coke was originally a tonic potion that was said to be able to cure all ills. If one ingested enough Coke, pain of any kind would subside quite nicely as the cocaine buzz took over. Merchants would travel with their wagon stacked full of different healing salves and drinks from all sorts of exotic places. There was no real controlling mechanism to maintain an ethical code amongst medicine merchants or doctors, and there was no way to ensure patients that they would be receiving proper medical care, or that the drugs they were using were safe. Many people died, and are still dying today, because they were misdiagnosed and/or given bad drugs for their ailment.

Studies of Marijuana

> When it comes to cannabis, one hears anything and its opposite. While in some areas more research is needed and in others research results are contradictory, there exists nevertheless a strong basis of information contradicting many of the myths that continue to be perpetuated.
>
> (*Canadian Senate Special Committee on Illegal Drugs, Cannabis*, p. 15)

The first published account of cannabis in medical literature comes from China 4000 years ago under the rule of Hen Nun. It was said to be good for malaria, constipation, rheumatic pains, "absent-mindedness" and female disorders. Another early record is found in the Herbal, the prototype of the U.S. Pharmacopoeia, which was written about 450 B.C. It wasn't until 1753 that Linnaeus named the plant *Cannabis sativa*, though most everyone continued to call it Indian hemp.

> Viewing the subject generally, it may be added that the moderate use of these drugs is the rule, and that the excessive use is comparatively exceptional. The moderate use practically produces no ill effects. In all but the most exceptional cases, the injury from habitual moderate use is not appreciable.
>
> (British Army in India, *Indian Hemp Commission*, 1894)

In the last hundred years, there have been a number of studies, completed by several different nations, looking at the use of cannabis from different sociological perspectives. Some studies on cannabis include the "British 1893-4 Indian Hemp Drugs Commission," the 1944 La Guardia Report, titled "The Marijuana Problem In The City Of New York," and the "2002 Canadian Report of the Senate Committee on Illegal Drugs." Many study results are erratic and misleading because proper testing methods had not yet been developed when they were completed. Another problem with early tests was the fact that the euphoric sensation induced with the ingestion of THC was an unfamiliar experience to most individuals. Some of the people in experiments reacted negatively to exposure to non-ordinary reality, i.e. hallucinations, that can occur with eating high doses of THC. Hence, many had intense trips after smoking or eating large amounts marijuana in settings that were not necessarily created for comfort and relaxation. Those who did not deal well with it were often diagnosed as having mental problems.

> Over the last century, published scientific investigations conducted by the governments of India, Costa Rica, Jamaica, Greece, Canada and the City of New York have all concluded that marijuana is not only the safest recreationally used substance but also has unmistakably unique therapeutic properties. Since the 1960's marijuana has been the subject of thousands of studies by the US government, pharmaceutical companies and private agencies. Even though the investigations funded buy the US government and pharmaceutical companies set out specifically to prove the harmfulness of marijuana, the evidence was quite the contrary. Time and again untested and preposterous allegations have been highlighted in the press, such as, that marijuana caused birth defects, brain damage, lung cancer, and sterility. However, these accusations have been scrutinized and proven untrue. The last government-sponsored investigation began in the Nixon years and was finally completed during Carter's term. Marijuana was almost decriminalized at that time because the Commission could find no danger whatsoever issuing from its use, either for health or behaviour, but because of fierce political pressures from the hard-core conservative elements, marijuana remains stigmatized and illegal.
> (*The Benefits of Marijuana*, p. 22)

The LaGuardia Report was started by the mayor of New York in the late 1930s, soon after the passage of the Marijuana Tax Act, in an attempt to understand the social, medical, and economic impact of cannabis. While this study discredited most of the accusations made against cannabis when the 1937 Marijuana Tax Act was passed, it did not affect the federal government's position on the plant. Some conclusions reached by the La Guardia Report include:

1) Marijuana is used extensively in the Borough of Manhattan but the problem is not as acute as it is reported to be in other sections of the United States.

2) The introduction of marijuana into this area is recent as compared to other localities.

3) The cost of marijuana is low and therefore within the purchasing power of most people.

4) The distribution and use of marijuana is centered in Harlem.

5) The majority of marijuana smokers are Negroes and Latin-Americans.

6) The consensus among marijuana smokers is that the use of the drug creates a feeling of adequacy.

7) The practice of smoking marijuana does not lead to addiction in the medical sense of the word.

8) The sale and distribution of marijuana is not under the control of any single organized group.

9) The use of marijuana does not lead to morphine or heroin or cocaine addiction and no effort is made to create a market for these narcotics by stimulating the practice of marijuana smoking.

10) Marijuana is not a determining factor in the commission of major crimes.

11) Marijuana smoking is not widespread among school children.

12) Juvenile delinquency is not associated with the practice of smoking marijuana.

13) Indulgence in marijuana does not appear to result in mental deterioration.

14) Under the influence of marijuana the basic personality structure of the individual does not change but some of the more superficial aspects of his behavior show alteration.

15) With the use of marijuana the individual experiences increased feelings of relaxation, disinhibition and self-confidence.

16) Marijuana not only releases pleasant reactions but also feelings of anxiety.

17) Individuals with a limited capacity for effective experience and who have difficulty in making social contacts are more likely to resort to marijuana than those more capable of outgoing responses.

18) The publicity concerning the catastrophic effects of marijuana smoking in New York City is unfounded.

(Mayor Laguardia's Committee on Marijuana, 1944)

Top: New York Mayor Laguardia
Bottom: Founder of San Francisco CBC, Denis Peron

Other studies have shown that the moderate use of marijuana has little to no long-term negative side effects.

In its position paper, Use of Marijuana as a "Medicine", the California Narcotics Officers Association refers to "10,000 studies [...] documenting the harmful physical effects of smoking marijuana." This myth has been effectively debunked in a letter to Dr. Lester Grinspoon from NIDA's marijuana research librarian at the University of Mississippi, Beverly Urbanek, who writes, "We are totally in the dark as to where the statement that there are 10,000 studies showing the negative impact of marijuana could have originated." She explains that while her library has some 12,000 citations on cannabis, they cover a broad spectrum of economic, legal, horticultural, enforcement, and other non-health issues, and are not categorized according to negative or positive effects.

(*Marijuana Medical Handbook*, p.220)

Experienced drivers who are experienced smokers usually find that they drive more slowly, pay greater attention to other vehicles, and take fewer risks. However, inexperienced drivers who are just beginning to smoke cannabis are just as dangerous as a drunk driver. While estimates vary, approximately 3% to 5% of people who try cannabis become technically addicted for at least a brief time in their lives. Clinical addiction is consumption of over one gram per day. The negative side effects from addiction to cannabis can be loss of memory, concentration skills, and motivation. Though these effects are not felt by all heavy cannabis users, they are also felt by inexperienced users. Smoking cannabis does not degrade moral character and therefore does not contribute to criminal acts, besides breaking the cannabis laws. Cannabis use does not lead to use of other drugs in the vast majority of cases, and is often used to help people stop using alcohol, tobacco, cocaine, heroin, and crystal meth. Chronic smoking can cause lung and throat irritations, including bronchitis.

The data on the adverse effects of marijuana are more extensive than the data on its effectiveness. Clinical studies of marijuana are difficult to conduct: researchers interested in clinical studies of marijuana face a series of barriers, research funds are limited, and there is a daunting thicket of regulations to be negotiated at the federal level (those of the FDA, and the DEA) and state levels. Consequently, the rapid growth in basic research

> on cannabinoids contrasts with the paucity of substantial clinical studies on medical uses. The profile of cannabinoid drug effects suggests that they are promising for treating wasting syndrome in AIDS patients. Nausea, appetite loss, pain, and anxiety are all afflictions of wasting, and all can be mitigated by marijuana. Although some medications are more effective than marijuana for these problems, they are not equally effective in all patients. A rapid-onset (that is, acting within minutes) delivery system should be developed and tested in such patients. Smoking marijuana is not recommended. Terminal cancer patients pose different issues. For those patients the medical harm associated with smoking is of little consequence. For terminal patients suffering debilitating pain or nausea and for whom all indicated medications have failed to provide relief, the medical benefits of smoked marijuana might outweigh the harm.
> (*Marijuana and Medicine: Assessing the Science Base*)

One must take into consideration, while looking at most of the studies and research programs done with cannabis, that those conducting the experiments and the patients were often unfamiliar with recreationally smoking or eating the herb. Patients need to be prepared for the sudden rush of perception and feeling of euphoria in order to comfortably use cannabis. Evidence suggests that getting high in sterile, cold atmospheres such as hospitals and laboratories is too disturbing for some people. Efforts must be made in future experiments to ensure patients who use cannabis are in comfortable, preferably green, settings with qualified, reassuring physicians and researchers. By qualified, I mean people who are familiar with cannabis intoxication themselves and have the interpersonal skills to help patients deal with experiences of non-ordinary reality. If appropriate precautions are taken in the research projects, the results should be in favour of using cannabis. Most research done on cannabis in North America comes from government controlled facilities that have strict limits on THC percentages, therefore limiting the potential medical benefits.

> Since 1995, The Multidisciplinary Association for Psychedelic Studies (MAPS) has disbursed over three million dollars to worthy research and educational projects. Medical marijuana has been a major part of MAPS' research efforts. At present, the National Institute on Drug Abuse (NIDA) has a monopoly on the supply of marijuana that can be used in research, provides low-potency material, and only makes it available to projects it approves. MAPS needs its own independent source of supply since NIDA's arbitrary and lengthy review process for providing marijuana essential to research can derail any drug development plan. NIDA has refused to supply marijuana to two MAPS-sponsored protocols that the FDA had already approved.
> (MAPS.org)

Doctor watching old man smoke

The penalties associated with producing or distributing resins, oils or extractions from cannabis are greater than having the dry herb in most countries. This makes it even more risky for any organization to produce and distribute a smoked or edible cannabis product with a high concentration of THC and/or other cannabinoids. This is an ironic and unfortunate circumstance because these products often provide greater relief of symptoms than the unprocessed herb.

There are a number of pharmaceutical products being tested and marketed that contain synthetic cannabinoids and endo-cannabinoids that are intended to provide medical benefit without the same psychoactive effect as smoking. New pills, patches, salves, and even intravenous forms of cannabis have been created in laboratories around the world. Some products, like Sativex from GW Pharmaceuticals, are alcohol-based inhalers that contains THC and CBD, and are actually made from living plants. Drugs made with one or two cannabinoids do not contain the full spectrum of chemicals available in the cannabis plant and therefore have different and limited benefits, often with side-effects not known to regular cannabis consumers. The synthetic THC pill, Marinol, began to be prescribed by oncologists beginning in 1985, and by 1989 over 100,000 doses had been given out.

> Nevertheless, concentrated THC was a powerful psychoactive drug and many patients didn't like it. They complained that it caused intense anxiety, or that it kept them from carrying on normal activities for up to six hours at a time. Patients also complained about the price of Marinol. A year's supply can cost as much as $15,000, too high a price to pay, some said, for a flawed version of a common weed easily grown in anyone's backyard. There were many other complaints about Marinol, as well.
>
> Patients experiencing extreme nausea find it difficult to swallow any medication in pill form. Some patients vomit when trying to swallow the capsule and are unable to use it. When Marinol does work, many patients claim it takes over an hour to relieve their symptoms. This probably results from the fact that the THC passes through the liver before reaching the receptors in the brain where psychoactive reactions and nausea suppression take place. Because Marinol takes so long to reduce nausea, some patients have complained that they are at risk of overdosing when they are driven to get quick relief from their violent symptoms.
>
> One of the reasons many patients prefer smoking marijuana to swallowing Marinol is that it allows them to precisely regulate the amount of THC they take into their systems. Because smoking permits an almost instantaneous transmission of the THC in the marijuana to sites in the brain where it works to control nausea, patients are able to simply continue smoking until the nausea subsides. This allows some to stop smoking before they get high. When the antinausea effect wears off, they can smoke a little more if they need to. Since individuals respond differently to different doses, smoking allows patients to determine the proper dose for themselves. As a result, they can avoid taking too much, which is not possible with Marinol.
>
> It has been suggested by researchers that cannabinol, one of the 460 known compounds in marijuana smoke, actually reduces some of the anxiety brought on by THC in its pure form. While some patients report feelings of anxiety or discomfort after using either drug, these feelings generally cease to occur in those who repeatedly administer smoked marijuana. Patients who were unfamiliar with smoked marijuana initially, describe more pleasurable feelings after they are acquainted with, and can anticipate, its effects. With Marinol, on the other hand, many patients report that it has an unpleasant and debilitating effect on them even with continued use.
>
> (*Is Marijuana the Right Medicine for You?*, p. 22)

The effectiveness of any drug has a lot to do with the attitude taken towards the effects. Another reason it is difficult to study the effects of cannabis is because people can have various reactions when using cannabis at different times. Many who believe marijuana is bad before they try it may actually block positive effects from consciously

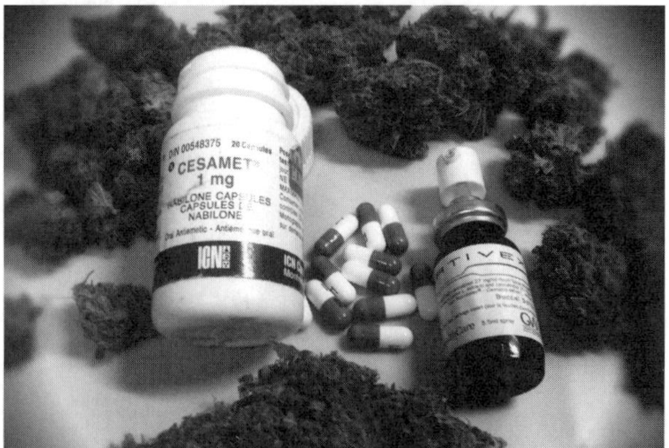

Legal cannabis pharmaceutical products and raw herb

occurring. Other negative cannabis experiences can occur if the smoker is not physically comfortable or in an awkward situation, or not prepared for the physical and emotional effects of the herb.

> Oral administration leads to almost complete (90 to 95%) uptake of THC from the gastrointestinal tract but absorption into the systemic circulation is variable and slow because of extensive metabolism during transit through the liver, so that only 10 to 20% of the administered dose reaches the systemic circulation. THC is widely distributed in body tissues, with extensive uptake in fatty tissues; consequently, low levels persist over a prolonged period with the time taken for 50% loss (the half-life) being 24 to 36 hours. As a result, some of the effects of THC, such as appetite stimulation, persist for 24 hours or longer, although psychoactive effects start at 30 to 60 minutes after oral administration, peak at 2 to 4 hours and last for 4 to 6 hours. Activity is also due in part to an active metabolite, 11-hydroxy-Δ9-THC, which is present in similar concentrations to THC. The licensed commercial product, dronabinol, which is THC dissolved in sesame oil, is suitable for oral administration. The other routes which have been advocated and which are the subject of current research include inhalers, sprays, skin patches and suppositories, and eyedrops for glaucoma. No clinically-useful intravenous formulation is available.
>
> (Royal Pharmaceutical Society of Great Britain: Report on Cannabis, Response to the House of Lords, Science and Technology Committee, May 29, 1998)

The effect a person gets from using cannabis depends upon a number of factors, including diet (or lack thereof), the quality and quantity of the herb, past consumption and tolerance of other mind-altering substances, the setting and people nearby, the amount of misinformation a person receives concerning negative effects of marijuana, and, of course, the extent of experience with the plant a person has. A sense of lightness, a lack of focus, loss of time, clarity of thought, intense sounds and colours and a calm inner peace are all signs of a good stone. Most people can learn to experience a wide range of pleasant sensations by smoking cannabis.

> The federal government has done a number of clandestine research projects in New Mexico and elsewhere using Vietnam veterans suffering from Post-traumatic Stress Disorder (PTSD), with significant findings that have not yet been made readily available. Many veterans who first experienced cannabis in South-east Asia have found it to be quite useful in dealing with the flashbacks and sudden fits of anger, anxiety, and depression that are associated with the disorder. Curiously enough, veterans of the 1991 Persians Gulf War also report that the effects of Gulf War Syndrome appear to be mitigated by the use of cannabis. Recent evidence indicates that these troops were exposed to doses of nerve gas a number of times during the conflict. The exact nature of the neurological benefits of cannabis in both these situations may not be properly understood until the government ends its cover-up of what really happened to these veterans.
>
> The U.S. Department of Veterans Affairs conducted a secret study of marijuana use among veterans suffering from PTSD, to determine the reasons for marijuana use and how side effects differ from marijuana differs between diagnostic categories of psychiatric patients. Preliminary data suggest both similarities and differences in why mental health patients from all diagnostic groups reported use of marijuana to help relax and to socialize. The PTSD group more often used marijuana to help with sleep, decrease nightmares, prevent bad memories of the past, and improve self-esteem. Bipolar patients often reported to use marijuana to stabilize their mood. Depressed patients often reported use for "fun." Schizophrenics reported more unpleasant side effects than did patients with other diagnoses.
>
> (*Hemp for Health*, p.65)

While there is some evidence suggesting that marijuana can trigger, not cause, schizophrenia in some youth, there is also living proof that symptoms of this illness can be controlled with the moderate use of cannabis. For many seriously mentally ill people, cannabis does little to help and can aggravate problems, inhibiting their capacity to focus and problem solve. When eaten or smoked, cannabis can have a calming effect upon violent people. While some see the use of cannabis as a means of distraction, escapism and avoiding problems, others see these effects as important tools in dealing with stress. Many people struggling with forms of depression, anxiety, obsessive-compulsive behaviour, attention difficulties, stress, and other mental issues find that cannabis helps subdue feelings of extreme emotions, though other people dealing with mental illnesses can have terribly bad reactions. Usually the only time smoking marijuana causes these people a problem is when they run out of herb.

The effects of cannabis use upon short and long-term memory are interesting and depend upon the mental capacity of the individual in question almost as much as the quality and quantity consumed. Experienced users can develop a tolerance to the loss of short-term memory, the effect of which on first-time smokers has generated much laughter while causing some students a problem. A person who smokes cannabis will not forget very important matters, at least not like someone under the influence of alcohol, though it can make remembering trivial things, like names, more difficult. The brain, though, is much like a muscle, and if fed and exercised properly with constant reading, debate, and active living/learning patterns of behaviour, mature adults usually find the use of mind-altering substances like cannabis helps release creative energies, explore personal feelings, and relax from the pressures of modern life—without affecting memory long-term.

> Discussions on the health effects of cannabis have often been the lynchpin of the other key debate on the legal status of cannabis. Indeed, it has been argued that the scientific investigation and deliberation on the health effects would resolve decisions on whether to legalise or not. The papers in this issue on the legal, social, psychological, pharmacological and therapeutic aspects of cannabis indicate the complexity of the debate which clearly has no simple right or wrong answer. There is mounting evidence of the adverse physical effects and the psychological effects of cannabis. However, while there is need for an awareness of the negative effects, they are not impressive compared to the adverse effects of tobacco and alcohol misuse. This is not to argue that cannabis should be given the same status as tobacco and alcohol but to recognise a factual comparison. There is a tendency among the proponents of cannabis legalisation to argue that cannabis is devoid of adverse health effects and to ignore the evidence that cannabis itself can induce significant levels of dependence.
> ("Cannabis and Health")

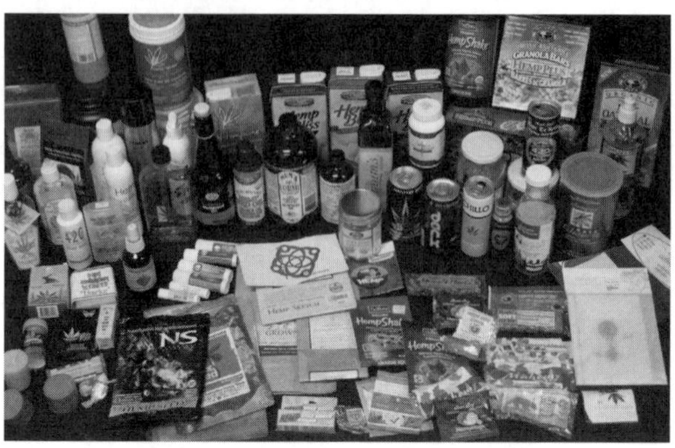

Many hemp seed food and skin products are available now

Seeds of the Future

The nutritional value of hemp seeds, and the oil which can be pressed from them, is a very important component of cannabis that is being rediscovered. Historically for many farmsteads, hemp seeds were a staple food over the long, hard, winter months. No matter how poor the growing season was, there were always hemp seeds at the end of the year. They did not know it at the time, but hemp seeds are the most nutritional food on the planet, containing all the essential amino acids and essential fatty acids necessary to sustain our lives.

Not only that, but the ratio of oils in the seeds, with 80% essential fatty acids (EFA) and 8% saturated fat, is perfect for the human digestive system. These EFA's have been the focal point of a lot of scientific inquiry. Many professionals believe that degenerative diseases may be a result of a lack of EFA's in our diet. This is because most convenience foods are systematically cleaned of EFA's in order to prolong their shelf life. Hence, the faster hemp oil is consumed after being extracted from the seeds, the better it is for you. Hemp seed oil should never be heated and should be kept in the refrigerator.

> Seeds of the hemp plant contain all the essential amino acids and essential fatty acids necessary to maintain healthy human life. No other single plant source provides complete protein nutrition in such an easily digestible form. More importantly, hempseed contains the oils essential to life in a perfect ratio for human health and vitality. Hempseed oil (35% of total seed weight) is the richest source in the plant kingdom of these Essential Fatty Acids (EFAs). The lustrous oil contains 80-81% EFAs, and is among the lowest is saturated fat content, at 8% of total oil volume. Marijuana seeds are nature's perfect food for humanity.
> (*Green Gold*, p. 407)

An exciting new process was developed in 1986 that extracts hemp seed oil in absence of heat, light, and air. This allows the oil to be pressed into a bottle without being contaminated with oxygen, which causes it to go rancid. This oil is very effective for sunburns and to prevent peeling, as it is absorbed into the skin cells instead of just coating them. Many ancient recipes use hemp oil and crushed hemp root in their healing potions, massage rubs, and salves. EFAs act as lipids in the membranes of all body cells, preventing the build-up of arterial plaque. EFA's structure the very base of our immune system. Consumption of EFAs has proven to be beneficial in the fight against AIDS.

> Hemp oil contains 57% linoleic (LA) and 19% linolenic (LNA) acids, in the three-to-one ratio that matches our nutritional needs. These are the essential fatty acids (EFAs)-so called because the body cannot make them and must get them from external sources. The best sources are oils from freshly ground grains and whole seeds, but EFAs are fragile and quickly lost in processing. EFAs are the building blocks of longer chain fats, such as eicosapentaenoic (EPA) and docosahexaenoic acid (DHA) that occur naturally in the fat of cold-water fish like sardines, mackerel, salmon, bluefish, herring, and, to a lesser extent, tuna.
>
> Adding these foods to the diet seems to lower risks of heart attacks because omega-3 fatty acids reduce the clotting tendency of the blood and improve cholesterol profiles. They also have a natural anti-inflammatory effect that makes them useful for people with arthritis and autoimmune disorders.
>
> (http://www.ratical.org/renewables/TherapHoil.html)

Hemp seed is especially high in minerals. It has plenty of calcium, magnesium, phosphorus, potassium, and sulfur, while being low in heavy metals such as strontium, thorium, arsenic, and chromium. It is low in vitamins, as most grains are, so fresh vegetables are necessary to maintain a healthy diet. It is not clear if sterilization, which we will discuss further, affects the vitamin content of the seed. The only plant to have higher protein content than hemp seed is soybean, although the complex proteins in soybeans make them harder to digest. Many scientists claim that hemp seed could treat malnourishment and help prevent many diseases in all Third World countries.

Soy oil contains 50% LA (Omega 6, linoleic acid) and 9% LNA (Omega 3 linoleic acid), while hemp oil contains 57% LA, and 19% LNA, a substantially higher ratio. The ratio of three to one, LA to LNA, was figured out by scientists to be the healthiest possible combination of acids before hemp oil was tested. A careful mixture of other oils would be needed to come close to the perfect, natural balance hemp oil provides to our body. The recommended daily requirement of LA is three grams daily, and LNA, two grams a day. Of the dozen fatty acids we usually eat; only a couple have proven to be essential to human life, LA and LNA being the two most important. Flax oil has become a six million dollar a year industry through growing awareness about the health benefits of LA and LNA, but the taste of it is not as good as hemp oil.

Hemp oil also contains 1.7% GLA (Super Omega 6, Gama Linolic Acid). Although the nutritional value of GLAs are still scientifically undetermined, many people take a supplement in pill forms of evening primrose oil, black current oil, and borage oil. GLA is not considered an EFA and included in the daily requirements because the human body, unless subjected to stress from autoimmune diseases, alcohol abuse or other imbalances, can produce GLA from LA.

> Recent scientific research indicates that essential fatty acids (EFAs) cannot be manufactured by the human body and deficiencies can cause undesirable chronic conditions such as obesity, cardiovascular disease, osteoporosis, and eczema. Therefore, hemp seed and its by-products can be used to supplement diets poor in EFAs in order to maintain health. One by-product, hemp seed oil, contains 30% of its weight in EFA-rich oil, delivering an ideal combination of omega 3 and omega 6 fatty acids for long term use. Hemp seed oil may have potential health benefits for diabetes, cancer, lupus, asthma rheumatoid arthritis, depression and hypertension. Hemp is one of only two plants that contain both EFAs as well as gamma linolenic acid (GLA). GLA has been found to have many properties ranging from anti-inflammatory to anti-depression. It can lower cholesterol and help to correct dyslexia, dyspraxia, and hyperactivity (ADHD). Approximately one-third of the population lacks the enzyme to metabolize GLA from omega 6 and must take GLA from an outside source to maintain good health, and hemp is an excellent way for them to do so.
>
> (Agriculture and Agri-Food Canada)

An energy field is created throughout the entire body with the ingestion of EFAs, as they produce a bio-electric current very similar to static electricity, essential to nerve, muscle, heart, and membrane functions. This is our very life-force—that stimulates the most active tissues in our brains, retinas, inner-ears, and adrenal and testicular cells. The high energy created by LA, LNA, and the highly unsaturated fatty acids the body makes

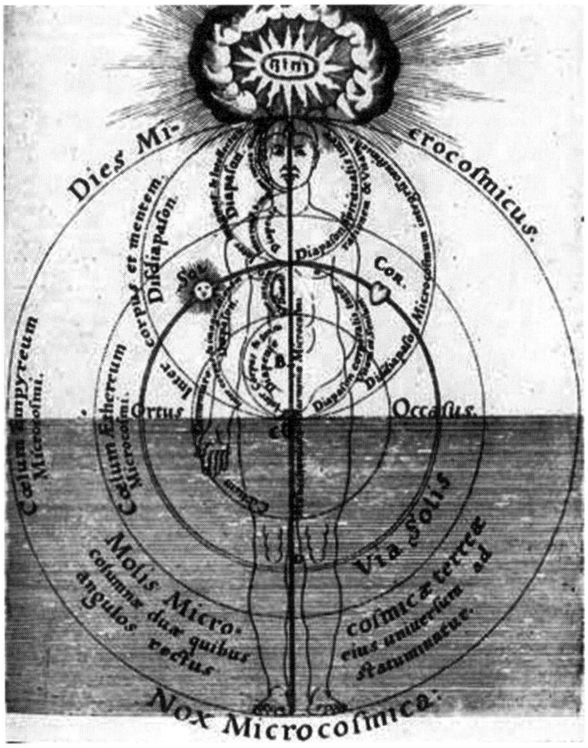

Man is a Microcosm, Robert Fludd, 1617

from them, ensures a high oxygen content to body cells, helping life-force energy travel. LA is thought to be able to transform solar energy into chemical energy, in a sense creating photosynthesis within human cells, and LNA transports that energy.

When the 1937 Marijuana Tax Act was put in place, a concession had to be made for bird owners, who demanded access to hemp seeds for their pigeons and poultry. Under the condition that the seeds were steamed at a temperature of 160°F, permission was granted to allow the importation of hemp seeds. This does not crack the shell of the seed causing the oil inside to go rancid, but it does destroy the seeds ability to germinate. Since the recent increase in both interest in and the consumption of hemp seeds has been so dramatic, the U.S. government has increased the temperature, dry heated at 300°F, which is just enough to crack the shell and cause the seed to go rancid if not consumed soon enough. The imported seeds are also fumigated with methylene bromide, which works like a carbon dioxide, suffocating all living matter while still being inert enough not to react with the seeds.

All produce brought into North America must undergo this treatment so that no living insect or plant pest can travel across international borders via human foodstuffs. Although the methylene bromide used as a fumigant is only a small portion of what is used on farms themselves, if any of it is released into the atmosphere, it rises, eventually depleting the ozone layer. Hemp nuts avoid this process because they are not viable seeds.

Meanwhile, hemp seeds are being eaten all around the world as you read this book. In China, toasted hemp seeds are sold by street vendors like popcorn. In parts of the Ukraine, hemp seed recipes using the seed, oil, and flour ground from seeds, are passed down from generation to generation. The Japanese use hemp seeds for condiments. The Polish use them in holiday treats. In North America, there is a surging interest in hemp seeds being fuelled by the production of hemp food products in Canada. Soon restaurants will begin popping up all over specializing in hemp seeds.

Hemp seeds can especially help those who suffer from immune diseases—AIDS, for example. It is obvious, however, that a health oriented public, eating nutritional foods, using environmentally responsible goods, and living healthy social lifestyles, would be detrimental to several large drug companies and medical suppliers. The reason most of this information about EFAs and the nutritional value of hemp seeds has been suppressed is because food, drug, and chemical companies make vast amounts of money from unhealthy consumption patterns.

Cannabis Helps With...

We will now examine medical problems cured, controlled, or subdued by the ingestion of cannabis either by applying topically, orally, or by smoking. First, we will look at cancer. Over the past few decades, more and more people seem to have died from a variety of forms of cancer which, to our knowledge, have never appeared before in history. Why, you might ask? Well, there are several possible reasons why usually inert cancer cells, which everyone has inside their body, become triggered and begin eating healthy cells. Most of these reasons centre around the waste and pollution we have produced in our industrial countries over the past few centuries, and the chemicals we continue to eat, breath, and drink every day in our food, water, and air.

The following statement was taken from a decision made by the DEA Administrative Law Judge Francis Young, Sept. 6, 1988. Unfortunately this decision was later overturned by the U.S. government.

> There is another reason why DEA should not be guided by FDA criteria in ascertaining whether or not marijuana has an accepted medical use in treatment. These criteria are applied by FDA pursuant

to Section 505 of the FDCA, as amended. When the FDA is making an inquiry pursuant to that legislation it is looking at a synthetically formed new drug. The marijuana plant is anything but a new drug. Uncontroverted evidence in this record indicates that marijuana was being used therapeutically by mankind 2,000 years before the birth of Christ.

Uncontroverted evidence further establishes that in this country today "new drugs" are developed by pharmaceutical companies possessing resources sufficient to bear the enormous expense of testing a new drug, obtaining FDA approval of its efficacy and safety and marketing it successfully. No company undertakes the investment required unless it has a patent on the drug, so it can recoup the development costs and make a profit. At oral argument Government counsel conceded that "the FDA system is constructed for pharmaceutical companies. I won't deny that."

Since the substance being considered in this case is a natural plant rather than a synthetic new drug, it is unreasonable to make FDA-type criteria determinative of the issue in this case, particularly so when such criteria are irrelevant to the question posed by the Act: does the substance have an accepted medical use in treatment…

The overwhelming preponderance of the evidence in this record establishes that marijuana has a currently accepted medical use in treatment in the United States for nausea and vomiting resulting from chemotherapy treatments in some patients. To conclude otherwise, on this record, would be unreasonable, arbitrary and capricious.

(*Cancer Treatment & Marijuana Therapy*, p. 330)

Recent cancer research has proven promising in some areas, especially in chemotherapy. Every few weeks, patients are injected with chemotherapeutic agents that attack both cancerous cells and non-cancerous cells alike, often causing serious side effects. Cisplatin (Platinol) can cause life-threatening kidney failure or deafness. Isofamide (Ifex) causes bleeding and bruising. Doxorubin (Adriamycin) kills heart muscle cells. There is cyclophospamide (Cytoxan) a drug that disturbs the entire immune system. Other drugs delivered by needles, such as melphan (Alkeran) and chlrorum (Leukeran), are nitrogen mustard derivatives that are so toxic they literally eat all flesh they come in contact with, occasionally resulting in the loss of a patients limb from a single misplaced drop. Most of these drugs also cause hair loss, may trigger a second form of cancer in the patient, and must be safely administered. An overdose could cause kidney, heart, or respiratory failure. Relief can be obtained for many cancer patients by taking standard anti-emetic drugs like prochlorperazine (Compazine) or ondanstron (Zofran), which are now considered the better medicine, though it is administered intravenously at a very high cost. These drugs do not always work and their effects may lessen and disappear over time.

Books about cannabis

In about December 1977, the previously underground patient practice of using marijuana to control emesis burst into the public media in New Mexico when a young cancer patient, Lynn Pierson, began publicly to discuss his use of marijuana. Mr. Pierson besought the New Mexico legislature to pass legislation making marijuana available legally to seriously ill patients whom it might help. As a result, professionals in the public health sector in New Mexico more closely examined how marijuana might be made legally available in meeting what now appeared to be a widely recognized patient need.

In many cases doctors have found that, in addition to suppressing nausea and vomiting, smoking marijuana is a highly successful appetite stimulant. The importance of appetite stimulation in cancer therapy cannot be overstated. Patients receiving chemotherapy often lose tremendous amounts of weight. They endanger their lives because they lose interest in food and in eating. The resulting sharp reduction in weight may well affect their prognosis. Marijuana smoking induces some patients to eat. Doctors have found the benefits to be obvious. There is no sig-

> nificant loss of weight. Some patients will gain weight. This allows them to retain strength and makes them better able to fight the cancer. Psychologically, patients who can continue to eat even while receiving chemotherapy maintain a balanced outlook and are better able to cope with their disease and its treatment.
>
> (*Cancer Treatment & Marijuana Therapy*, p. 317)

In a study printed in the *New York State Journal of Medicine 88* (October 1988) called "Inhalation of Marijuana as in Antiemic for Cancer Chemotherapy," it was discovered that 78% of a group of cancer patients who received no help from legal medicine became symptom-free after smoking marijuana. Growing, eating, drinking and smoking cannabis, in appropriate amounts and combinations, can help people fighting cancer with severe nausea, pain relief, appetite stimulation, sleep enhancement, boredom, stress and depression. Some research has even indicated that tumour growth stopped and actually reversed with both benign and malignant (cancerous) tumours.

Some research showing potential positive results have been buried, like the now infamous mice experiment in the 1970s called "Anti tumor Properties of Cannabinoids". When mice received delta-9-THC, delta-8-THC or cannabinol, after being injected with cancer cells, the size of the tumours decreased, depending upon the size of the dose and duration of treatment, from 25 to 82%, with a relative increase in the life expectancy. Other studies done with animals have yielded similar results, though no human research has ever been done.

AIDS is a disease that has had such a dramatic impact upon civilization that it is difficult to comprehend the full extent of its reach. Since 1981, 150,000 Americans have died from this illness. Nearly 2 million have the human immunodeficiency virus (HIV), and about 250,000 are dying from it today. Those who are infected with HIV and don't have access to expensive modern drugs are almost certain to become infected with AIDS, with the average incubation period being between eight to 10 years. Once the immune system is defunct, all types of infections and cancerous growths (neoplasm) attack the body. These can be combated with the proper treatment, though often a simple cold can last for months. Zidelovadine (AZT) attacks the virus itself, though it suppresses the production of red blood cells by the bone marrow, decreases the number of white blood cells, and causes many problems in the digestive system. On top of that, AZT causes intensified nausea in patients already suffering semi-starvation and weight loss. Between HIV and AIDS is a phase called ARC, the symptoms being fatigue, pain, diarrhoea, nausea, fever, and swelling of the lymph nodes. This stage can last for years or weeks, and the standard drugs usually prove ineffective. As well, 20% of AIDS patients develop cytomegalovirus retinitis, a blinding eye infection. Foscarnet (Foscavir) effectively treats this disease though it causes nausea.

Glaucoma is an eye disorder that afflicts someone if the intraocular pressure within the eyeball builds up, causing it to lose its almost perfect spherical shape. This can occur if the eye produces too much aqueous humor, the internal fluid, or more commonly, if the channels that excrete the aqueous humour are gradually blocked. Glaucoma is the second most common cause of blindness, next to old age, afflicting 1.5% of the population over the age of 50, and 5% at 70. It is usually treated with eye-drops containing beta-blockers, which effectively control the activity of epinephrine (adrenaline) but also may cause depression, aggravate asthma, slow the heart rate, and increase the chance of heart failure. Other epinephrine-like eye-drops are also effective, though they irritate the white of the eye, aggravate hypertension and may cause heart disease. In the past, patients were usually given miotics such as pillocarpine, which are safer for the heart, respiratory, and digestive systems but can cause blurred vision, loss of night vision and cataracts. Pills containing a carbonic anhydrase inhibitor may also be used, though they may cause lose of appetite, nausea, diarrhoea, headaches, numbness, tingling, depression and fatigue, kidney stones and, rarely, a fatal blood disorder. Fifteen percent of glaucoma patients cannot handle any of these drugs.

It wasn't until the L.A. Police Department tried to prove that marijuana dilates the pupils that it was officially discovered that THC actually slightly constricted, rather than dilated, the pupils. When eaten or smoked marijuana reduces inocular pressure, with no serious side effects, for four to five hours. It has been confirmed that THC is a much more effective medicine to help most glaucoma patients than any other drug currently developed.

Epilepsy is a strange disease that has plagued humankind, and some other highly intelligent animals, for a very long time. Many myths and rumours about people being possessed by the devil and cursed by the gods could likely have an epileptic as the main character. It can be caused by physical damage to the epileptic focus, a specific grouping of brain cells, at birth, by accident, or otherwise by an over-stimulation of that area, which can cause minor to very violent muscle spasms, loss of consciousness, or a varied combination of the two. Patients usually develop a recurring symptom—i.e. grimacing, excited eye movements, hand, foot or mouth movements—that is in some patients nothing more than a smell, anxiety, dizziness, or deja-vu. It is hard to classify the different types of epileptic seizures, as each patient seems to have their own unique type of attack, and even patients with similar appearing attacks react differently to the same drugs.

Anticonvulsant drugs, phenytoin (Dilation), primidone (Mysoline), and phenobarbital (Dilantin) help epileptics about 75% of the time, with focal seizures and temporal lobe epilepsy being hard to treat, though they soften bones, reduce the production of red blood cells (pernicious anemia), cause the gums to swell, and create emotional disturbances. If too much is taken, or a negative reaction occurs, the results could be anything from rapid uncontrollable eye movements (nystagmus), loss of co-ordination and balance, coma, or even death.

The use of cannabis to treat this ailment has been known for millennia in some parts of the world, though its therapeutic use has been ignored almost completely in current Western medical literature. Although not all epileptics are cured using cannabis, with some patients showing no improvement at all, quite a few do completely stop having seizures with a relatively small prescription of marijuana. Some have dramatic decreases in the regularity, severity (or both), of their seizures.

Montel Williams uses cannabis for MS

Multiple Sclerosis occurs when the body's immune system goes haywire and treats the myelic, the protecting covering of spinal brain and nerve cells, like a foreign invader, destroying the thin skin and disrupting the nerve fibres and signals. Symptoms include, but are not limited to, severe depression, skin ulcerations, constipation, urinary tract infections, loss of bladder control, tremors, weakness or paralysis, fatigue, loss of co-ordination and balance (ataxia), painful muscle spasms, difficulty speaking, impaired vision, numbness, and tingling. These symptoms usually occur in early adulthood, and come and go without warning or mercy, until the attacks stabilize or the patient dies. The average age of survival is 30 years, though injury, stress, or other illnesses may rapidly stimulate the deterioration of nerves.

> A survey of cannabis-using MS patients in the USA and UK by Consroe and colleagues (1997) reported improvements after cannabis use in spasticity, chronic pain, acute parozysmal phenomena, tremor, emotional dysfunction, anorexia/weight loss, fatigue, diplopia, sexual dysfunction, bowel and bladder dysfunction, vision dimness, dysfunction of walking and balance, and memory loss (descending rank order). While the authors of this study discuss the potential shortcomings of the survey design, this report suggests that cannabis may significantly relieve signs and symptoms of MS such as spasticity and pain along with a number of other complaints.
>
> In the 19th century, O'Shaughnessy (1842) used hemp extract in treating muscle spasms associated with tetanus and rabies. Reynolds (1890) reported using cannabis to treat muscle spasms, as well as for epilepsy, migraine, and other indications. While medicinal cannabis use continued in the years after the work of O'Shaughnessy and Reynolds, little was published concerning cannabis and spasticity until the 1970s.
>
> ("Cannabis in Multiple Sclerosis: Women's Health Concerns")

The options for people with MS are not very pleasant. The drugs adrenocorticotropic hormone (ATCH) and prednisone, known as corticosteroids, help with the most acute symptoms, but cause mental problems and weight gain. Muscle spasm drugs like diazepam (Valium), baclofen (Lioresal) and damtrolene (Dantrium) are used; though Valium can be addictive, cause drowsiness and must be used in heavy doses over long periods of time; Lioresal causes dizziness, weakness, and confusion; and Dantrium can cause fatal liver disease, drowsiness, dizziness, weakness, general malaise, abdominal cramps, diarrhea, speech and visual disturbances, seizures, headaches, impotence, tachycardia, erratic blood pressure, clinical depression, myalgia, and feelings of suffocation and confusion.

> The conclusions of Dr. O'Shaughnessy were repeated in a report issued by the Ohio State Medical Society in 1860. This report, in effect a monograph of the medical opinions of the time, declared that marijuana was effective in treating spasticity. So common was marijuana's use for this purpose during the 19th century that Dr. J.R. Reynolds, personal physician to Queen Victoria, stated in the Lancet published in 1890, that "(marijuana), when pure and administered carefully, is one of the most valuable medicines we possess." Listing the maladies for which the drug was useful, Reynolds asserted that marijuana was quite effective in treating spasms, violent convulsions, and other forms of spasticity.
>
> Unaware of this medical history, most patients suffering from spasticity discover marijuana's medical utility serendipitously. Valerie Cover, for example, first realized that marijuana, unlike any other drug she had been prescribed, successfully treated her spasticity resulting from MS after smoking with a neighbour. One puff of a marijuana cigarette, she found, relieved the shakiness that she had felt deep inside since the onset of the disease. Her limbs were easier to control and she could walk again...
>
> Despite the fact that marijuana proved to have a dramatic and obvious effect upon their conditions, patients frequently discounted the responses of their own bodies and initially attempted to convince themselves that marijuana was not actually working. Thus, nearly all patients stopped marijuana in order to test its medical utility. This rejection appears to be a characteristic of many nervous diseases, particularly MS, and results as well from the negative stigma associated with marijuana smoking. Likewise, since marijuana is expensive and often hard to acquire- it is an illegal drug- patients frequently have been forced to interrupt their treatment due to lack of finances or inability to locate a supplier. Upon cessation of use, patients experienced resumption of spasticity.
>
> (*Muscle Spasm, Pain & Marijuana Therapy*, p. 157)

Most MS patients hear through the grapevine about marijuana's use in treating this horrible disease. There is a lot of evidence proving that THC can not only stop the symptoms of MS almost immediately, but that it can also repair the myelic and return crippled MS patients to normal, productive lives.

Paraplegia occurs when disease or injury to the spinal cord causes weakness or paralysis in the lower body. If the injury is from the neck down it is called quadriplegia, permanently condemning it's victim to a wheelchair. Pain and muscle spasms, which usually accompany this ailment, are treated with opioids, baclofen, and diazepam. The reasons for paraplegics using marijuana for pain relief and to control muscle spasms are much the same as the reasons given by MS patients. Not only are the tremors stopped and motor coordination improved, but the ability to retain an erection and orgasm is quite often returned, as is bladder control.

Other people suffering from joint, muscle, and bone problems also find the anti-inflammatory, muscle relaxing, and pain numbing effects of cannabis to be extremely useful. This includes a wide range of diseases and injuries from arthritis to fibromyalgia, to anckolysis spondylitis to lupus, from knee problems to tendonitis. Most of the medications available to individuals with these types of issues cause stomach problems.

Idiopathic dystonia is a group of disorders causing prolonged muscle spasms or muscle contractions that look like abnormal postures or movements. Quite often, this disease is a side effect of the neuroleptic drugs used to treat chronic psychotic disorders. Cannabis can be very useful in controlling the spasms, pain, and shaking that comes with this disorder.

Pruritis is a strange inflammatory skin disorder, atrophic dermatitis. It is probably caused by an allergic reaction that makes a person have very itchy patches of inflamed skin on mostly the hands, face, neck, legs, and genitals. The treatment is a combination of corticostroids (anti-histamines) and ointments, though they are only partially effective. Steroids work, too, though long-term use causes serious side effects. In most cases, these drugs are not enough to stop the itching, and many patients end up in the hospital from infections caused by this disease. Patients who smoke marijuana find that the urge to scratch disappears almost instantly, and cannabis salve is by far the best ointment to use on the skin.

Chronic depression and other mood disorders are diseases that we know very little about. They seem to be able to suck the very life out of people to the point where many consider suicide, or just give up on life entirely. While most people can snap out of a lethargic and negative mood after a few hours or days, others get trapped into that mindset for years. Loss of appetite and sleep loss, or over-eating and weight gain, headaches, backaches, upset stomachs, constipation, and chronic fatigue are all physical symptoms of depression. For many, it is simply a matter of trying to escape from the world to live inside their own shell. Many lose all interest in life, no longer feeling pleasure.

The most popular drugs for treating depression are antidepressants called tricyclics (Tofranil), amitryptiline (Elavil), and desipramine (Norpramin), whose side effects include dry mouth, weight gain, blurred vision, constipation, difficulty urinating, and orthastatic or postural hypotension (dizziness from loss of blood in the brain), which can make them dangerous for patients with heart problems. Monoamine oxidase (MAO) inhibitors, isocarboxazid (Marplan), tranylcypromine (Parnate), and phenelzine (Nardil) can cause dizziness, insomnia, and impotence if certain foods are eaten at the same time. Fluoxetine (Prozac) is another drug on the market, though it is far too addictive to use over the long term, putting the patient in a "loose-fitting emotional straight jacket." Smoking marijuana is the best treatment for many of these people.

Asthma is the medical term for repeated attacks of breathlessness and wheezing caused by allergic reactions to pollen, dust, feathers or animal hair, cold air, infections, exercise, or air pollutants, during which the bronchioles (small airways in lungs) close up. More common in children, this disease kills over 4,000 Americans every year, as a chronic cough can develop from the swollen, inflamed, and phlegm-filled linings of the bronchodilators. Treatment is usually beta-agonists, used to relax the bronchial muscles, which opens up the lung airways, or synthetic steroids to reduce inflammation, the former causing possible sleeplessness, jitteriness, and nausea, the later causing bone loss, seizures, and bleeding. Other non-inflammatory drugs cause more serious side effects. There is evidence to suggest that some of these drugs are associated with high death rates in asthma sufferers.

It has been proven that THC acts as a bronchodilator in both healthy and sick people, allowing more cannabinoid-laden oxygen into the bloodstream, while reversing bronchial restriction in asthma patients. Compared to a standard bronchodilator, isoproternol, THC worked for a longer period of time, though it worked slower and had a less dramatic peak effect.

Last century it was common for women to use marijuana to ease menstrual cramps and labour pains, though almost no literature proving this is available. Many women today claim that smoking a joint greatly relieves the discomfort caused by these natural processes.

Hyperemesis gravidarum is a rare form of intense morning sickness in which the pregnant mother is never free of pain, often leading to abortion. Recently, this has been treated with hospitalization and intravenous nutrition. Smoking marijuana everyday is a viable option these women have, if they want a healthy baby. Though taking any drugs at all during pregnancy is risky, cannabis is more than likely one of the safest, if not the safest, of any drug.

> This presentation supports the proposition that cannabis has been employed historically for legion complaints in obstetrics and gynecology. To list briefly, these include treatment of: menstrual irregularity, menorrhagia, dysmenorrhea, threatened abortion, Hyperemesis gravidarum, childbirth, postpartum hemorrhage, toxemic, seizures, dysuria, urinary frequency, urinary retention, gonorrhea, menopausal symptoms, decreased libido and as a possible abortifacients.
>
> It is only recently that a physiological basis for these claims has been available with the discovery of the endocannabinoid system. Limited research to date supports these claims in terms of cannabinoids analgesia, antispasmodic, and anti-inflammatory. activities, but requires additional study to ascertain mechanisms and confounding variables.
>
> (*Cannabis Treatments in Obstetrics And Gynecology*, p. 28)

As an antibiotic, cannabis may in fact prove to be the most effective and diverse ointment known to humanity. Cannabiolic acid attacks strains of micro-organisms that resist penicillin and other antibiotics, treating such conditions as ear infections, cuts, and open sores. Cannabis, specifically THC, even treats the symptoms of herpes. In a shampoo, cannabis gets rid of dandruff, kills tics and other pests, while revitalizing dry hair. This, too, is an area that needs more research to be done, especially if the number of diseases that cannot be helped with penicillin keeps increasing at the current rate.

> Between 1950 and 1965, a series of papers appeared in the Czech scientific literature discussing the potential of cannabis as an antibiotic. Having

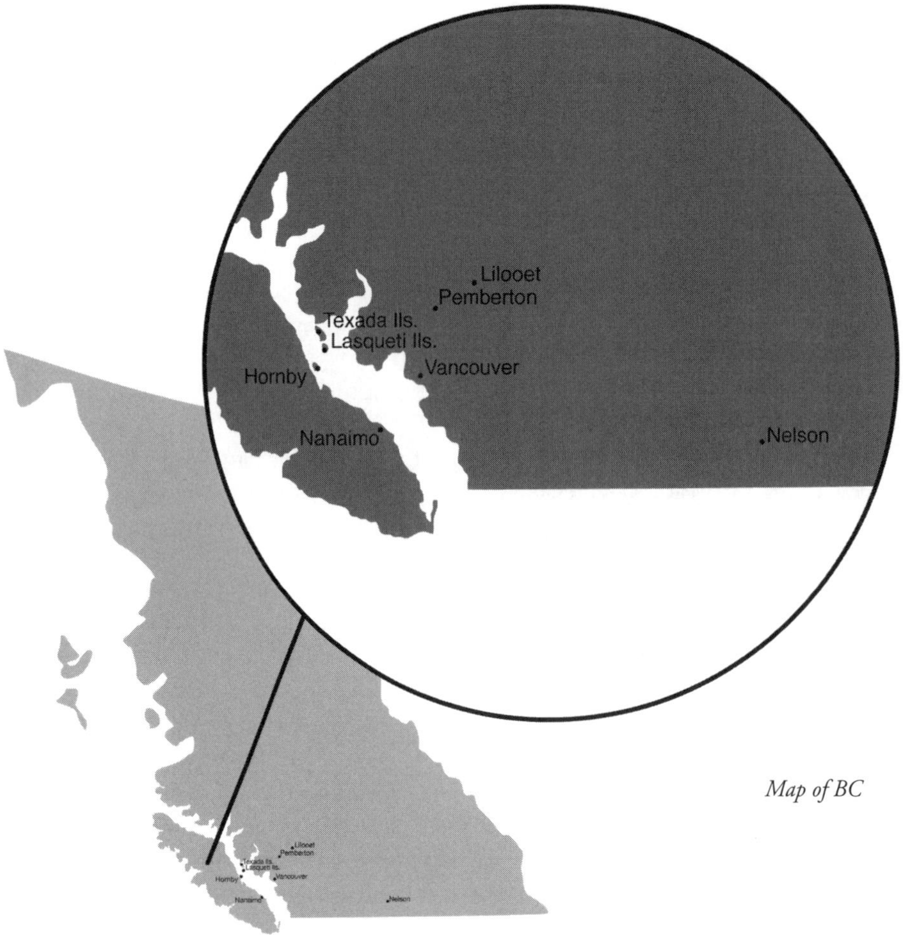

Map of BC

studied many plants in a search for those with antibiotic action, these scientists found that preparations made from cannabis were quite effective when applied to the skin or mucous membranes as a poultice, salve, or spray.

Among the conditions successfully treated were herpes labialis (an acute skin inflammation caused by a virus) and otitis media (inflammation of the inner ear). Irrigation with cannabis also healed infection caused by chronic bone disease. Cannabis also was reported to reduce pain from second-degree burns. A study published in 1976 reported that both THC and cannabinol halted the growth of certain bacteria in test-tube experiments.

(*Marijuana as Medicine*, p.122)

Over 4.5 billion sleeping pills were sold in British Columbia, Canada alone in 1994, causing a variety of medical problems, and in some cases death. Cannabis has a long history of putting people at ease, mellowing them out and making them go to sleep. Those with insomnia, or those who have smoked a joint late at night after a hard day's work, will agree that nothing puts you to sleep as nice and gently as a puff of a good indica. Since many medical problems interrupt a full night's sleep, this benefit of cannabis use is extremely important.

Another quality of marijuana is also the largely unexplored area of the suppression of violent impulses and actions. Whereas alcohol and cocaine can stimulate violent rages in certain people, smoking marijuana is traditionally a globally accepted means of calming people down. Although no public research is available to date, there is no doubt about this in the minds of those who, like myself, have seen alcoholic bastards turn into loving pot-smokers, without needing to seek professional help. The number of deaths, injuries, and general negative energies which tend to result from alcohol stimulated violence and accidents is staggering.

Likewise, it has been found that cannabis is a very useful harm reduction tool for those trying to stop using alcohol or other hard drugs. This effect is completely the opposite of the gateway theory that prohibitionists love to promote. While it is true that some individuals can become addicted to cannabis to the point of being unproductive, and that the first intoxicant that some youth experiment with is cannabis, there is every reason to believe that those who go on to use harder drugs are risk takers who were very likely to rebel and engage in poly-drug use. Without cannabis to use as a relaxant and intellectual stimulant, many former alcohol and drug addicts would have difficulty dealing with stress, painful memories, and occasional physical discomforts. My last drink was May, 1996.

Modern Medicine and Marijuana

One wonders why more research hasn't been done with cannabis after only one or two of these remarkable medical statistics, until you realize that the people paying for current research are large pharmaceutical firms that cannot patent a plant as common as cannabis. It was estimated in Nov. 1980 by *Omni Magazine* that legal cannabis could eliminate 40% of the drugs we sell in drug stores—that was before AIDS and Hep C appeared, and before cancer became as common as it is today.

> Toward the end of the 1970s, the general public was hearing about the medical potential of marijuana and related drugs. As is frequently the case when word spreads of a promising new treatment for a specific disease, patients searched for additional information. Those with cancer who were undergoing chemotherapy learned several facts: (1) early studies indicated that THC was effective as an antiemetic; (2) federal law prohibited prescribing marijuana or THC; (3) many people who were using illicitly obtained marijuana as medicine were having positive results; (4) obtaining illicit supplies of marijuana was risky, expensive, and- for many- difficult or impossible; (5) although federal law permitted patients to use marijuana or THC in an approved research project, few physicians were in a position to design and conduct such studies, given the demands of their medical practices.
>
> Chemotherapy patients who turned to their physicians and were advised to smoke marijuana to prevent nausea and vomiting "if you can get it" on the illicit market, felt angry at the risks involved and faced the difficulty of justifying illegal behaviour. Many of these patients, along with their doctors and others, began to organize to lobby for changes in government policy.
>
> (*Marijuana as Medicine*, p.6)

Doctor in a blind fold

Some patients who benefit medically from smoking cannabis claim that, although the side effects of the legal drugs may be devastating, they have no choice but to use them because of moral obligations, fear of arrest, or social, religious, and personal repercussions. Unfortunately, many patients are unaware of the potential cannabis has for relieving the side affects of their prescription drugs, and the symptoms of their medical problems, because their doctors are misinformed or misguided.

In times past, the doctor was almost the last person in the world one would admit smoking marijuana to. An open dialogue between doctors and patients can only begin when prohibition is over. Most doctors who support the medical use of marijuana have done so because a patient has been very honest with them regarding their use of the herb, and the doctor has monitored their health as it improved resulting from using cannabis. Doctors who smoke pot themselves are less likely to stand forward because they are risking both their professional career and personal lives. Patients need to help educate doctors about the benefits they receive from cannabis.

Though western doctors are only now re-discovering the many medical applications of cannabis, physicians from other parts of the world are much more familiar with it.

> The country with the harshest drug laws in the world is Malaysia. "There, hemp is completely illegal, and anyone convicted of possessing more than 200 grams is sent to the gallows" (Haag 1995:102f.*). As a result, both the hedonistic and the medicinal uses of hemp have declined significantly in recent years. The psychoactive effects are well known to Malay healers, shamans known variously as bomor, pawing, or poyang (Eliade 1975:329*). A number of hemp preparations are included in their store of traditional medicines. Hemp is a component of a narcotic, aphrodisiac mixture used in Kelantan (Gimlette 1981:220). A Chinese hemp recipe was introduced to Malaysian medicine at the turn of the twentieth century. The medicine, known as tai foong chee, consists of seeds from Hydnocarpus anthelmintica Pierre and Cannabis indica. It is used to treat leprosy (Gimlette and Thomson 1968; Lu 1991:142).
>
> In Laos, Cambodia, and Vietnam, hemp is legal as medicine and is available to all. Throughout the region, it is regarded as a means to obviate pain and to relax, especially in cases of migraines and stiffness. These properties are recognized in both folk medicine traditions and in the government pharmacopoeias of these countries (Martin 1975:70).
>
> In Cambodia, hemp is not solely an agent of pleasure. The entire dried plant is freely sold in the markets, for it is an important ingredient in the spicy, stimulating soups (sngao, sngao moon) that are offered in numerous Cambodian restaurants and consumed with gusto (cf. Huu 1987). The Khmer consider smoking marijuana (leaves and flowers) a sign of good manners, and it is a mandatory part of social events (Haag 1995:94f.*; Martin 1975:74). Marijuana is primarily regarded as a medicine, no matter whether it is used prophylactically (hedonistic and recreational use) or as part of a therapy. Sick persons, irrespective of the cause of their ailments, often receive small amounts of marijuana mixed into the rest of their medicines. This makes them feel better and also stimulates their appetites. They may also be given a decoction of the entire plant to drink twice daily (before lunch and dinner) or a joint to smoke (Haag 1995:95f.*; Martin 1975:70).
>
> Cigarettes made from hollow stems of the chkae sraeng plant (Cananga latifolia, a ylang-ylang plant) stuffed with hemp foliage are smoked daily to cure nasal polyps; they recede and then disappear entirely. A smoking blend of hemp and tobacco is said to inhibit excess bile flow. Malaria sufferers are advised to add 500 g of male and female flowers to a water bath and inhale the vapors twice daily (Haag 1995:97*; Martin 1975:70,71).
>
> (*Marijuana Medicine*, p. 52)

It is obvious that there are many medical benefits that can be derived from the cannabis plant, and that it is a relatively safe recreational substance to use. Individuals who experience these benefits and compare them to the effects of various prescription drugs often find that their health is better using cannabis, and quit using synthetic drugs unless absolutely necessary. Unfortunately, most of the governments in the world have regulated the production of health care products so much that it is difficult, if not impossible, to quickly include cannabis as a prescribed medicine without major changes in policy.

Chapter 5 Prohibition

2,500 Years of Religious Oppression

> And the Lord God commanded the man, "You are free to eat from any tree in the garden; but you must not eat from the tree of knowledge of good and evil, for when you eat of it you will surely die."
> (Genesis 2: 16-17)

It is ironic that the root of the prohibition of cannabis is based in religious prohibitions meant to suppress women and force citizens to stop worshipping deities other than God, and not based upon the actual effects of the herb. The original prohibitions were intended to force citizens to consolidate their resources behind one spiritual leader and one god. Ultimately, though, these prohibitions became tools to suppress plant-enhanced spiritual exploration and the cultures that used naturally occurring intoxicants to heal or achieve heightened states of awareness. Whether it was to monopolize the use of incense or stop the use of hemp as paper and fuel, the prohibition of cannabis has always been enforced to support the economic agenda of a few, while the masses are convinced it is for their own good.

> And the serpent said unto the woman, "Ye shall surely not die. For God doth know that in the day ye eat thereof, then your eyes shall be opened, and ye shall be as the gods, knowing good and evil. And when the woman saw that the tree was good for food, and that it was pleasant to the eyes, and a tree to be desired to make one wise, she took of the fruit thereof, and did eat, and gave also unto her husband with her; and he did eat. And the eyes of them were opened, and they knew that they were naked; and they sewed fig leaves together, and made themselves aprons.
> (Genesis 3: 4-7)

Eve eating forbidden fruit

The Old Testament was originally written to record the oral stories and traditions of Jews living as slaves in Babylon. This forced the authors to censure the information contained within these documents, as to openly reveal the secret practices of the group in literature would be to invite suppression and possibly death. A system of writing developed using parables to communicate complex, and sometimes revolutionary, themes. These written stories were used in public to spread the ethical behaviour promoted within the simple parables. Those who understood the actual meaning of the words contained within the Bible, and other texts written using this method, knew how to interpret words in ways that explained much more than morals. By the time of Jesus writing and understanding parables became an art, as phrases with multiple meanings were used to educate the masses while stimulating the enlightened.

> Thus on a seal from[...]ancient Uruk[...]the king offers two fruitful branches to two caprids, which reach up to feed. The panel is significantly flanked by symbols of the fertility-goddess Ishtar, who may thus be symbolized by the sacred tree[...] This conception of the king as the medium of fertility through the fertility-goddess is expressed in Assyrian sculpture, where the king is touched by a protective genius with a cone dipped in some fertility substance, either pollen or oil[...] The fertility is communicated by the king to a stylized version of the Tree of Life.
>
> Like 'Messiah', the 'son of man' is a royal title derived from the ideology of the king of the House of David during the Monarchic period in Judah, where it is attested to in Psalm 80:17 from the liturgy of the fast, where it stands parallel to 'the man of thy right hand', obviously the king, who was enthroned at the right hand of God. The 'Son of Man' takes us back to the old Mesopotamian conception of the king as the representative of the community tending the Tree of Life in the Garden of God, which symbolizes at once man's service of God and the king as the mediator of God's blessing in nature to the community. The Mesopotamian conception of the king tending the Tree of Life in the Garden of God has been democratized in the Hebrew conception of Man in the Garden of Eden with its Tree of Life. But the denunciation of the king of Tyre in Ezekiel 28:12-19 as the executive of God, His signet, in 'the Garden of God' probably reproduces the conception of the king as the archetypal man in the Garden of Eden, created in the image of God, is a theological democratization.
>
> (*Near Eastern Mythology*)

The Tree of Life is an example of a term with many meanings used in the Bible. In the book of Genesis, Adam is instructed by God not to eat from the Tree of Knowledge of Good and Evil. God creates prohibition because he fears that the human will open his eyes and see like God. Though God does not specifically tell Adam to eat from the Tree of Life, God certainly did not say he should not. God told Adam to eat from all of the seed bearing plants upon the Earth, except for the Tree of Knowledge of Good and Evil.

> The records of the Tree of Life [in the bible] are the sublimest proofs of the unity and continuity of tradition, and of its Eastern tradition, and of its Eastern origin. The Earliest records of the most ancient Oriental tradition refer to a Tree of Life which was guarded by the spirits. The juice of this sacred tree, like the tree itself, was called Soma in Sanskrit and Hoama in Zend: it was revered as the life preserving essence.
>
> (*Keys to St. Peter*)

Tree of Knowledge and good and evil

The parable of Man's exit from the Garden of Eden, in my opinion, explains the religious prohibitions carried out by Moses, followed by the Jews and Roman Catholics. The Tree of Knowledge of Good and Evil is a representation of the multitude of religions that used mind-altering plants to push consciousness beyond a dualistic interpretation of the material world and enter a unified state of awareness. The Tree of Life is a representation of the cannabis plant and the Goddess Ashera. It is interesting to speculate that it was not the use of cannabis that resulted in an awakening within humans that God felt threatened by, but it was the use of mushrooms and other hallucinogens. Adam and Eve were only told they could not eat from the Tree of Life after they had eaten from the Tree of Knowledge of Good and Evil. By ultimately banishing the use of both mind-expanding substances, the Jews, and later Christians, were able to stop their followers from directly experiencing altered states of awareness that could lead to personal knowledge of the divine. This was no easy task because the physical appeals of the pagan religions were tempting to a people who were constantly escaping from enslavement.

> The Canaanite [and Near Eastern] pantheon[...]included goddesses, such as Ashera, consort of El and Baal. She[...]was a nature deity, symbolizing sexuality and fertility. In some passages in the Old Testament there are references to an asherah as a wooden pillar, an object of cultic devotion. This is clearly a phallic symbol, occupying a place similar to the Hindu lingam in the Temple of Shiva[...]All of [the] gods and goddesses worshipped by Israel's neighbours near and far were intimately and organically related to nature and the various forces and powers encountered there. For the most part they appeared in male/female pairs and were pictured in the myths and legends creating the world by copulation. They had special responsibilities for fecundity and fertility of all sorts of conditions. Their worship apparently required a kind of imitative magic in which male and female devotees yoked their bodies sexually and spilled their seed upon the field they desired to yield bounteous crops. Orgies involving the use of intoxicants and indiscriminate sexual activity played an important role in these cults, and many Israelites gladly became apostates to these weird and wondrous religions. The inexperience of the nomadic Hebrews in the task of agriculture in their new homeland made them easy converts to the local Baals who promised good harvests. The exotic character of the cult with its mystic roots extending far back into antiquity, together with the highly sensual pleasures afforded in the worship, combined to make it an attractive type of religious experience. Any such temple in modern society would encounter no difficulty in attracting large numbers of devotees[...]
>
> (*Sex and Love in the Bible*)

There are five times in history, in theory, when pagans, or anyone caught worshipping a deity other than God, were all killed. The first time, according to Christian mythology, was when everyone but Noah's family was killed in The Flood. The second massacre occurred when Moses came down from Mount Sinai to find many of his followers practising ancient fertility cult rites. The next time the Jewish people killed thousands of its own people for engaging in any religious activities that closely resembled the ceremonies of their former captors, was around 600 B.C. Almost 1,000 years later the Roman Catholic Church began to seek out and murder anyone caught practising religions that were not Judeo-Christian. The fifth and final wave of massacres occurred during the witch hunts that lasted from the 1200s to 1800s. Despite all the stories of prohibition, at the end of the Bible, in Revelations, it is written that at the end of time the Tree of Life will be growing upon the banks of the rivers.

Kill the Pagans

In the struggle to survive after leaving Egypt, Moses tried to convince 70 Israeli elders to agree to live under one God. This was an attempt to consolidate control over the religious practices of the tens of thousands of nomads, who were quickly using the group's resources, by making sacrifices to a number of deities. After being reintroduced to the ancient pagan traditions of their homeland, the Israelites were experimenting with a number of other types of worship. The Israelites that escaped Egypt were quickly using their resources and losing their identity. While Moses and 70 elders were "communing with God" as he appeared in a cloud of smoke, the rest of the Israelites converted back to their ancient pagan roots.

> Anath's brother consort, Baal, often depicted as a bull, is referred to often in the Old Testament. The bull, of course is often credited with

> tremendous sexual power. When Aaron told the Israelites to make a golden calf and worship it, he was encouraging them to enact the rites associated [Baal's consort] Anath[...]This would account for the fact that the participants in the ceremony were naked and apparently holding an orgiastic feast when they were discovered by Moses.

Moses with tablets

(*The Mythology of Sex*)

The first documented wave of violently enforced prohibition of worship of deities other than Yahweh occurred in Exodus after Moses came down from Mount Sinai to find the Israelites practising other religions. All of the problems the Israelites were experiencing in the desert were blamed upon the worship of other deities. According to Exodus 33:28, about 3,000 men, and probably many more women and children, were killed by Moses and his followers to show God's wrath for worshipping other gods and goddesses. It is not clear exactly how long this prohibition was enforced with death, but by the time of King Solomon the worshipping of more than one god was again a common practice.

When Moses was on Mount Sinai God instructed him in the making of anointing oil and gave him these special instructions.

> And thou shall anoint Aaron and his sons, and consecrate them, that they may minister unto me in the priest's office. And thou shall speak unto the children of Israel, saying, This shall be an holy anointing oil unto me throughout your generations. Upon man's flesh shall it not be poured; neither shall ye make any other like it, after the composition of it: it is holy, and it shall be holy unto you. Whosoever compoundeth any like it, or whosoever putteth any of it upon a stranger shall be cut off from his people.
> (Exodus 30:30-33)

From that time forward, the Jewish priesthood did not allow the anointing oil to be used by the general population, though the burning of incense to Yahweh was allowed until 387 AD. Though Moses tried to eliminate the worship of idols, with God's instructions he later created a brass serpent that was to be worshipped by the Israelites to heal themselves from poison from snakes that God had sent amongst them for questioning him. Many modern medical symbols can trace their beginnings to this event.

> And the Lord said unto Moses, Make thee a fiery serpent, and set it upon a pole: and it shall come to pass, that every one that is bitten, when he looketh upon it, shall live.
> (Numbers 21: 8)

This brass serpent was kept for centuries with the Ark of the Covenant where incense was commonly burned. It is obvious that the mythologies in Genesis had not yet been created, or any association with a snake would have been seen as Satanic. It seems likely that Moses was using an ancient symbol of knowledge and healing to secure his followers. There are other clear stories in the Old Testament that indicate that the Hebrews and Jews slipped back into polytheistic worship.

> King Solomon, who reigned from 960-925 B.C., made 20,000 gold censors for the temple of Jerusalem and 50,000 others in which to carry burning incense. Solomon's temple was modeled after the much larger ziggurat at Babylon. The temple and the vestiges that filled it were designed and constructed by artisans from the Phoenician city of Tyre. In addition to the Tyrian sun god Melek or Heracles-Melkart (biblical Molech), Solomon burnt incense to Ash'-toreth (Astarte) and Che-mosh in the temple at Jerusalem, and his wives "burnt incense and sacrificed to their gods" (I Kings 11:5-8) the gods common to the people of the Near East.
> (*Green Gold*, p. 83)

Ashera feeding followers

Female deities and women were given credit in ancient times for discovering wisdom and knowledge, as well as with having the spiritual capabilities to communicate with Nature. In a complete reversal of thinking, women were blamed by the Hebrews and the Roman Catholic Church for having created evil, and therefore had to be controlled by men for the good of humanity. Solomon's wives, for example, were said to have stirred God's wrath by worshipping so many other deities that he caused the Hebrews to be imprisoned by the Assaryians for hundreds of years. While it is difficult to speculate why individuals like Peter and Paul seemed to have such negative views of women, there can be no doubt that their insatiable quest for power was to set the standard for other fanatics to use Christian dogma as a means to gain control over the practices of women. Women became easy targets for those looking to place blame for all of the world's ills.

The Fear of God

The next violently enforced prohibitions began in Jerusalem in 621 BC. The Hebrews had temporarily regained control of Jerusalem, with some returning from Assyria and other regions. The Assyrians, like most other cultures of the time, worshipped cannabis as the Tree of Life. The Assyrians held the Hebrews as slaves for years. A fanatical sect had grown within the Jewish community that professed that Yahweh alone should be worshipped, as Moses had once attempted to declare. All other gods and goddesses were considered false and impotent, leading to the demise of the Jewish people and humanity as a whole. They claimed that the Hebrews were defeated and taken from their homeland in the first place because some Hebrews paid tribute to deities other than Yahweh.

In 621 BC, a lawyer wrote a document that was conveniently found by a priest within the Temple in Jerusalem. After it was confirmed as legitimate by a priestess, it was taken to King Josiah who quickly swore to obey the Word of God as was written in this newly "discovered" book of Moses, which has not been recovered yet in modern times. This "Book Of Law" is recorded in the Old Testament in chapters 21-26 and 28, of the Book of Deuteronomy. This piece of fiction contains a number of historical errors and inconsistencies that show that Moses could not possibly have been the author of the work. This forgery was created because the restrictive Hebrew religion of Yahweh was not receiving as many offerings as the other temples, and the Jewish priests wanted a religious monopoly. King Josiah immediately began forbidding the burning of incense to deities other than Yahweh, destroyed altars and images of gods and goddesses, levelled temples, desecrated graves, killed religious leaders, demolished ancient Jewish and Hebrew artifacts, and forbade the worship of deities other than Yahweh. These actions are recorded in depth in the Old Testament in Kings II 22:3. These acts of religious rebellion were only possible because the once powerful Assyrian empire was temporary distracted by trying to stop its inevitable dissolution.

> He did away with the pagan priests appointed by the kings of Judah to burn incense on the high places of the towns of Judah and on those around Jerusalem- those who burned incense to Baal, to the sun and the moon, to the constellations of the starry hosts. He took the Asherah pole from the temple of the Lord to the Kidron Valley outside Jerusalem and burned it there. He ground it to powder and scattered the dust over the graves of the common people. He also tore down the quarters of the male shrine-prostitutes which were in the temple of the Lord and where the women did weaving for Asherah.
>
> (2 Kings 23: 5-7)

Even though King Josiah of Judah abolished the practice of burning incense to deities other than Yahweh in 621 BC, most of the people living throughout the known world at the time continued to burn hash incense, drink bhang, and use cannabis oils while worshipping a host of deities. It was only in the small kingdom of the Hebrews, which only lasted a couple of decades, that a monotheistic religion dominated anywhere in the world.

After the Hebrews lost control of their homeland, they were held as slaves by the Babylonians for a long time. It was during this time that the Old Testament was collected and the book of Genesis written. This was also when hatred towards the Tree of Life as worshipped by the Assyrians and Babylonians grew in the Jewish people because of the harsh treatment they received as slaves. The Hebrews resented the power the Tree of Life appeared to give the rulers of these empires. In Genesis, when Adam and Eve were kicked out of the Garden of Eden and banished from the Tree of Life and the Tree of Knowledge of Good and Evil, it was also meant to imply that the worship of any religion that acknowledged these sacred trees was no longer allowed by the followers of God. Pagan worshipping was no longer acceptable to the Jewish elite.

Taken in this context, the Genesis story about man being expelled from the Garden of Eden has many more meanings than the awakening of the human mind and the creation of clothing. The ancient kingdoms of Mesopotamia, Assyria, Babylon, and Sumer had sacred gardens where cannabis resin was collected by the kings in religious ceremonies. Leaving the Garden of Eden behind represents the attempt to stop Hebrews from practising many ancient religious traditions associated with their sworn enemies. Becoming civilized, according to the Hebrews and later Christians, means to stop worshipping plants, animals, seasons, and other natural, procreative forces. By leaving behind many ancient religious practices, the Hebrews were attempting to separate themselves from all other prevailing "uncivilized" religions of the time, claiming to have essentially grown out of primitive pagan ceremonies.

> It (the Pentateuch), no less than Homer, contained some things which, at least on the surface, seemed inconsistent with morality. To it, no less than Homer, was applicable the theory that the words were the veils of a hidden meaning. The application fulfilled a double purpose: it enabled educated Jews, on the one hand, to reconcile their own adoption of Greek philosophy with their continued adhesion to their ancestral religion, and, on the other hand, to show to the educated Greeks with whom they associated, and whom they frequently tried to convert, that their literature was neither barbarous, nor unmeaning, nor immoral.
>
> (*The Influence Of Greek Ideas On Christianity*, p. 66)

During the time of Jesus, the Jewish priesthood continued to burn hash incense and anoint with cannabis oil, though any connection between cannabis and the Tree of Life had been publicly severed within their community. The rest of the Jewish population was denied using cannabis incense and anointing oil, though the punishments for using them are not exactly clear. The Romans had no problem using cannabis in any way at the time of Jesus, and the plant was used by every major religion in every large city in the known world.

Catholic Killers Convert Rome

In 325 AD, Constantine formed the Roman Catholic Church as the official Church of Rome, even though he only had a vague impression of its doctrines and its conflict with his other practice of worshipping the Unconquered Sun God, Apollo. When Constantine began forming the Roman Catholic Church, the Roman Empire seemed near the verge of collapse. After consolidating his power over the provinces, Constantine resorted to controlling the Roman citizens and the rest of the world by creating a religion that would eventually control the spiritual practices of the people. His real objective was to convince the masses that paying taxes to Rome was a morally responsible thing to do. The original Roman Catholic doctrines that were created during Constantine's reign did not include the prohibition of worshipping other deities. Roman Catholics only lived peacefully along with pagans for a short period of time.

> Among the barbarians, both men and women seem to have enjoyed the cult of Dionysus: but in Greece, it was particularly a religion of women. The reason for this, we may surmise, was perhaps that women were then, as some say they now are, more religious than men; but we believe rather that in the Dionysiac mystery women found the means to throw off the heavy domination of their husbands which had come with the end of primitive communism, the establishment of private property, monogamic marriage, and the concomitant requirement of chastity among wives, all of which was of such recent origin that the memory of their former freedom, economic independence, and social dominance was still vivid in their consciousness.
>
> (*The Religion of the Occident*, p. 48)

About 50 years after Constantine formed it, the Roman Catholic Church, under the leadership of emperor Theodosius, opposed and condemned worship of the Mother Goddess in any form. In 387, at the Council of Nicea, the Roman Catholic Church and Theodosius decided to eliminate anyone caught practising religious ceremonies that they did not sanction. Once the Christian fanatics were given endorsement from the state to condemn all other religions, the damage that they did to the relics and statues within the temples of the ancient world is only comparable to the damage sustained in the two World Wars. They destroyed every altar upon which incense was burned and tore apart ancient forest groves within each city, which is where most god/dess and earth worshipping ceremonies took place since the beginnings of civilization. Christian zealots murdered the philosopher/sage Hypatia, who taught her lessons at the Museum of Alexandria, in 415 AD, while denouncing all other women from teaching or learning. They ruined hundreds of enormous, beautiful, ancient temples; destroyed libraries, religious artifacts, and ancient writings. Christian scholars conjured up myths and legends concerning religious martyrs to create a false history of Christian faith, and forced Roman citizens to convert to Christianity, denouncing publicly their former pagan religions, usually under the threat of torture or death.

> It was Theodosius who dealt the death blow to paganism, for his Draconian decrees prohibited the most offensive old customs: the burning of incense and the lighting of a fire at home in honour of the house-god, the pouring of wine with a similar intention and the adoring of trees. Many of these rites were hardly connected with the pagan cult[...]
>
> Such rites, or rather traditions, were punished by confiscation of the house and prosecution for high treason. The new laws were reinforced sternly by magistrates and judges. The third of a field in which a pagan fire had been kindled was confiscated, even though its owner had not participated in the rite. 'Prejudice disguised itself in religious fervour, and many accused their neighbours of paganism in order to despoil them.'
>
> (*Magic, Supernaturalism, and Religion*)

The ancient temples that were too large to deconstruct had large pits dug out from underneath their foundations, after which the logs used to prop up the temple were burnt so as to cause a collapse of the structure. Theodosius not only killed all those opposed to his new laws, he as well had the properties confiscated of anyone found practising forbidden activities before he prosecuted them for high treason. This was the first time that the use of cannabis was completely forced from public view anywhere in the world.

It is no wonder that the Roman Catholic Church grew so powerful quickly. However, many people acknowledged Christianity in public while continuing to practice other religious traditions behind closed doors. Eventually, though, many ancient secrets were lost from the public. Punishment for practising pagan activities was so great and intense that people forgot their earlier beliefs over long periods of time during which they refrained from earth-worshipping ceremonies and could not openly speak ancient words. The fear of God ruled over the populace.

The Roman Catholics wrote and edited the New Testament about 367 AD. There is much debate about when the first four books, Mathew, Mark, Luke, and John, were written. By this time, the original teachings of Jesus and the early Christian Gnostics had been so distorted that only subtle remnants of their ideologies actually remained in the Christian doctrines. The Catholics rewrote the Old Testament to suit their purposes. They discarded scrolls and teachings that did not favour the history or ideology of the ruling Roman statesmen, the first of many "new translations." The extent that the Roman Catholic Church used the teachings of ancient, secret societies in its formation is exemplified in the selection of December 25 as the birth of Jesus, a date which was previously celebrated by the worshippers of Mithra, who claim their God was born from a rock on that day.

Since the formation of the Roman Catholic Church, prohibition, in many forms, became rampant. While the prohibition of worshipping different deities and using some substances has probably been recurring for thousands of years within a broad range of different, unconnected cultures, we can be especially critical of the Roman Catholic Church because it is so well documented, recently in historical terms, and still prevalent in today's society. The severe oppression brought upon its membership was only shadowed by the murderous genocide the clergy periodically directed towards other non-Christian societies. For hundreds of years, writing and reading were restricted to a select few. Priests were sanctioned to conceal, destroy, or rewrite history according to the beliefs and principles of the Church and the Pope. At certain times, everyone except the clergy and ruling caste was prohibited under threat of death for having any written material except the Bible. Sexual behaviour was seen as unclean, unless for the sole purpose of procreation, with young girls being strongly encouraged, if not forced, to stay a virgin until marriage. Any erotic same-sex relationships were considered to be sins that would be punished in hell.

In order to maintain control over the masses, the Christians did not allow the use of mind-expanding plants, like mushrooms or cannabis, but encouraged the use of alcohol, which has a tendency to dull the mind and spirit. Hemp was grown for rope, canvas, and seed, though its psychoactive properties were never publicly discussed. Those who continued to use plants to heal or gain enlightenment celebrated their ancient pagan ceremonies in secret, using all sorts of codes, symbols, and secret words with double or triple meanings, to conceal their activities, yet still communicate with each other.

The Holy Wars

Christians who desired control of the Holy Lands launched the Great Crusades in 1096. The Christian warriors took control of Jerusalem in 1099, after much ugly bloodshed. In 1118, Hugh de Payns founded the Order of the Knights of the Templar in Jerusalem, to protect travellers going between the lands conquered during the Great Crusades and the homeland in Europe. Every one of the Knights Templar had to be first ordained as a Catholic priest before being given the title of knight. The Knights Templar quickly became very organized and influential, not only building large, beautiful castles to live and worship within, but also by gathering about them a fleet of ships, huge tracts of land and a strong, fierce army of devoted followers. They were in many ways the first bankers of the world, as they would guard money and goods while in transit, protect and store valuables, and loan money. They also created the cheque, as it was easier to transport signed papers across vast areas of land than actual gold or coinage. The Knights Templar learned many languages, interacted with many religions, and learned about local myths, histories, and healing practices across the known world and beyond. The Knights Templar slowly developed ties to the Haschischins and Sufis and quietly worshipped the Mother Goddess in the form of the Virgin Mary, while striving to put women and femininity back to its rightful divine place in society.

A Knight with a Muslim

> The Order of the Knights of the Temple was founded in the Holy Land in 1118 A.D. Its organization was based on that of the Saracean fraternity of "Hashishim," "hashish-takers," whom Christians called Assassins. The Templars first headquarters was a wing of the royal palace of Jerusalem next to the al-Aqsa mosque, revered by the Shi'ites as the central shrine of the Goddess Fatima.
>
> Western Romances, inspired by Moorish Shi'ite poets, transformed this Mother-Shrine into the Temple of the Holy Grail, where certain legendary knights called Templars gathered to offer their service to the Goddess, to uphold the female principles of divinity and defend women. These knights became more widely known as Galahad, Perceval, Lohengrin, etc.
>
> (*The Women's Encylopedia of Myths and Secrets*, 1986)

The tradition of these warriors lives on in the stories of King Arthur and the Knights of the Round Table. The origins of these myths can be traced back to the Order of Knights of the Templar. The names Perceval, Galahad, and Lohengrin are accredited with not only with being valiant defenders of women, but as also being mystics, sages, saints, wizards, and alchemists. The search for the Holy Grail was the symbol for humanity's search for the life-serving knowledge that flowed from Christ's cup. The turning of lead into gold represented the ability to transform the leaden mind of an ordinary person into the golden mind of an enlightened human being. This transformation is the very crux of alchemy. Unfortunately, it is these beautiful qualities and practices that the Church felt most threatened by. They accused the Templars of witchcraft and Satan worshipping, not to mention homosexuality, a practice that the sexually repressed Catholics still feel especially threatened by.

> The Knights Templar were involved with the Saracen fraternity of the Hashish-Takers. One of the original purposes of the Knights (before the Inquisition when the Powerful Church wrenched them away from the service of the "Lady" and coerced them to fight for the Church), was to aid and uphold the feminine goddess, which included the practice of a secret form of Tantra. This spiritual quest was degraded by the Church's attempt to remove the power of the Goddess by making her the mother of God, and relegating her to a secondary position.
>
> (*Undoing Yourself With Energized Meditation and Other Devices*)

During this time, other religions were slowly gaining in popularity in parts of Northern and Eastern Europe, where many ancient traditions continued. The Cathar religion was for a long time larger and more openly defiant towards the Catholics than the Templar's organization. The Cathars worshipped the Mother Goddess. Both men and women were preachers who taught that direct personal experience with the Creator was more authoritative and important than any ideology or doctrine. It is not known exactly how or when the Cathars started, but in all probability they began with nomadic traders who brought hashish from the Near East, along with the proper knowledge of how to induce mystic states of extra-ordinary experience with it. The Cathars were very well read—studying Hebrew, Arabic, Cabala and other esoteric philosophies—at a time when most other European nobles and aristocrats were illiterate.

Saint Dominic Guzman, founder of the Dominican Order, tried for years to convert the Cathars into the Roman Catholic Church. They laughed at him. The Church's ideology was ridiculous to them. They knew that the cross was a symbol for Christianity picked years after the death of Jesus, used to stir up feelings of guilt and sin. To the Cathars, the idea of living with a spiritually and intellectually inferior religion was ludicrous. When Guzman saw that they would not be converted, he sent in the army and the Holy Wars began. In 1204, an army 30,000 strong destroyed the Cathars, laying waste to French towns, cities, and villages, killing at least 15,000 men, women, and children.

Eventually, the Templars openly denied the crucifixion of Jesus, saying they had proof that he lived a full life after his public death on the cross. This was more than enough for the Roman Catholic Church to want to kill them all. They also practised a seven stage initiation process, much like the Mithraic and Gnostic religions, and may have secretly worshipped a mysterious head. The Sufis used the phrase Golden Head to refer to someone who has reached a higher state of consciousness after consuming the required amount of cannabis. It has been put forward in Chris Bennett's book Green Gold the Tree of Life: Marijuana in Magic and Religion, that this mysterious head of the Templars was a drinking cauldron from which the knights drank bhang, the holy grail of enlightenment.

Unfortunately, we may never know, because on Friday October 13, 1307, about 15,000 of the French Templars were rounded up, imprisoned, and tortured. Many were burned at the stake. Most died in jail without ever having a chance to defend themselves. This is despite the fact that many had previously denounced their Goddess worship in public. In a small French port, several large sailboats full of Templars escaped. These surviving Templars may have formed the basis for the first international ex-military pirates. These former Templars robbed the Catholic Church and French Monarchy at every opportunity. Ex-Templars in hiding may have also been behind the Peasant's Revolt in England in the late 1300s. The history of the Templars ended with this heinous crime on the first Friday the 13th, with the few surviving Templars joining the secretive Masonic Lodges throughout Great Britain for protection.

Masters of Thought Control

All this time, the alchemists continued to practice their arts throughout Europe under the watchful and deadly eye of the Church. Alchemists convinced the Church that they were conducting tests in search of a means to turn lead into gold—a perfect cover to grow and collect rare and forbidden plants while operating extravagant laboratories to conduct experiments. It was an excellent diversion from their real purpose of turning the dull, dark minds of humans into bright, beautiful companions in the Youniverse. The symbols and codes of these alchemists kept their objectives hidden, for the most part, and an underground network of brilliant physicians and scientists stayed in contact for hundreds of years, right under the eyes of watchful authorities. A rich volume of texts is available from this time period, though most of what was produced has been lost. Many incredible pieces of art and literature that the Church found were destroyed as quickly as they were discovered or captured. This includes manuscripts from alchemists, religious criticism and observations, paintings, prophecies, scientific theories, literature, poetry, and philosophical arguments. Nostradamus, for example, wrote in coded words, though never about his use of hashish. However, most of the pictures and words done by alchemists were so immersed in symbology that interpreting the information is still more of an art than a science.

The first scientific societies in Italy and France were full of cannabis inspired members. These worldly scholars worked together to found both science and medicine as separate, established organizations from Church and State by creating universities across Europe. Though knowledge of hashish, mushrooms, and mystical experience remained hidden, Europe became flooded with old forgotten texts from the ancient world. Reading and writing was rediscovered by the masses as being a pleasurable and worthwhile experience. Knowledge of history, philosophy, and the human condition was considered an asset, for the first time in over 1000 years. New artistic expressions flourished. Though the pagan rituals were forgotten, the use of cannabis was not.

> Pagan Gnosticism was condemned and prohibited. But the Magian and the Hermetic Gnostics withdrew from philosophical and mystical debate, many sages having previously retired into the kitchen laboratory to kindle the Mystery hidden in matter—to make it manifest. The language of debate held in such high esteem in the golden age of Alexandria underwent a metamorphosis in the kitchen laboratories of the sages: the inscrutable lexicon of Alchemy was born from it. Without the key to the alchemic lexicon the Christian high priests—bishops—thought alchemy was nothing more than formulas for making gold from lead or other worthless items.
>
> (*Green Gold*)

Witches and warlocks, older women, suspicious looking strangers, homosexuals, disfigured people, and some children, did not fare very well during certain time periods. They were sought out by the Church, and tortured and burned on a stake whenever an unfortunate incident occurred. Crazed religious fanatics had no problem condemning and killing any suspicious suspect whenever evil seemed to appear in the community.

There is really no way to calculate the number of

The Mystery of the Hermetic Arts

people killed by the Church during the Holy Wars, the Inquisition, and witch-hunts that followed. It continued on for centuries, spanning as far as the United States. The most accepted theory puts the number of deaths around 9 million people, with 85 percent being women. The witch burnings began around 1233, soon after the end of the Albigensian Crusade that wiped out the visible Cathar religion, and continued to kill innocent people until the early 1800s. Christians tortured and killed all worshippers of the Mother Goddess, making them confess to crimes they did not commit. One popular method of discerning the pagans from the "true followers of Christ" was to force their heads under water for 5 minutes. If they lived they were burned as witches, and if they died they were given burials as faithful Christians. There are countless horrible stories of the suffering, both of innocent people accused of paganism by vengeful neighbours and those who worshipped the Mother Goddess.

The early universities in England and France in the 12-1300s were created by people who wanted to wrestle the authority to confirm the legitimacy of knowledge, science, and law away from the church and monarchy. However, public education became a favourite tool of prohibitionists, who used it to force their will upon the masses. After hundreds of years of restriction in academic and scientific exploration, the Renaissance of the 16th century opened the gateway to knowledge and wisdom kept secret for over 1000 years. A renewed interest in ancient knowledge generated a resurgence of creative thought and art, especially in the upper class. For the first time in a long while, intellectuals not affiliated with the Church became prominent figures in the State and society. However, the efforts of these enterprising men were quickly channelled towards empowering the wealthy.

After the French Revolution of 1592, the Church and monarchies of Europe reorganized to maintain a tight grip upon the populace, but the damage done to the credibility of these power structures could never be completely repaired. Governments began forming around the world to wrestle power away from monarchs and churches so the wealthy could manage society's affairs. It was in the 1800s when the State began to formally take control of the education system from the Church, for several different purposes. The main reason behind this move was to create better citizens for the State. This meant perfecting techniques of manipulation and deceit that the Church had used to subdue its membership from birth. The education system also serves to further separate youth from spiritual connections of any kind, distracting young, active, intelligent minds from the practice of studying any philosophy or ideal that does not serve the purpose of State. With control of the education system, the State gained the ability to manipulate productive young people from the general population, turning them into good soldiers and consumers.

Prohibition in the 1900S

Coffee was actually made illegal in England for a brief time in the 1600s, because the King believed that the drink was partly responsible for discussions about revolution that were occurring in the coffee houses of the time.

The British started selling opium to the Chinese in the early 1700s, causing addiction and draining silver from the domestic economy. Some of the first well-documented examples of smuggling occur after the Chinese authorities attempted to stop public sales of opium.

> By the time company officials added privately produced Malwa opium from western India to the trade in 1830, a refined system of smuggling was well established. In a legal sense, company officials could argue that their hands were clean. Private buyers from Calcutta purchased company opium and sent it on consignment to agency houses at Canton, such as the British firm, Jardine, Matheson, and Company. Agents, dealing with what was still in theory a legitimate commodity, never actually sold opium in China. When the brown mud in the holds of the ships reached the costal waters nears Canton, it became contraband. Chinese merchants then transferred the opium to floating warehouses, clandestinely sold the precious cargo, and then turned the profits over to the agency houses. Some 5,000 chests of opium, each weighing 145 pounds, reached China in 1820; the annual average for the next decade was more than three times that amount. And in 1834, the final year of its monopoly of the China trade, the East India Company sent as many as 20,000 chests of opium to Canton- all quite legally.
> (*Opium and Foreign Policy*)

In March of 1839, Chinese authorities sent a letter to Queen Victoria demanding the end of the opium trade. When this did not happen they began confiscating opium. The British declared war to protect their economic interests. After defeating the Chinese in a couple years, the resulting Treaty of Nanking established Hong Kong as a smuggling port for opium and other British interests for more than a century. Soon after the British created a market for opium in China, other groups became involved in the trade. Chinese warlords began forcing peasants to grow more poppies than food, often paying mercenaries in opium. In the early 1900s, the Japanese became involved in the industry because the profits were high and the use of opium was seen as a means to make the Chinese docile and lazy so they would submit to eventual assimilation by the Japanese. People began growing opium around the world, transporting the drug to China or any other large city with a sizeable Chinese population. Eventually the practice of smoking opium spread throughout the world, with many respectable monarchs and politicians indulging openly.

However, this century saw a change in attitude towards opium. After anti-Asiatic riots in 1907 in Vancouver's Chinatown, Mackenzie King visited Canada's west coast to review the situation. In 1908, he introduced the Opium Act, which prohibited the manufacturing and sale of opium and its derivatives morphine and heroin, without expressed consent from the government for medical reasons. These laws were used to arrest Asians

Top: Opium den
Bottom: Women's groups lead fight against alcohol prohibition

when local authorities felt the desire to impose their will. While many Asians in North America did use opium before prohibition, they did not commit crimes, generally speaking. That is, not until the violent enforcement of the laws forced the prices of pure heroin artificially high. In 1911, King introduced legislation to include cocaine on the schedule of prohibited drugs. For the first time, the simple possession of an illegal substance became a criminal offence. Religious puritans, fledgling pharmaceutical companies, racists, lawyers, police, and black market entrepreneurs had huge incentives to support prohibition, while women's groups wanted substance abuse and violence stopped.

In 1919, in the U.S., the 18th Amendment prohibited the sale, manufacture, or distribution of alcoholic beverages, an action that turned respectable, honest citizens into criminals if they wanted to drink. Bars turned into lawless, underground drinking holes, with shootouts and robberies occurring continually between rival bootleggers. Organized crime exploded in size, as the excitement of breaking the law and earning a lot of money drew in aimless youth and hardened criminals. The alcohol itself was completely unregulated, causing blindness and even death due to poor quality or tainted products. By the time alcohol was reintroduced to the U.S. market on Dec. 6, 1933, large gangs of criminals owned legitimate businesses that they had created to launder illegally obtained money through. Though alcohol abuse is still a very serious issue today, it could be greatly countered, in my opinion, if marijuana were legally available.

Today, liquor continues to be a far more harmful drug than marijuana, both in terms of the physical and psychological damage done to the individual's body after prolonged use, and in terms of the social costs. In 1988, for example, 48,000 U.S. citizens died directly from alcohol abuse, as compared to 3,000 people who died from the abuse of illegal drugs, none of which were a result of marijuana use. Alcohol, though, is the favorite tool of the establishment to subdue and discourage the public from rediscovering their connection to Mother Earth.

While it is commonly thought that the laws prohibiting smoking cannabis were first meant to punish Mexicans, it was actually for herb-loving Mormons coming back from Mexico that the first anti-cannabis laws were brought into effect in Utah in 1915. With a large number of poor Mexicans in the southern U.S., other states seized upon the idea of marijuana prohibition as a means to convince them to go home. Possession of cannabis became illegal in Wyoming (1915), Texas (1919),Iowa (1923), Nevada (1923), Oregon (1923), Washington (1923), Alaska (1923) and Nebraska (1927).

The main reason legislation prohibiting cannabis was passed was that the economic entities who that felt threatened by hemp were able to channel these racist and puritan ideals into political action. "Reefer Madness" was the term most commonly used to describe the campaign waged against marijuana, and the public was motivated into action with false information, racist accusations, and religious pressure. Images of non-white rapists wandering the streets in violent rages while under the influence of marijuana were drilled into the public's mind. Poverty was blamed on the drugs ability to relax the mind and ease the daily discomforts in life, turning the lower classes into lazy, unproductive slackers pulling down society.

The Hearst Newspaper Company, the largest newspaper chain in North America, had heavily invested in the timber industry to maintain a constant supply of cheap wood pulp. People who desire to control the conscious behaviour of the multitudes own the media, and prohibition quickly became a favourite theme of editorials. The people behind this slanderous campaign completely deceived the public as to the true intentions behind these laws, and the repercussions of this campaign are still very apparent today.

William Randolph Hearst began his campaign against cannabis in 1916 by literally inventing the word marijuana to describe the weed smoked by Mexicans. After investing massive resources into timber acreage, the Hearst Paper Manufacturing Division was about to lose millions of dollars to the cheaper, higher quality hemp paper if something was not done about it. He was very clever in his creation of the word marijuana, as no one understood that he was actually referring to the cousin of hemp and no one could foresee the two plants being prohibited together. Hearst was able to quickly gather allies in his campaign against cannabis, starting with the chemical industry as hemp paper uses a quarter of the sulfur-based acid chemicals used in the production of pulp paper.

Since the cannabis culture was only prominent in poor, black communities in larger cities like Chicago, no pot smoker could seriously defend their rights and freedoms. It was a reoccurrence of the suppression of blacks, a step taken by certain religious, economic, and political forces in government because some free black people had gained money, power, and respect in some areas of the country. This threat was to be controlled by prohibiting the use of marijuana. Since herb was used by most members of radical black organizations and musicians, and many were arrested for possession. Numerous false stories circulating during these times concerning the horrible effects of marijuana smoking were obviously directed at blacks, Hispanics, and the poor. This form of propaganda is still used today, though it is being disproved time and time again.

> [...]Macleans's Magazine published the first of Mrs. Murphy's articles on the illicit drug traffic in Canada. The stated purpose of the series was to arouse public opinion to pressure the government for stricter drug laws. Mrs. Murphy's ability to blend statistics, anecdotes, popular racial bias, fables and sensationalism gave her writings wide public appeal. The public's profound ignorance of drug use and the lack of objective information enhanced her apparent expertise. Newspapers across Canada seized on the drug issue and publicized her views. Her writings were extremely influential in shaping Canadian drug laws which underwent significant changes throughout the 1920s.
>
> (Introduction to *The Black Candle*)

The first female judge in the British Empire, Emily Murphy was a fierce advocate for women's rights and has been considered one of Canada's greatest women. On the other hand, she was a racist who believed that lesser humans should be sterilized. Her writings were very influential in Canada where laws prohibiting cannabis were passed without debate in 1923, 14 years before the laws were passed in the U.S. Britain passed cannabis prohibition laws in 1928.

> In 1923, marijuana was criminalized with a simple declaration in the House of Commons: "There is a new drug in the schedule." There was a unanimous passage of this addition and no debate. Marijuana had been associated with Mexican migrants and black jazz musicians, and was said to be connected with madness and promiscuity.
>
> Alcohol was also a much discussed and debated drug during this period of history. Temperance unions were formed, spurred on, at least in part, by women who had experienced drunken beatings at the hands of husbands. In a national referendum on prohibition in 1898, a slender majority of Canadians endorsed the principle of an alcohol-free society; Wilfrid Laurier, a proponent of a "wet" Canada, declined to transform this majority view into legislation. While the temperance movement was ultimately successful in accomplishing a short-lived national prohibition in 1918, as part of the war effort, it was never really as powerful as anti-opium, cocaine, or marijuana organizations. By the late 1920s, each province had repealed its prohibition

> legislation, and the popularity of alcohol began to climb, along with the power of the industry and the power of government to raise revenue from sales.
> (*High Society*, p. 9)

In the U.S., the Pure Food And Drug Act of 1906 was the first set of laws written with the intention of regulating cannabis, along with other mind-altering substances. The Harrison Act of 1914 was intended to tax and strictly regulate the use of cannabis, though only opium and coca products became controlled with this legislation. The first laws of this century prohibiting the distribution of cannabis by pharmacists were passed in the Louisiana legislature in 1911. The cities of El Paso, Texas, and New York passed laws banning the possession of cannabis in 1914. By 1923, many states had passed laws prohibiting the use of cannabis. The Marijuana Tax Act was introduced seven years after the Federal Bureau of Narcotics was created under the guidance of Harry Anslinger, in 1930, partly to employ thousands of officers formerly focused upon alcohol prohibition.

One of the brains behind cannabis prohibition was Andrew Mellon. He became very wealthy from working in the banking industry before founding Gulf Oil. After becoming the richest man in America, he became U.S. Secretary to the Treasury, giving him control over the country's fiscal policy. He was also the prime banker for the DuPont Company, which was developing fuel additives like tetraethyl lead, sulphate for pulp paper, as well as nylon and other plastics. Andrew Mellon loaned DuPont money to buy General Motors while pushing for tax breaks for oil companies. While it is rumoured that he did not like his nephew, who joined the family by marriage, when Andrew Mellon hired Harry Anslinger he knew he needed an arrogant, pushy, bull-headed leader to do the job. When Harry Anslinger began his campaign to eradicate cannabis as head of the Bureau, 16 states had mild laws prohibiting the use of the herb. By 1937, though, Harry Anslinger had convinced everyone that cannabis was a dangerous drug that had to be eliminated, even though the American Medical Association testified before Congress against the Marijuana Tax Act.

> Cannabis and its preparations and derivatives are covered in the bill by the term "marihuana" as that term is defined in section 1, paragraph (b). There is no evidence, however, that the medicinal use of these drugs has caused or is causing cannabis addiction. As remedial agents, they are used to an inconsiderable extent, and the obvious purpose and effect of this bill is to impose so many restrictions on their use as to prevent such use altogether. Since the medicinal use of cannabis has not caused and is not causing addiction, the prevention of the use of the drug for medicinal purposes can accomplish no good end whatsoever. How far it may serve to deprive the public of the benefits of a drug that on further research may prove to be of substantial value, it is impossible to foresee. The American Medical Association has no objection to any reasonable regulation of the medicinal use of cannabis and its preparations and derivatives. It does protest, however, against being called upon to pay a special tax, to use special order forms in order to procure the drug, to keep special records concerning its professional use and to make special returns to the Treasury Department officials, as a condition precedent to the use of cannabis in the practice of medicine.
> (Williams, W.C., Legal Counsel testifying to Congress, American Medical Association, July 10, 1937)

> On the day the Marijuana Tax Stamp Act was enacted—Oct. 2, 1937—the FBI and Denver, Colo., police raided the Lexington Hotel and arrested Samuel R. Caldwell, 58, an unemployed labourer and Moses Baca, 26. On Oct. 5, Caldwell went into the history trivia books as the first marijuana seller convicted under U.S. federal law. His customer, Baca, was found guilty of possession. Caldwell's wares, two marijuana cigarettes. Caldwell was sentenced to four years of hard labour in Leavenworth Penitentiary, plus a $1,000 fine. Baca received 18 months incarceration. Both men served every day of their sentence.
> *(Bourrie, Mark, National Post, Jan 11, 2002)*

In 1938, a number of arrests were made, with huge piles of confiscated pot being burned for the media to watch. Most arrested were visible minorities. Since the main goal of the program was actually to eliminate hemp, these arrests were never serious attempts at stopping the use of marijuana. Up until recently, thisplan has been successful, with the media still creating confusion about the issues to stall the reintroduction of cannabis.

From the Anslinger papers and the Washington, D.C., DEA Library, containing the old FBN (Federal Bureau of Narcotics) papers and memos, we have this: From 1943 to 1948, Anslinger ordered all of his agents throughout the country to watch and keep marijuana criminal files on virtually all jazz and swing musicians; but not to bust them until he could coordinate all the jazz busts of the same night!

His goal and dream was to bust them all in one giant nationwide sweep! This would garner the front page of every newspaper in America, and make Anslinger more famous than J. Edgar Hoover. The jazz and swing musicians would be shown to the youth of America for what they really were "dope fiends."

Anslinger ordered his agents to keep files and constant surveillance on the following "low life" Americans and other bands, swingers and comedians: Thelonius Monk, Louis Armstrong, Les Brown, Count Bassie, Cab Calloway, Jimmy Dorsey, Duke Ellington, Dizzy Gillespie, Lionel Hampton, Andre Kostelanetz. Also under surveillance were the NBC Orchestra, the Milton Berle show, the Coca-Cola program, the Jackie Gleason program, and even the Kate Smith program. All people we think of today as musical innovators and wonderful Americans.

(*The Emperor Wears No Clothes*, p. 90)

For four decades Harry Anslinger lead drug prohibition efforts

Though we will discuss this further in the chapter on the revival of cannabis, it is worth noting here that we owe the return of marijuana and hemp in part to the U.S. government. For it was during the 1940s and 1950s that the White House began secretly conducting all sorts of weird tests upon criminals, the mentally and physically handicapped, students, volunteers, and soldiers, some of which involved experimentation with LSD. These experiments, combined with a renewed interest in the ancient, aboriginal use of psychoactive drugs and medicinal herbs, lead to an intellectual whirlwind of exciting possibilities. Many rebels in the 1950s, and even 1940s, smoked pot in an act of defiance.

In 1961, after years of effort by Harry Anslinger, the UN Single Convention on Narcotics was signed by most countries in the world, leading to a renewed interest in curbing international drug trafficking. This was followed by the 1971 Convention on Psychotropic Substances and the 1988 Convention against Illicit Traffic. All of these conventions were intended to establish a system of drug regulations where only scientific and medical uses of various prohibited substances (coca, opium, cannabis, and LSD) were permitted. Despite these international laws, drug use continued to rise in the 1960s causing great public concern. When Richard Nixon began using the term "War on Drugs" the American public felt society was starting to fall apart, and blaming drugs was easier than dealing with greed and corruption.

Throughout the decades since Richard Nixon first proclaimed a war on drugs in 1971, the United States has repeatedly made a "drug war exception" in its foreign policy toward repugnant and repressive regimes. Policy toward Burma has been by no means an aberration. The United States adopted a similar approach to Panama's dictator, Manuel Noriega, Peru's authoritarian president, Alberto Fujimori, and even Cuba's dictator, Fidel Castro. Incredibly, Washington even sought to cooperate with the infamous Taliban regime in Afghanistan and praised its professed effort to eradicate the cultivation of opium poppies. The willingness of U.S. administrations to collaborate with the most odious dictatorships in the war on drugs is long-standing and continuing. It is more than a little distressing to see the U.S. government betray America's values in that fashion. Moreover, it has been a myopic, utterly futile policy. In case after case, Washington's ostensible partners in the anti-drug crusade have themselves been extensively involved in drug trafficking.

(*Unsavory Bedfellows*)

Prohibition Now

Every country has different laws regarding the possession, sale, and cultivating of cannabis. Most countries have followed the lead of the U.S. and prohibited the use and sale of cannabis with harsh punishments since the 1920s. In some countries like India, Morocco, and Iran, it is still customary for citizens to smoke hash or drink cannabis in bhang while tourists need to be more careful of law enforcement. Many countries have punished cannabis traffickers more than the U.S. Though the death penalty is available to cannabis traffickers in the U.S., it has never been used. Other countries like Saudi Arabia, China, Indonesia, Thailand, Singapore, Malaysia, and the United Arab Emirates do execute cannabis growers and dealers in public displays and street justice killings. The Philippines only stopped executing people caught with over 500 grams of cannabis in 2006, when the death penalty was abolished. China executes about 500 drug dealers per year, though it is not clear how many are cannabis traffickers.

In 1996, Republican Newt Gingrich (who has himself admitted to using cannabis) proposed to introduce a mandatory death penalty for a second offence of smuggling 50 grams of cannabis into the U.S., in the proposed law H.R. 4170. Luckily, this proposal failed. Current federal law (1994 Crime Act) sets the threshold for a possible death sentence for marijuana offences at 60,000 kilograms or 60,000 plants (which includes seedlings) regardless of weight. An individual can also be sentenced to death for running a continuing criminal enterprise that distributes marijuana and receives more than $20 million in proceeds in a year, with the weight of marijuana involved not factoring into it.

In Oct. 2004, Australian Schapelle Corby was arrested in Indonesia and sentenced to 20 years in jail after 4.2 kilos of cannabis was found in her baggage. This is in contrast to Australia where cannabis has been decriminalized because it is not considered a major health or social problem. Many European countries have reconsidered harsh punishments for cannabis use, with the Netherlands leading the way. Laws prohibiting the use, sale, and production of cannabis still exist in Holland; however, the police have decided to allow cities to license cafes selling hash, cookies, and other cannabis products. Italy, Spain, and Switzerland have decriminalized cannabis, while the U.K. reclassified cannabis in 2001, so that simple possession can no longer lead to jail. In Germany, Jamaica, and Belgium, the law is not strictly enforced. Mexican politicians tabled a bill in April of 2006 that would have decriminalized the possession of small amounts of all drugs (up to 5 grams of cannabis). Pressure from the U.S. made Mexican President Vincent Fox send the bill back to be rewritten. In Norway, Sweden, and France, though, penalties for possessing cannabis still include jail.

> But in practise, the French law system is so harsh that it has even been condemned recently in the European Court of Human Rights in Strasbourg. The reason is as follows: the use of illicit drugs (of any nature) is a minor offence, up to 1 year in jail—"minor", a question of speaking[...]—while possession and trafficking can lead to 20 year sentences, even life sentences—according to the new Penal Code of 1994. But it happens that someone that is caught with tiny amounts of cannabis can easily be prosecuted under the term of "detention of illicit drug with intent to trafficking by way of networked crime." And the Penal Code says that under this charge the police can keep you in custody for 4 days. Usually for a common crime, or even serious one the custody is fixed at 1 or 2 days. So the police have the power to impose this 4 days of custody (without the presence of their lawyer) for the possession of cannabis for personal use. Europe has developed a legal system under the European Convention on Human Rights—which

Steve (2nd from left) and Gary (right) Tucker in jail with visitors courtesy of Shattered Lives: Portraits from America's Drug War

> is a protection system for the convicted people. The European Court of Human Rights is based in Strasbourg, and recently it has condemned France for illegally convicting a man for possession of Cannabis. The Court said it was unfair to confine someone during 4 days without his lawyer's help, for the sole reason that he was in possession of illicit drugs. Unfortunately this decision doesn't force France to change its law.
>
> (Cannabis And Marijuana Laws And Law Enforcement In Europe, NORML Annual Conference, 2000)

Many states in the U.S. have decriminalized cannabis for recreational users, or attempted to legalize its use for medical purposes with referendums like Proposition 215 in California, in 1996. In 2005, the United States Supreme Court ruled in Gonzales vs. Raich that the federal government's drug laws supersede state medical cannabis laws, thus allowing DEA agents to raid clubs where local officials refuse to do so. Many jurisdictions continue to resist the U.S. federal government and the DEA, particularly California.

> After three decades of increasingly punitive policies, illicit drugs are more easily available, drug potencies are greater, and drug barons are richer than ever. The war on drugs costs Washington more than the Commerce, Interior and State departments combined- and a strangled court system, exploding prisons, and wasted lives push the cost beyond measure.
>
> (*Smoke and Mirrors*)

In Canada, the federal government has come close to passing bills to decriminalize cannabis, once in the 1970s under Pierre Trudeau, and again early this century. However, the current Conservative government is backtracking from any moves to decriminalize cannabis, and has cut funding for medical cannabis research while holding friendly press conferences with the U.S. Drug Czar, John Walters.

> In a sample of Vancouver marijuana growing operations "busted" by the police, most of those who were convicted received no jail time: 55 percent. Five more percent were sentenced to a single day or less and another 8 percent received sentences of between one day and 31 days, while still another 8 percent received 60 days. Some 11 percent were sentenced to 90 days. Of those who are repeat offenders, half are reconvicted within the year. Of the 35 percent who were fined, the average fine amounted to less than $1,200: a small amount considering the size of most marijuana operations. While police resources are spent to destroy nearly 3,000 marijuana growing operations a year, the consequences are relatively small for those convicted.
>
> (*Marijuana Growth in B.C.*)

Every country in the world has prohibited drugs in an attempt to manipulate the behaviour of citizens by controlling which substances are legally available. By giving illegal organizations a virtual monopoly in the unregulated supply and distribution of some expensive, powerful, mind-altering substances through the government's policy of prohibition, we are combining two very dangerous factors: drug use and violence. When drugs are only available on the black market, the substance is often mixed with harmful chemicals, and because some addictive drugs are so expensive, addicts use the most effective method of maximizing the high they can receive for their money. This causes many addicts to use needles when getting high, increasing the chance of death from overdose and/or contracting a disease. Violence created by prohibition has become a huge problem because addictive drugs like cocaine and heroin are only available from large criminal organizations who are willing to commit serious crimes like murder, kidnapping, extortion, torture, and theft to protect their economic and political interests. Also, many people addicted to cocaine and heroin resort to violence to obtain the cash to support their habit.

> We conclude from these observations that the international regime for the control of psychoactive substances, beyond any moral or even racist roots it may initially have had, is first and foremost a system that reflects the geopolitics of North-South relations in the 20th century. Indeed, the strictest controls were placed on organic substances—the coca bush, the poppy and the cannabis plant—which are often part of the ancestral traditions of the countries where these plants originate, whereas the North's cultural products, tobacco and alcohol, were ignored and the synthetic substances produced by the North's pharmaceutical industry were subject to regulation rather than prohibition.
>
> (*Report of the Senate Special Committee on Illegal Drugs, 2002*, p. 31)

Prohibition has created different problems for different countries. Excessive profits can be made selling illegal drugs, especially cocaine and heroin, which has lead to the formation of paramilitary drug cartels and street gangs. These drug networks spend vast resources corrupting, threatening and paying off local and state officials to protect their crops and processing facilities. Several terrorist groups use the profits from illegal drugs to support random acts of violence against innocent civilians from developed countries. Good farmland is used to produce opium and cocaine using a great deal of chemical fertilizer and pesticides. Many poor nations are overwhelmed with violence from competing drug cartels and gangs. On the other hand, in the U.S. many police estimate that about 50 percent of thefts and assaults that occur in cities are from people stealing for drugs or fighting over them. As a result, no one in the world is truly safe from violence that is related to the war on drugs.

> The pursuit of prohibitionist foreign policies can generate serous consequential harms in the countries where those policies are imposed - defoliation and other environmental harms due to crop eradication, adverse health consequences from the use of herbicides on drug crops, loss of livelihood for already desperately poor farmers. Because prohibition is often enforced selectively, production and trafficking by some ideologically favoured groups is tolerated, enhancing their power. This enables them to brutalize the population and destabilize the otherwise democratic governments. Colombia is perhaps the best example. Both the left-wing guerrillas and the right-wing paramilitaries in Colombia are known to profit extensively from the trade in cocaine. Thus, prohibitionist policies both empower those domestic terrorist groups that are able to profit from the drug trade and often create other hardships within the countries on whom those policies are imposed.
>
> (*How Drug Prohibition Finances and Otherwise Enables Terrorism*)

"In captivity" by Calvin Treiber, 1993 courtesy of Shattered Lives: Portraits from America's Drug War

This scenario allows governments to create sweeping laws, often violating the rights and freedoms of citizens, and hire legions of drug enforcement agents, prosecutors, social workers, and prison guards. New by-laws by municipal governments fine landlords who do not inspect rentals for growing cannabis every couple of months. A conviction for simple possession of cannabis can lead to loss of education, employment, and ability to travel. Drug testing is becoming more common in the workplace and schools. Testing positive for illegal drugs like marijuana can lead to suspension from professional and amateur sports.

> The prohibition of drugs is premised upon the vast number of negative consequences that are thought to arise from their use. Once focusing on the moral corruption of the individual, today there is an emphasis on the pharmacological effects of the drugs themselves, including the possibility of addiction, adverse psychological conditions and physical illness. Aside from damage to the individual, advocates of prohibition also indicate the extensive social costs that are borne by the community at large—such as health service provision for addicts and the crime that is often generated by the need to finance a habit. As the criminological community has pointed out for many years, efforts to control these risks through prohibitionist policies have generated their own sets of problems and paradoxes. Most prominent in the literature are discussions of the emergence of black markets, criminal subcultures and organized crime, the financial and community costs of law enforcement and dilemmas in the administration of effective public health strategies.
>
> ("The Problem of Drug Prohibition For Drug Users")

With no regulation governing the production of drugs, both youth and adults are vulnerable to contaminated substances, sometimes leading to overdoses or other serious medical problems. Intravenous drug use has caused a series of health and social problems, ranging from the Hep C epidemic occurring in East Vancouver and in the prison system, to discarded, infected needles sticking into people in parks. Families are torn apart by the drug war in many ways, with children being taken from parents who use illegal drugs in many countries, and access to children denied or restricted after even an accusation of illegal drug use. People with physical and mental health problems often resort to trying illegal drugs in an attempt to kill pain or block out bad memories, sometimes leading to poly-drug addictions. Every country in the world has problems related to the war on drugs, though few of those problems are the result of the actual use of the drugs themselves.

> In Britain, Canada and in the U.S. a new punitiveness toward women drug users, especially single parents, has emerged since the 1970s. These women are depicted as producing social problems and draining already strapped social, medical and criminal justice services. Their perceived unwillingness to work, to follow doctor's orders, to refrain from using drugs not approved by the medical profession and justice agents, and their unfitness to parent justifies cutbacks in social and economic services and increased criminal justice spending[...] Women who are suspected of using drugs are vulnerable to inter-locking and competing spheres of formal and informal control. However, not all women are impacted similarly, poor women and women of color are most vulnerable to state and nonstate intervention. In addition, although state and nonstate intervention is patriarchal, women are also instrumental in regulating and punishing women constructed as "less moral" than themselves. Women in Third World nations such as Columbia and women of color and Aboriginal women continue to be negatively affected by colonization in all its diverse effects. The punishment of women who use illegal drugs, especially pregnant women, challenges the rights and reproductive autonomy of all women.
> (*From Witches To Crack Moms*)

Though a stated purpose of the war on drugs is the protection of children and traditional family values, ironically, many of the real effects of this war are exactly the opposite of the intended goals. In the U.S., where the war on drugs has been waged more than anywhere, hard drugs are readily available to children as soon as they have a disposable income. For several reasons, prohibition may actually encourage drug use in youth. First, the unregulated illegal drug industry allows underage consumers and distributors to enter the market. Young people have few means of earning a good income, but the buying and selling of small quantities of drugs can be an easy way to earn money, become popular, and support a lifestyle of recreational behaviour. Youth learn from the drug war to disassociate from adults because being honest about illegal drug use could result in a loss of household privileges, or even forced institutionalization for drug rehab, something more common in the U.S. Youth can get very confused about morality when they see adults they respect using drugs despite the law, questioning everything they are told by the government, and distrusting authority as a result. Rebellion and defiance are often feelings provoked when using drugs against the law, especially in youth. Youth quickly develop cynicism toward their country if they are told they are free yet are not allowed to consume the substances they want. One strategy used by prohibitionists has been to distort the negative impacts of drugs, especially cannabis, to youth in an attempt to scare them into not using drugs. However, many youth have realized that they were lied to, while others become curious after school presentations.

Violence in the illegal drug trade seriously affects children if their parents are producing or distributing.

Arthritis patient Will Foster serving 20 years for growing courtesy of Shattered Lives: Portraits from America's Drug War

While many children whose parents are involved in the industry never see or hear any violence, there is always the threat of robberies and bad deals in situations where the police cannot be called to handle the problem. In many countries like Jamaica and Columbia, the gang and paramilitary violence that controls regional production and distribution networks can affect entire communities, not just those involved in the drug industry. Many families suffer the loss of an innocent loved one due to random violence in the drug trade. The violence that the state can impose upon families in the name of the drug war is also devastating. Children can be used as informants against their parents if they admit to school officials that mommy and daddy smoke pot and grow some in the backyard. In some states in the U.S., women who are caught using illegal drugs while pregnant are charged with endangering the life of their child, and are often thrown into prison while their child is taken away forever by the state.

> Although the proportion of our citizens using illegal drugs is spread across all segments of society, a vast majority of those imprisoned for drug related crimes are the poor and the minority populations. Citizens released from prisons having served their time for drug related offences carry the stigma of "drug felon," limiting their ability to find work, obtain a mortgage, or receive federal college loans. Children are being lured or coerced from school to the streets to participate in a drug economy, which offers an (unrealistic) opportunity to become rich. The double problem of the addicted citizen and the crime-related economy supporting that addiction imposes a cost on society which must be paid using the same resources needed for improving education, public safety and quality of life. As a result, a small segment of society is holding the remainder hostage in an environment of danger, fear, low educational attainment, and low job opportunities.
>
> (White Paper, City of Hartford, Oct. 2005)

In the U.S., it is a common practice to send youth caught using cannabis or other illegal drugs to a drug rehab facility, and to require youth living at home to submit to random urine tests. The impact on a child of losing a parent to jail can be very painful and confusing, which can lead to anti-social behaviours and loss of identity. If an illegal drug user is caught they can lose their job, social status, family, and volunteer positions, along with their right to vote (in the U.S.) often with little or no recourse. Even if the illegal drug use is for a medical purpose, there is usually too little sympathy extended to people caught with illegal drugs, especially single mothers. People using or addicted to illegal drugs are often treated differently from those using or abusing legal drugs by family, social workers, medical staff, and the criminal justice system. Some families, especially Christians, have placed allegiance to the laws of the country over commitment to their own brothers and sisters, shunning and sometimes even informing upon them if they are even suspected of using illegal drugs. Ultimately prohibition, not drug use, is causing more harm to families and western society.

Prohibition takes away from a person's dignity since the State has decided that since a few people cannot control their use of some substances, no one should be allowed legal access to them. When respect is shown towards our youth and tax-payers that credits them with having the intelligence to make healthy, proper choices regarding the substances they use, then, and only then, will we begin to see some improvements in the disturbing patterns of drug use we see today under prohibition. Laws cannot eliminate non-violent action, self-medication or human nature.

Ironically, while lawyers writing lies may have been the original foundation of prohibition, the courts may be the final burying ground for these laws. In Canada, for example, the government, under the leadership of the pot-smoking Pierre Trudeau, has created a document called the Charter of Rights and Freedoms that is being used by activists, like myself, to argue that the laws are unreasonable, arbitrary, and malicious. The Charter enshrines the rights of the individual against the rights of the state, and this is where the laws ultimately fail. For just as the state has no right to enter the bedroom, it has no right to enter the minds and bodies of its citizens by prohibiting mind-altering substances.

Without a doubt, the prohibition of drugs is the most disastrous set of international laws ever established. The War on Drugs has wasted precious government resources, strained the environment, hampered economic development, and damaged or destroyed many lives in the process—with few positive results. Drugs have become a problem in society, but prohibition amplifies, if not creates, many of these issues, and the War On Drugs makes it virtually impossible for drug abuse to be seen as primarily a health issue. As long as prohibition remains the dominant international policy regarding naturally occurring mind-expanding plants and fungi, the multitude of problems faced by people around the world because of the War on Drugs will continue.

Chapter 6 Counter-Culture Revival

The Discovery of LSD

The discovery of LSD is a very important factor affecting the revival of the cannabis culture. The use of psychedelics stronger than cannabis paved the way for social acceptance of the herb, and changed a few minds about the value of a totally sober life. Dr. Albert Hofmann worked at the Sandoz Pharmaceutical Company in Basel, Switzerland, in 1938, when he developed Lysergic acid Diethylamide - 25 (LSD). He was trying to create a stimulant for blood circulation from ergot, a fungus that contains many interesting alkaloid chemicals. Although the initial tests performed by the company upon animals proved unsuccessful, five years later, April 16, 1943, Albert picked his creation up to perform some more tests, and accidentally dosed himself with a very small amount in the process. Three days later, he decided to first try inhaling vapours without effect. He then tried drinking two hundred fifty micrograms in a water solution, a relatively small dose of material for a clinical test. LSD was born!

This first trip on acid has since become a classic example of the initial feelings induced by LSD. First, Albert had a strange bicycle ride home from the lab, experiencing time and space distortions. Then, after being examined by a physician, who assured him that aside from enlarged pupils he was fine, he was overcome with feelings of death and doom. He came down later to see a world of intensified colours, visualized sounds and flowing energies. Upon waking from a refreshing night's sleep, Albert found a brand new world full of beauty and mystery around him. While not entirely pleasant, this experience changed Dr. Hofmann forever.

Dr. Abby Hofmann

"As far as I can remember, the following symptoms were strongly marked during the height of the crisis, which had already passed when the doctor arrived: dizziness and defective vision; the faces of those present seemed to me like coloured masks; strong kinetic disturbance alternating with paralysis; my head, my whole body and limbs seemed at times very heavy, as if filled with lead; cramps in my legs, my hands sometimes cold and numb; a metallic taste on my tongue; my throat dry and contracted; a feeling of suffocation; I was alternating bewildered and in clear understanding of the situation, so that I sometimes stood outside myself as a neutral observer as I shrieked half madly or babbled unintelligible nonsense."

Stoll notes that the doctor found a somewhat weak pulse, but in general normal circulation. Six hours after taking the drug, his condition had improved definitely.

"The visual distortions were still pronounced. Everything seemed to waver and be out of proportion, like the reflection in an agitated sheet of water. Moreover, everything was soaked in changing, unpleasant, mostly poisonous shades of green and blue. With my eyes closed, colourful, ever-changing fantastic images invaded my mind continuously. It was especially remarkable how all sounds- for instance, the noise of a passing car were transposed into visual sensations, so that with each tone and noise a corresponding coloured image, changing in form and colour like a kaleidoscope, was produced."

(*The LSD Story*, p. 33)

The LSD experience has since transformed many, many lives. Dr. Hofmann has worked hard, breaking through the barriers of consciousness and historical prejudice with mind-expanding drugs and reasonable thinking. Aside from discovering LSD, he has isolated the active ingredients in magic mushrooms, Psilocybin and Psilocin. He also found lysergic acid arnide in morning glory, or ololuiqui seeds, a substance very similar to LSD, which may have been used by the Greeks in the Eleusian Mysteries' ceremonies and by ancient Egyptians. He has maintained an intelligent position towards the use and distribution of LSD since the beginning.

In the early 1950s, the English psychiatrist Dr. Humphry Osmond and two Canadian colleagues were discreetly using mescaline to treat patients with schizophrenia in a state mental hospital in Saskatchewan, Canada. Aldous Huxley learned about the results of Dr. Osmond's research in certain medical and scientific journals, and soon invited Osmond to meet him. Dr. Osmond administered mescaline to Aldous Huxley in May 1953. Dr. Osmond and Huxley's wife observed while he had his first mescaline experience.

Huxley did not hallucinate. He saw familiar objects in a wonderfully compelling and aesthetic way. He was back in a world where the infinite "Inner Light" shone through furniture[...]where the doors of perception were cleansed enough to allow him a glimpse of a "sacramental vision of reality" (Bedford 1974: 538). Huxley's reflections on this experience were published within a year in *Doors Of Perception*. This rather intellectual little book sparked considerable controversy and paved the way for the psychedelic movement. Several other notable anthropologists and scientists, among them James Mooney, Weston La-Barre, and William James, had ingested peyote or mescaline long before Huxley. But, none of them had Huxley's literary reputation, or his ability to make personal mystical experience attractive to the general public.

Why did this famous writer wish to ingest a "mind-expanding" chemical used in the treatment of mental illness? Huxley evidently believed that mescaline, in addition to mystical enlightenment, emotional shock, aesthetic experience, and disease, could facilitate an expansion of mind beyond the narrow confines of the utilitarian, conventionally real world. He assumed that drug-induced experiences could help attune people to a primordial reality which had been bypassed by focusing on the exigencies of survival. Huxley's "Mind at Large Theory" explained human consciousness from a survival-oriented psychological perspective, one rather unlike the cultural relativism espoused by Castaneda. Believing that psychedelics were one of several ways to satisfy the "universal desire for self-transcendence," Huxley advocated widespread dissemination of a "new drug which will relieve and console our species without doing more harm in the long run than good in the short"

(Bedford 1974: 542).

Although Huxley mentioned the limitations and contraindications associated with mescaline use (Bedford 1974: 542-43), he claimed it was almost completely innocuous for most people, and clearly preferable to alcohol, tobacco, marijuana, and barbiturates. To his credit, he abstained from the psychedelic sensationalizing so vividly illustrated by Timothy Leary. In 1956, Huxley declined to participate in a series of half-hour television shows to be aired on CBS. He warned Dr. Osmond that television would reveal the most remarkable mysteries of mescaline and the mind to an enormous plebeian audience. Huxley's experiences had convinced him that reaction from members of the "lunatic fringe" was excessive "even after[...]a two and a half dollar book." (Bedford 1974: 604).

Even without Huxley having to appear on TV, his book, *Doors Of Perception*, contributed significantly to the public's fascination with mind-expanding plants and chemicals. One assumes it was a reader inspired by *Doors Of Perception* whose letter to the editor appeared in *LIFE* magazine in 1957, just after it had published Wasson's extraordinary account of his encounter with Maria Sabina's magic mushrooms in a Mazatec Indian village in central Mexico.

"Sirs: I've been having hallucinatory visions[...] in my New York apartment for the past three years[...]produced by eating American-grown peyote cactus plants[...]from a company in Texas[...] for $8 per 100 buttons." (Stafford 1983: 116)

But by the late 1950s, LSD was already eclipsing peyote and mescaline as America's most preferred psychedelic. Throughout the 1950s, medical and scientific research with LSD generated little publicity. The prominent psychedelic researcher, Dr. Oscar Janiger, believes the research of Dr. Sidney Cohen, a psychiatrist affiliated with the Veterans Hospital at UCLA, stimulated demand for recreational LSD use among the elite of Los Angeles. By the late 1950s Janiger himself was participating in a new institution, social gatherings devoted to recreational use of LSD. These small gatherings held in private homes brought together researchers and celebrities, including Aldous Huxley. LSD-using groups were also being assembled by avant-garde inhabitants of Greenwich Village, New York (Stafford 1983: 42). By 1960, LSD and mescaline had shed their association with insanity and alcoholism. Thanks in part to Huxley and Wasson, LSD had acquired mystical, artistic, and creative connotations among elite on both coasts.

(*Carlos Castaneda, Adademic Opportunism and the Psychedelic Sixties*, p. 14)

Timothy Leary

Timothy Leary, a psychology professor from Harvard University, paraded around the country, giving away acid while promoting its use as a mind-expanding, thought-enhancing drug. Timothy has the distinction of being called "the most dangerous man alive" by Richard Nixon. In fact, he was, for the counter-culture that was forming around Leary and his friends contained the potential to expose government weaknesses, question authority, change consumer purchasing patterns and disrupt society in general. Non-conformity exploded through western society.

The C.I.A. was quick to hear about the creation of LSD. After a few failed attempts to convince Albert to share his secret, they formed Operation Bluebird. This project was in part an attempt to keep Nazi scientist's from Communist influences after WWII and involved the smuggling of Nazi scientists out of Germany, especially those specializing in chemical weapons. The U.S. government, while publicly denouncing nuclear, biological and chemical weaponry, was quietly developing the largest, deadliest arsenal of killing tools in the world, using the expertise of the fallen Nazi regime. In LSD, military leaders saw the potential for mass mind control.

The CIA's official programs included Operation Bluebird, Operation Paperclip, and Operation Artichoke, or MK-ULTRA (MK for Mind Kontrol). These organizations co-ordinated the secret "ratline" which transported Nazi officials across the globe under CIA protection, created twenty-six thousand drugs, including lethal nerve gases, blister agents, "riot control" gases, and an eighty hour dysphonic, incapacitating agent called BZ (quinucldinyl benzilate)—a derivative of LSD. These drugs were stockpiled for possible future use, and were used to conduct mass tests with military officers and civilians without written consent, or any consideration of the negative affects the testing had upon their human guinea pigs. These toxic substances still sit ready for use. Although the smuggling of Nazi intelligence into the United States is slow in being uncovered and exposed, the effects of these devious schemes hampered the cause of social control more than it did to help it.

> Three years later (after the discovery of LSD in 1943), the first LSD experiments in the U.S.A. were conducted under the direction of Dr. Max Rinkel at the Massachusetts Mental Health Center. Rinkel concluded that, "LSD has no therapeutic value whatsoever" (Kobler 1963). In 1953, the year Huxley first took mescaline, the first public LSD clinic in England was opened. The clinic, in a small English mental hospital, was administered by Dr. Ronald Sandison. And, in April 1953 the United States' Central Intelligence Agency became involved in LSD research.
>
> The CIA had $300,000 to study this new and powerful mind-altering drug. Research was partly motivated by the fear that the Soviet Union might acquire this potential chemical weapon. Dr. Sidney Gottlieb was assigned to direct the MK-ULTRA research project. The CIA's mission was to determine whether the behaviour of an individual secretly dosed with LSD could be changed and directed.
>
> The extent of CIA involvement in early psychedelic experiments may never be known. Army, Air Force, and Naval intelligence were also interested in LSD. LSD tests administered by the U.S. Army alone may have involved 1,500 individuals (Furst 1990: 73). Years passed before Dr. Hoffman admitted that during the 1950s the U.S. Army had been contacting him every two years to request his assistance in military experiments (Stafford 1983: 45). In 1953, CIA agents were sent to Sandoz laboratories to negotiate the purchase of enough LSD to "turn on" 100 million people (Stafford 1983: 45). Sandoz laboratories agreed to supply as much LSD as possible to the CIA, and keep them informed of the identities of all other purchasers.
>
> (*Carlos Castaneda, Adademic Opportunism and the Psychedelic Sixties*, p. 20)

The tests using LSD and its derivatives, some of which cause serious mental and physical problems, were conducted in sterile, even hostile environments, with cold demanding doctors drilling questions at the patient, in undecorated and unfamiliar hospitals. Some who were submitted to these harsh experiments committed suicide, others became incapacitated for life, and some completely suppressed their conscious memory of the experience. However, no one has ever died directly from the ingestion of LSD, and many who tried LSD in these experiments, and in their personal lives, became more enlightened, caring human beings.

Soon LSD was introduced to people in and out of the CIA. The academic and medical reports proving its success in helping alcoholics and schizophrenics began surfacing from Switzerland. People like Dr. Humphrey Osmond, Captain Alfred "Cappy" M. Hubbard, Dr. Ronald Sandison, Aldous Huxley, Oscar Janiger, Cary Grant, Anais Nin, Alan Watts, Timothy Leary, Allen Ginsberg, Richard Albert (who later changed his name to Ram Dass), Ralph Metzner, Dr. John Bereford, Micheal Hollingshead, and Ken Kesey, just to name a few of the early pioneers, all took it upon themselves to make personal quests to spread LSD. These psychedelic voyagers have proven that for some, the proper use of pure LSD is a healthy, creative, and life-enhancing experience.

Ken Kesey

Cary Grant has taken LSD and has sung its praises. Television producer Ivan Tors has taken LSD and liked the experience. The late Aldous Huxley was wild about LSD. Author Budd Shulberg, philosopher Alan Watts, poet Robert Graves, writer Alan Harrington, Beat poet Alan Ginsberg and a host of other notables and not-so-notables have tried LSD and did not find it wanting. Cults have sprung up overnight. College kids have stopped jamming themselves into phone booths, showers and Volkswagons long enough to go tripping through their own subconscious. Newspapers and magazines have discovered more mileage in LSD than in LBJ. Intellectuals rhapsodize over LSD. And there are those who look upon LSD as the harbinger of the end of the world. There seems to be no middle ground.

No less than three United States Senate subcommittees have investigated LSD. They heard experts say LSD has precipitated a crisis. They heard experts say LSD has not precipitated a crisis. They heard experts say LSD is bad. They heard experts say LSD is good. Then they went on to pass more laws to control LSD, whether it needed more controlling or not.

(*The LSD Story*, p. 33)

Leary and his friends were supplied with LSD by the World Psychedelic Center in London, England, which mailed acid all over the world. When the FDA started to restrict LSD in medical experiments, Leary and his crew moved to Mexico and set up the International Federation for International Freedom—later named Castalia—which was soon kicked out by Mexican officials. After a few brief stints on Caribbean Islands, they ended up in a Mansion in Millbrook, N.Y. owned by William Mellon Hitchcock, a wealthy oil man who sympathized with Leary.

While this was attracting media attention worldwide, the Merry Pranksters were causing even more trouble on the West Coast. Kesey turned a log cabin outside of Palo Alto into a center for psychic exploration, La Honda. He, along with Neal Cassady, Ken Babbs, Allen Ginsberg, Hugh Romney, and others, joined together to create a world of peace, love, and freedom through the ritual use of LSD. In 1964, Kesey and the gang bought the magic bus, with a sign on the back saying: Caution—Weird Load, and one on the front saying: FURTHER. With Cassady, a.k.a. Speed Limit, behind the wheel, these wacky and wonderful characters drove across the country to visit their idols, lead by Leary, in New York, who found the Merry Pranksters too weird, even for him. So the Pranksters went home to California, where Augustus Owsley Stanley III was waiting to offer his services as one of the world's best acid makers.

Public "Acid Tests" were organized during which hundreds of people would drop Owsley's LSD and trip out to sound and light productions specifically designed to create a mind-expanding environment. Bands like the Grateful Dead began playing in the San Francisco neighbourhood of Haight-Ashbury, where many "Acid Tests" were held. Newspapers dedicated to this increased influx of sense perception investigations were also brought into existence for a time.

The San Francisco neighbourhood of Haight-Ashbury became the focal point for the movement on the West Coast. Rock concerts were organized by the Family Dog, featuring all sorts of LSD influenced music and lots of Owsley acid. The scene revolved around a communal feeling of love and respect, creating a wealth of imaginative art and writings that continue to inspire us today. In 1966, however, things were to change for the worst, as LSD was made illegal by Congress. The hippies replied by getting a few hundred people together to drop acid in Golden Gate Park, calling it a Love Pageant Rally. The first human be-in, which was basically an afternoon in the park with a large crowd of stoned people, was held in January of 1967, later to be repeated in New York City and other places across North America.

Merry Prankster's bus spread cheer across USA

So the proselytizing goes on, and the cultists expand their sphere of influence and the sphere of influence of the drug itself. The seeds are falling on fertile ground. Alan Watts explained it to his interviewer this way:

"There is the psychedelic revolution, which is the vast increase in use not only of LSD but marijuana as well, by people who have never used it before; by intellectuals and people from higher levels or social classes. People are using these substances as they never did in the past.

There is a spiritual, or religious, or even metaphysical hunger among young people which standard brand religions just don't satisfy. For one thing, the standard brand religions have had a cardinal defect for centuries now. They preach. They tell you what you ought to do, but they are not sources of power. In other words, they do not transform the way you experience your own existence or your own identity. They just talk and urge.

This is one of the great lessons of history. Preaching doesn't work. The only way to change someone's behaviour is to woo, not to preach."

The proponents of LSD as a religious experience are doing exactly that. They aren't trying to preach some strange doctrine to which they are only privy; they admit they can't translate the experience into words. They are offering everyone the experience for themselves. Just take the LSD and see, they say. Don't take our word for it, try it! There will be some bad reactions, but the glories of the experience are worth the risk- besides the risks are minimal if you take the LSD in a favourable setting. This "favourable setting," as defined by those of a mystic or religious bent, is definitely not under a doctor's care in his office or clinic. "Such surroundings," says one supporter of LSD as a religious experience, "are not conducive to a good trip."

(*The LSD Story*, p. 70)

The rock and roll scene in Haight-Ashbury was taken over by rock promoter Bill Graham, who sought to exploit the economic potential developing in the corresponding industries. The media built up all of the hype about the problems of drugs, the drug culture, and the teenage runaways getting sucked into San Francisco because of the scene. This press only served to draw more freedom-fighters into Haight-Ashbury, along with every runaway in the country. The drug problems claimed by the press in '66 and '67 proved to become a self-fulfilling prophecy later on. When Charles Manson showed up on the scene with his love-cult of drugged killers, the media and government were given perfect justification to condemn drug users. When Jim Morrison, Janice Joplin, and Jimi Hendrix left this world, the music industry, too, experienced a sudden shift in momentum. The Woodstock festival became the symbol of the 60s, the perfect ending to a crazy decade—ten years which saw blood, sweat, and tears flow through the streets of America every single day.

In the 1960s, the New Age exploded in almost every sphere of human thought and activity. Though many at first chose to suppress, deny, downplay, or ignore new developments in culture, science, and historical perspective, others fully embraced these alternative non-violent ideas, living in defiance of cultural norms and repressive institutions. A wave of love and inspiration swept across the United States, and throughout the world, generating a renewed interest in ancient arts, healing practices, environmentalism, and communal living. A reconnection to Mother Earth, sexuality, and the power of love, along with, of course, LSD, magic mushrooms, mescaline, marijuana, and a variety of plants, pills, and hallucinogenic substances, gave birth to a new sub-culture. The music industry's incredible assortment of inspirational material became a focal point for youth searching for intoxicated ecstasy. All of these factors did not come together at any one time or under one banner-head, but they did have one thing in common: rejection of the rigid authoritative social structures which became consolidated by the U.S. government after WWII in order to contain the public within specified boundaries of intellectual and spiritual exploration.

Smoking cannabis became much more popular in North America after the Vietnam War for a variety of reasons. The soldiers were introduced to the herb by

Asians who saw an opportunity to make extra money. Soldiers smoked cannabis to relieve the mental strain of warfare without slowing the senses down as much as using alcohol or heroin. Injured veterans returning home found that using cannabis helped deal with the physical pain and post-traumatic stress of war. Many veterans' hospitals continued to allow their patients to use the herb, sometimes right in bed. Others began smoking pot as an act of open defiance against the American government and society.

American soldier smoking cannabis

Another factor contributing to the spread of cannabis use beyond specific minority groups is the increase in international travel among United States citizens, and not only among civilians; World War II, and, to a great extent, the Korean War and present Vietnam-Cambodia-Laos "War" have introduced many young (and a few not-so-young) individuals to an entirely different attitude toward the use of cannabis from that which prevails in the United States. The general equalizing or socio-leveling effect of the multicultural military experience (for the typical G.I.) has had some effect in breaking down many of the customary barriers that exist between various minority groups and the huge American middle class.

In both 1925 and 1931 the Army conducted investigations concerning soldiers' use of cannabis in the Panama Canal Zone, largely on accounts of pressure from anti-marijuana advocates. The two reports reached practically identical conclusions: marihuana was found to be not habit-forming, and it was reported as the cause of no deleterious influence on those soldiers using it. But the Army findings created much concern in non-military newspapers and magazines, which "attacked them viciously for they saw one of their most lurid topics of reportage snatched away from them." The Army in turn responded with an article entitled "The Marihuana Bugaboo" which stated in part that "the smoking of the leaves, flowers and seeds of *Cannabis sativa* is no more harmful that the smoking of tobacco or mullen or sumac leaves[...] It is hoped that no witch hunt will be instituted in the military service over a problem that does not exist." The military chose to decide there was no problem, but openly admitted that many soldiers stationed abroad were turning on. During World War II and the Korean War the widespread but not truly large-scale use of marihuana among the troops was regarded as a trivial issue; indeed it was minor compared to the problem of opium addiction, especially for soldiers stationed in the Far East. But the period following World War II saw a decided change. The civilian and especially ex-G.I. use of marihuana was no longer limited to various underprivileged or unprivileged groups, with a small sprinkling of users among "the bohemian fringe of writers, intellectuals, artists, and musicians. [...] Many of the young men who had fought in the war returned with more than their battle experiences; a good number of them had sampled marihuana. [...]A decade had passed since the 'Marijuana Menace' scare of the thirties and, although the propaganda of the anti-marijuana groups still hung heavily in the air, the war veterans studying on the GI Bill spread its usage to campuses across America. The drug entered a whole new stratum of society. College students now encountered marijuana users of their own social class." And, perhaps as important, the students met marihuana users of their own skin colour.

(*Marihuana Reconsidered*, p. 195)

A large number of Americans dodged the Vietnam draft and came to Canada. Many of these draft-dodgers came to British Columbia where they hid in the mountains and grew cannabis in the summer. Apparently, it was this influx of determined growers who learned how to produce cannabis indoors, partly because they had the entire winter to experiment, partly because they had no other socially acceptable form of income, but mostly because they loved the herb and wanted to overgrow the government with it.

> Tough laws might have been in force at home, but American troops in Vietnam were smoking potent marijuana to alleviate a dismal situation. The use of cannabis was more common during the war; it was nearly universal. One well-known writer on the war beat reported that 75% of the soldiers stationed in Vietnam had used cannabis. Some soldiers smoked cannabis habitually because it helped them overcome fear- that is, they felt it made them better soldiers. But others smoked it for precisely the opposite reason, as writer William Novak found when he interviewed veterans for his book *High Culture*. "We knew that stoned soldiers were not aggressive, alert and effective soldiers," one veteran told him, "and because we opposed the war in a way that nobody but a grunt could experience, we used to say that smoking dope was a political statement[...] We enjoyed the idea that by getting high we were frustrating the President, Westmoreland, and all those war-mongers in the rear." When the U.S. officials decided to abandon the war effort, the growing resistance of the fighting core was a prime consideration.
> (*The Great Book of Hemp*, p. 167)

The year 1969 proved to be very important in our history for many reasons. The "Summer of Love," as it became affectionately termed, was a turning point for Western society, not just because the sub-culture had awakened a significant proportion of society to new states of health, activism, and awareness, nor because the anti-establishment movement was able to offer intelligent, feasible alternatives to the current political and economic problems. Western society changed because that fateful summer many rich, influential businessmen and politicians became convinced that something drastic had to be done about youth before the militant control that the U.S. government had effectively spread across the globe during the last century was dismantled by peace activists and student rioters at home. Men sitting behind closed doors making important economic and political decisions correctly realized that not only was the Vietnam War getting out of hand, but the population was becoming aware of government secrets that exposed corruption and eroded public trust. Ideas of peace, equality, love, transparency, and freedom are extremely hazardous to the health of many financial and military institutions. Though they could not directly attack those ideals, they could exclude, discredit, imprison, threaten, or even kill, those who were voicing these revolutionary themes.

Cannabis on the Run

Many factors converged in the late 1960s and early 1970s that led to a conservative backlash that gained full power during the Reagan era in the 1980s. Most of the world had not seen open religious use of mind-altering substances for thousands of years, if ever, and many powerful spiritual organizations began to attack drug use as being a tool of Satan. At other times, though, the drug reform movement was not entirely responsible, giving the authorities plenty of chances to condemn drug use

> It figures May 19 would be a bad day for the Nixon administration—it was the birthday of both Malcolm X and Ho Chi Minh. It was also, in 1969, the day the Supreme Court sided with drug guru Timothy Leary.
>
> Leary had been arrested four years earlier on a complicated charge stemming from the 1937 Marijuana Tax Act, a law that established federal control over marijuana not by banning it but by requiring possessors to pay a tax of $100 an ounce, a great deal of money in 1937. The thinking was that most people wouldn't pay it and then could be arrested for tax evasion.
>
> Customs agents on the Tex-Mex border had found a joint on Leary and charged him with failing to pay the $100-an-ounce transfer tax. Three months later, a federal judge in Texas sentenced him to thirty years in prison and a $30,000 fine.
>
> Leary argued in his appeal that had he paid the tax, he would have been admitting to marijuana possession, a crime in Texas. The tax requirement, therefore, constituted double jeopardy. Earl Warren's Supreme Court agreed, and suddenly, as Woodstock summer loomed, the federal government found itself with no control over the possession of marijuana.
>
> By coincidence it was two days later that Nixon nominated the conservative Warren Burger to replace Earl Warren as chief justice of the United States Supreme Court.
> (*Smoke and Mirrors*, p. 21)

In 1969, under the leadership of Richard Nixon, the U.S. government declared an official "War on Drugs." Protesting against the Vietnam War was not only causing civil unrest and disobedience, but it was also forcing some Americans to question the motives, indeed the very sanity, of those in charge of the military and the Pentagon. The owners of large multi-national corporations, the bishops and priests of organized religions, the military officers and war-loving mercenaries, the CIA and other intelligence communities, black market entrepreneurs, and the elected representatives in government, all realized individually that almost every aspect of their traditional way of life was threatened by this cultural evolution. They had better do something about it soon before it was too late. The War on Drugs was a perfect public relations campaign for the Nixon government to align itself with middle-class Americans.

One of the problems they started to tackle was the amount of cannabis that was flowing into the U.S. from Mexico. The Mexicans had done very little to stop the cultivation and exporting of cannabis, telling the U.S. government that the drug problem existed because of Americans demanding the herb. They refused to allow Americans to sponsor spraying cannabis crops with herbicides. All that changed in the fall of 1969, when American border officials began Operation Intercept.

> On September 21, 1969, the border suddenly squeezed closed. Customs inspectors who usually waved almost everyone through, began exhaustively searching every glove compartment, wheel well, backpack, and pocket. The result was predictable chaos, with lines of cars extending for miles. The Mexicans screamed blue murder, then pledged co-operation, and after twenty days the blockade was lifted.
>
> While few arrests were made, Intercept yielded two noticeable effects. First, aerial drug smuggling began on a scale never seen before. "Recently positioned radar installations showed the blips of intruding aircraft from the south," the New York Times reported. Second, Intercept succeeded at drying up marijuana supplies temporarily. Whether this was good news, however, is questionable. "I know of four kids—and they're really kids, like under 16—who've tried smack because they couldn't get grass," one Cambridge, Massachusetts, dealer told Newsweek. A doctor running the Haight-Ashbury Free Clinic in San Francisco noticed a sudden increase in kids strung out on stronger drugs than pot and was furious. "The government line is that the use of marijuana leads to more dangerous drugs," David Smith told reporters. "The fact is that the lack of marijuana leads to more dangerous drugs."
>
> (*Smoke and Mirrors*, p.24)

Part of the groundwork for interfering with trends in the sub-culture was partly laid through the 1960s with undercover police penetrating the Hells Angels Motorcycle Club. This loosely-knit organization has flooded the market with a variety of super-potent, dangerous drugs like speed and cocaine, while penetrating legal, political and economic special interest groups. Drugs were used to escape the realities of everyday life instead of being used to enhance awareness. Leary eventually sold to the Weathermen, who had helped him escape jail after a cannabis bust, and the Brotherhood of Eternal Love, a group that had taken over the world's production of LSD.

When the word came from the Pentagon to come down on the counterculture, it happened quickly with seemingly amazing results. A combined effort of several different organizations successfully pushed the cultural revolution underground. Activists were rounded up and imprisoned, with more than one being beaten, their books, possessions, offices, and homes destroyed. Propaganda in the media whitewashed the entire campaign, with all sorts of lies, half-truths, and cover-ups. Books were banned and store owners selling paraphernalia were shut down. Organized religions and psychedelic cults attempted to recruit ex-hippies, as many had lost faith in the sub-culture because the repressive forces converging upon it seemed too large and powerful to overthrow. Many decided that it was necessary to cut their hair, get a 9-5 job, and enslave themselves into normal society, while smoking pot in the privacy of their homes, living in constant fear of arrest, loss of a job or exile from the family. Others completely quit smoking pot and dropping LSD.

Growing pot was one of the few tax-free means by which these runaways could earn a decent living. Several commune-like organizations in the States began appearing in the 70s. Others followed the Grateful Dead back and forth across the country in a state of spiritual bliss and disorganization. Steven Gasket escaped from Haight-Ashbury to start The Farm in rural Tennessee. This hippie commune is still operating as a tribute to the real grassroots communities that are the result of a true union with Mother Earth and cannabis. Some who answered the call of the Goddess chose to go to places like The Farm or the Hogfarm, a Northern California commune that provided food and medical care to Woodstock. Thousands of other sub-culture farmsteads and squats grew throughout the world. Many attempts at living communally were not successful, but this could be mostly blamed upon the fact that our society has almost completely forgotten how to share. Those who experienced living communally, whether for a day or for a week, gained a sense of culture that can rarely be experienced in modern society.

The Emperor Wears No Clothes

For a while in the late 1970s, it appeared as though North American governments were about to change the cannabis laws to allow for simple possession. In 1973, the "LeDain Commission Of Inquiry Into The Non-Medical Use Of Drugs" was released in Canada after three years of public inquiry and debate about mind-altering substances. This report urged for the legal distribution of illicit substances and stressed the need for authentic education to replace fear tactics.

The most influential legalization organization is the National Organization for the Reform of Marijuana Laws, founded by 28 year-old Keith Stroup, in 1970, in response to the Nixon "War on Drugs." This group of lawyers, smugglers, and concerned citizens helped Oregon, California, Maine, Colorado, Alaska, and Ohio to end criminal penalties for possession of cannabis by the summer of 1975. By defending people with excessive jail sentences for cannabis offences, lobbying various political parties and levels of government, and organizing several public relations campaigns, NORML was able to fight the Nixon administration on this issue. Many bright, young lawyers joined the group. Things changed after NORML's 7th Anniversary party when the public found out that Peter Bourne, President Carter's senior drug policy advisor, snorted cocaine with Stroup and several others at the event.

> The Bourne incident simmered for months, seemed to have died out, then suddenly exploded into public view the next summer. It was a tragedy for Peter Bourne, but he was not the only person harmed by the affair. Keith Stroup, who contributed to Bourne's downfall, was soon under pressure to resign from NORML. Jimmy Carter was hurt politically by the scandal, once more embarrassed by a member of his inner circle. Finally, the Bourne affair hurt the movement for drug-law reform to which Bourne, Stroup, and Carter were all, in different ways, committed. There were larger political forces at work, of course, but the Bourne incident put the Carter administration on the defensive about drug policy. It destroyed NORML's political effectiveness and it emboldened the hard-liners who opposed any reform of the drug laws. The political pendulum, which had been moving toward reform throughout the 1970s, and which seemed to reach a peak with Peter Bourne's arrival in the White House, was swinging back the other way. "The drug-law reform movement vanished up Peter Bourne's nose," one participant later said bitterly.
> (*High in America*, p.23)

Some of the historical uses of hemp were known by a few people in the 1960s and 1970s, though the entire story of cannabis had not been put together on paper. While some of the individuals arguing for drug policy reform were sober intellectuals, the majority of people interested in cannabis were drug users. Stereotypes of hippy long-hairs smoking pot persuaded many average consumers to hide their use of cannabis. Though conservative forces in government were able to further entrench the drug war in the 1970s and 1980s, those who loved the herb continued to grow and smuggle more and more every year into North America.

> In 1973, when Jack Herer was thirty-three and an author on marijuana, he took an LSD trip with his friend and business partner, a head shop-owner called 'Captain Ed' Adair[...] They had decided to

Hemperor Jack Herer illustrated by Norman Soo

campaign for marijuana legalization and to do all they could to tell America that they believed it to be "good and fair."

After the publication of his book on marijuana connoisseurship, Jack had been approached by a number of readers telling him about an angle he hadn't covered: the fact that marijuana was formerly used to make paper. "I used to look at the little pot and wonder how they used that to make paper." They said, 'Did you know they used to use this to make clothing or sheets or pillowcases, or that 'canvas' is the Dutch pronunciation of Cannabis?' I just got absolutely 'How come I've been smoking for years, I've become a writer on marijuana, and I never knew it could be used like this.'"

He started going to libraries and teasing out information about the other use of cannabis as hemp, the fibre crop that had been cultivated in America until the mid-1950s and is still grown on a big scale in China, Eastern Europe and some former Soviet republics. He found old textbooks that praised hemp as a rotation crop and a US Department of Agriculture report from 1916 which argued that hemp could replace wood pulp as the raw material for American paper. The more research he did, the more uses he discovered for this versatile plant.

Then, as Jack and Captain Ed were still talking, stoned on acid, an idea descended on the pair simultaneously, and with the force of revelation. "Boom! In a millionth of a second it came to us that marijuana could save the world. It sounds so ridiculous, but as we came down from the acid we knew we were still right. It had been right there in front of our faces: so far in front of our faces that we couldn't see it. In this one night, in this one-millionth of a second, we were able to realize that it was the number one paper, fibre, fuel and food. It's the only single source that grows without pesticides and herbicides. It wasn't only greater than the other sources—it was greater than all the three million other sources on earth."

This thought bubbled away in his mind for a few years. Then in 1980 he wrote a four-page booklet on marijuana prohibition entitled The Emperor Wears No Clothes. The title comes from the Hans Christian Anderson story of the naked potentate who has been tricked into believing that he's magnificently clothed, and it reflects the author's conviction that his opponents were straw men, and that marijuana prohibition was a house of cards which would collapse once the facts were known. In 1985 the booklet re-emerged as a full-length book, published by Herer. It's now in its eleventh edition, having sold so far an astonishing 600,000 copies.

Since then "hemp shops" have opened in almost every American city, selling hemp clothing, cosmetics, foodstuffs and drinks. Calvin Klein's 1998 Spring/Summer collection featured a silk and hemp fabric. In 1996 Adidas launched a shoe called 'The Hemp' to draw attention to the uppers made from hemp fabric, and kept it on the market despite pressure from the White House's Office of National Drug Control Policy.

(*Cannabis Culture*, p. 115)

The influence of *The Emperor Wears No Clothes* spreads around the world. Activists and farmers in Canada and Europe were able to use the historical documentation provided in Jack's book to educate others about the history of cannabis prohibition, and the potential agricultural and industrial benefits of hemp. Others who used cannabis as medicine were inspired with the proof that cannabis had been legally used as a medicine in recent history. The introduction of *High Times* magazine, in 1974, by Tom Forcade, was another important step in the changes that were occurring during that time period. Many of the early stories and pictures focused on cocaine and other drugs. However, in 1988 a new editor, Steve Hagar, removed other drugs from the magazine and concentrated upon cannabis. That same year he organized the Cannabis Cup in Amsterdam, the most celebrated cannabis event in the world today.

The marijuana debate is an increasingly complex one, and there are many perspectives from which to view it: historical, scientific, economic, legal, cultural, sociological, political. My focus in this book is mainly on the politics of the issue and, beyond that, on its human dimension. As a writer, I have been fascinated by the mixture of comedy and tragedy that has surrounded the issue, and by the wonderful variety of people who became caught up in it in the 1970s. The cast of characters includes Stroup, an admirably flawed protagonist; Peter Bourne, a well-intentioned man who ventured beyond his political depth, Hugh Hefner, who scorned drugs for years, then suddenly found marijuana giving him unexpected pleasure, and a cocaine investigation causing him unexpected pain; Gordon Brownwell, a Ronald Reagan advisor who was transformed by psychedelic drugs into a pro-marijuana politician; Sue Rusche, a liberal Atlantan who became an anti-drug crusader; Tom Forcade, a smuggler turned Yippie who made a fortune with a pro-drug magazine; Frank Demolli, a college freshman whose love of marijuana won him a twenty-five-year prison term; and Robert Randall, a teacher who challenged the government to save his eyesight. I knew most of these people, and I thought them all caught up in political currents they could barely understand, much less control, currents that tossed their lives about, challenged them, defined them, and sometimes destroyed them. Few controversies in recent years have touched more American's lives than the drug issue, and to examine this issue is, I think, a way of looking at America in the 1970s, perhaps as good a way as any.

(*High in America*, p.8)

One of the changes in the North American cannabis community that began to occur in the late 1960s, and that exploded in the 1970s, was the number of plants being grown domestically. Most of the cannabis and all of the hash that was smoked in the 1960s came from Mexico, Columbia, Jamaica, the Middle East, or other countries. That changed in the 1970s. The art of growing cannabis indoors was discovered, and various methods were developed to maximize yield and quality. Despite the federal government's efforts, people everywhere decided to express civil liberties by smoking and growing cannabis.

In the mid-1970s America was seeing a boom in home-grown marijuana, from both back-to-the-land hippie families and returning veterans. The basis of Robert Clarke's research was field trips to out-of-the-way places: Indiana, Arkansas, the Ozark mountains of Kentucky. "It was mostly people who were growing for their own consumption. At that time there weren't a lot of people going out to make a bunch of money; it was Ma and Pa growing enough to sell some and make their life easier. It mostly started with a bunch of hippie drop-outs, organic vegetable growers."

These first-time growers were less set in their ways than their counterparts in other regions where they had been growing cannabis for generations. The Americans soon discovered sinsemilla; the best Mexican marijuana farmers boost potency by uprooting the male plants and harvesting the females without letting them set seed. Meanwhile people returning from the hippie trail brought seed from varieties that had never been seen in the New World. The most famous hybrid that resulted was "skunk," whose parentage included the pungent indica varieties from Afghanistan. A California-Afghan connection was first opened up in 1968 by the underground society of bikers-turned-psychedelic drug dealers called the Brotherhood of Eternal Love. Glen Lynd, a founder member, travelled to Kandahar and developed a lucrative connection with the Tokhi brothers who owned a rug shop there. A kilo of Afghan hashish which cost $20 in Kandahar could resell for $21,000 in California. A single shipment in an adapted van raised $400,000 for the Brotherhood to spend on distributing free LSD. Meanwhile, the community of growers felt sufficiently relaxed to inaugurate competitions for the best pot, held in the autumn as a kind of harvest festival celebration.

(*Cannabis Culture*, p. 134)

The intellectual community was frustrated by the majority's willingness to allow the continuation of the drug war when it violated civil liberties, had no scientific basis and did no have a realistic chance of success. The "Moral Majority" argued that drug use was a tool of Satan meant to enslave the spirit of those foolish enough to tempt fate.

Still, there has been progress. In the 1970s thanks to the efforts of, among others, NORML, the Marijuana Commission, and the Drug Abuse Council, America began to face up to the complexities of the marijuana issue. In just a few years we advanced from widespread arrest and jail for smokers to a national consensus that simple marijuana smoking should not be punished by jail, and towards serious debate of marijuana's eventual legalization. NORML's role in this was quite remarkable. There had been presidential commissions before, and Ford Foundation projects, but there had never before been a national lobby on behalf of people who were violating the law. For a few amazing years in the middle of the decade, largely because of Stroup's creativity and audacity, a well-organized pro-marijuana minority was able to seize political momentum and to pass decriminalization laws in a dozen states. Inevitably the anti-marijuana majority caught on to what was

> happening and a reaction set in, but the issues had been raised, progress had been made, and the debate would never be so one-sided again.
> (*High in America*, p.321)

Sensational media reports stirred many religious organizations and parents groups to focus upon eliminating illegal drug use. Though costs from alcohol related deaths, violence, addiction and disease have always been greater than all other drugs combined, the "Just Say No" campaign drove kids away from illegal drugs using inaccurate information, fear, and harsh punishments. That is not to say that many irresponsible drug dealers and users were innocent, because there were many visible social problems and accidental deaths from illegal drugs. By the time Reagan was elected, there was already a well-organized, well-funded movement working against the momentum that lead to so many states changing their possession laws.

> The crisis—youthful pot smoking—was already abating on its own. Lloyd Johnson's high school survey in 1981 showed the first decline in teenage marijuana smoking in six years. Likewise, teenage disapproval of marijuana was rising, which confirmed that the decline was real. Drug use historically rises and falls in cycles; people try a drug, like it, get bored with it, and then a new generation discovers it; this may have been a "boredom " stage. The parents' movement can probably take some credit, as can the overall conservative swing that put Ronald Reagan in the White House. "There is less adolescent rebellion now," Lloyd Johnson told reporters upon releasing the figures, "so youth is more apt to listen to the caution of their elders and less apt to use drugs as a form of social protest." Tobacco use was also in decline; kids may have been turning off the idea of drawing hot smoke into the lungs. For whatever reason, youthful marijuana use was diminishing. At that particular moment, with adolescent pot use dropping, cocaine a problem only for the very rich, and heroin off the national radar, there was as little need for a War on Drugs as at any time since Richard Nixon declared his in 1969.
> (*Smoke and Mirrors*, p.143)

However, the Ronald Reagan era forced all of the state governments, except Alaska, to establish penalties for cannabis possession that were harsher than the original laws. In Alaska, the only holdout, it was not until 1991 that laws forbidding the cultivation and possession of cannabis were enforced again. In Canada under Pierre Trudeau, it appeared as though the government was prepared to legalize the use of cannabis and possibly other substances in an attempt to curb other disturbing trends in society. In the end, though, Nancy Reagan and her mindless droves of supporters rekindled the War On Drugs, and the 1980s saw a decrease in the use of smelly pot, while cocaine use skyrocketed.

> Over the course of his eight years in office, Reagan spent $22.6 billion on his revived Drug War. Another major escalation was pushed through under George Bush, who spent $45 billion in a single term. Under Clinton, spending has continued to increase, with $16 billion for one year allocated in the 1998 fiscal budget. Those figures show federal spending only, not counting all unfunded mandates passed onto states.
>
> Spending at other levels of government adds up to approximately the same as the federal budget, so in 1998 you can expect to see well over $30 billion spent of the Drug War.
> (*Shattered Lives*, p.101)

Law enforcement officials found it very frustrating to know so many people were willing to risk horrible punishments to smoke and grow cannabis. Despite years of education campaigns aimed at discouraging citizens, especially youth, from using cannabis, the general public seemed content to tolerate the use of the herb. Stores began selling grow equipment and fertilizer that was specifically meant for cannabis, though the salespeople would never talk about the plant in the store for fear of police surveillance. This was a legitimate concern, as people are arrested to this day after being seen buying grow equipment at various stores. Thousands of raids on head shops have been conducted by various levels of law enforcement in North America in the last few decades. One of the largest multi-department raids occurred in 1989.

> The following day, the DEA conducted raids in forty-six states on retailers selling the kind of indoor-gardening equipment that could be used to grow marijuana—or orchids. The DEA selected the stores because they advertised in *High Times*.
>
> *High Times*, whose circulation floated around a quarter million, advertised drug paraphernalia. It ran a monthly "Trans-High Market Quotation," to track pot prices in various cities. Its photo

> spreads featured loving full-color photos of marijuana buds bursting with THC. These facts constituted "an open invitation to violate the drug law," in the DEA view. *High Times* also was a leading satirist of the War on Drugs, making fun of the DEA and William Bennett personally. The magazine called him the "Drug Bizarre" and ridiculed his cigarette addiction. WHAT JERKS! Ran one typical headline. BENNETT BLASTS POT WHILE AIDE HAS NICOTINE FIT!
>
> As word got out about the raids, *High Times* lost two-thirds of its advertisers. Though the DEA claimed it wasn't exercising unlawful prior restraint on *High Times* First Amendment rights to publish, harassing its customers was having the same effect.
>
> George Bush's first year in office ended with a rapid-fire series of explosive "drug" stories. Five days before Christmas, the United States invaded Panama and captured the onetime CIA asset and current Drug Enemy Number One, Manuel Noriega. The citizens of Kansas City, Missouri, running against a national tide of tax cutting, voted to boost their sales tax by 0.25 percent to beef up drug enforcement. Keith Jackson was finally convicted of selling crack to the DEA for President Bush to use as his speech prop. And the FBI paid a former girlfriend of D.C. mayor Marion Barry to lure him into a hotel bedroom and—over his repeated and fully recorded demurrals—offer him a crack pipe until he accepted. The grainy footage of the mayor smoking crack aired everywhere, an example, some pundits said, of the scope of this national tragedy.
>
> (*Smoke and Mirrors*, p.294)

Governments around the world continued to pour more and more resources into the prohibition of drugs as each decade passed. The introduction of crack cocaine devastated urban communities, and further entrenched division between drug users and the establishment. Smuggling, cultivation, distribution, and enforcement tactics constantly changed with technology, court decisions, and by the simple process of trial and error. For a variety of reasons, though, most people dealing illegal drugs always find a way to be one step ahead of the law.

Plant Power Prevails

Though corporate and government institutions have aggressively sought to eradicate cannabis in the last few decades, the benefits of using the plant have been great enough to encourage thousands of individuals to its defence. Many strong-willed people from all walks of life have declared war back against ignorance and superstition. While there are numerous intelligent, resourceful cannabis freedom fighters, it has not always been easy to get them to work together. One of the more controversial leaders in the movement is Ed Rosenthal, writer of many grow books and other material. In 1994, he published *Hemp Today*, a book that questioned some of the statements made in *The Emperor Wears No Clothes*, upsetting its author, Jack Herer.

> Confronted with this polemic, Jack Herer failed to appreciate, according to Rosenthal, that "my complaint is really a technical complaint. Maybe the market will decide that I'm wrong. He felt that it was a personal attack on him." When the two men were booked to appear at a legalization marijuana rally in San Francisco, Rosenthal says, he found Herer was passing out pamphlets denouncing him. "A couple of people tried to stop him; I went to help him hand them out. Now when I give a speech I tell people: 'Jack wants to save the planet; I just want to get you high.'" The irony, according to Rosenthal, is that he helped bring The Emperor into existence. "Jack earns a lot of money but he isn't a good caretaker for the money he earns. So when he said I 'wasn't hip to hemp', I financed the book." And in fact the joint introduction to its 1990-98 editions contains a dedication "to my selfless landlords Ed and Esther who extended me so much leeway in deferred payments so that this project, which they also believed in, would not cease or bog down because of lack of funds." Ed Rosenthal adds: "You have to understand why this got blown out of all proportion was that High Times magazine was using it to sell issues. It never got to the point where Jack and I weren't buddies or where we weren't speaking."
>
> (*Cannabis Culture*, p. 125)

It seems as though things can get blown out of proportion very easily in the cannabis movement. Another controversial figure is Marc Emery. He has been challenging the laws against cannabis in Canada since the early 1990s. First, he challenged the laws that forbade his bookstore in London, Ontario and other retailers from selling *High Times* and other information about cannabis. After he won that court battle, he sold his store and went to Asia for almost two years. When he returned he was disappointed that no one had started where he left off in the battle to bring cannabis to the Canadian public. He then proceeded to open Hemp B.C. on Hastings St., in downtown Vancouver. This store quickly became the focal point for cannabis activism in Canada, inspiring others to open stores across the country and drawing numerous activists together to plan rallies, write literature, and debate political theories. He began to publish a magazine that was first called the *Hemp And Marijuana Newsletter* after an old publication from the 1970s, which changed its name to *Cannabis Canada* before settling upon its current title, *Cannabis Culture*. In fact, the author of this textbook typed in the business directory in the first issue of *Cannabis Canada*. Hemp BC eventually shut down due to constant police raids, as did the Cannabis Café, which he opened after.

In 1995, Marc began selling seeds using his store, magazine, and the Internet. He used the money from the business, which eventually grew to about $3 mil-

The BC3: Michelle Rainey, Marc Emery, Greg Williams (bottom)
courtesy of cannabisculture.com

lion per year, to sponsor the Marijuana Party in several provincial and federal elections, support ballot initiatives in the U.S., operate POT.TV, and help cover the legal costs of several cannabis crusaders. In July of 2005, the B.C. Marijuana Party Store was raided, and Michelle Rainey and Greg Williams were arrested and charged with conspiracy to distribute marijuana seeds, conspiracy to distribute marijuana, and conspiracy to engage in money laundering, by the U.S. government. Marc was arrested in Halifax, N.S. at the same time, and charged with the same offences. Though neither Michelle or Greg spent any more time in jail, eventually Marc entered a guilty plea, and he is currently serving a five year jail sentence in the U.S.

In the early 1990s, another brave individual stepped forward south of the border. Denis Peron opened the San Francisco Cannabis Buyers' Club for people with serious medical problems in 1993. Denis lost his partner to AIDS, which inspired him to strive for access to marijuana for those in serious need because he saw first-hand the incredible medical benefits eating and smoking pot can bring.

> The nation's largest buyers' club was organized in San Francisco by Denis Peron in the wake of the AIDS epidemic, after the federal IND program was ended in 1991. Activists put together a city voter's initiative which was passed by voters three-to-one in 1992, expressing support for medical marijuana. Using that vote as a shield, Peron went on to establish his patient-operated club in a five-story building in the heart of the city, with over twelve thousand members and a staff that serviced thousands of clients each week in a casual smoking environment; part clinic, part social organization. To join, members submit a note from their doctor with a diagnosis of a serious health problem likely to be helped with cannabis. Many people are rejected for insufficient documentation, and bouncers make sure that nobody gets in without a photo ID card. City and county police refused to go after the club, which was prominently featured in many news reports. Activists gathered there to plan activities. Police operatives under Attorney General Dan Lungren infiltrated the club using forged documents, bought cannabis they claimed was for other patients buyers clubs, and brought minors into the building with them, then secretly videotaped their own illegal conduct. Using this evidence, agents got a warrant and conducted a heavily armed raid of the facility early one Sunday morning, with over one hundred agents, many armed with laser-guided automatic weapons. They humiliated patients and staff, took all the medi-

> cine and money, and closed the club to make sure it would serve no more sick and dying people. When the patients turned to the streets, several clergy members of the city opened the doors of their churches to help make up for the shortage. In January 1997 a judge allowed the club to reopen.
> (*Hemp for Health*, p. 171)

In November of 1996, voters in California passed Proposition 215, a loosely worded law that critics suggest is very close to legalization. At that time a number of States passed pro-medical marijuana laws, including Alaska, Washington, Oregon, Nevada, and Arizona. President Bill Clinton even admitted that he tried cannabis, though he "did not inhale!" This prompted U.S. Drug Czar Barry McCaffrey and the DEA into action.

> McCaffrey appeared everywhere on television, warning that the initiatives in California and Arizona were the narrow edge of the legalization wedge. It may turn out he was right. The California and Arizona campaigns provide new models for reform activists. In California, a broad-based coalition was slowly and noisily built during five years with local initiatives in San Francisco and Santa Cruz preceding the state-wide fight. Twice the legislature passed medical-marijuana bills only to have them vetoed by Gov. Pete Wilson. By the time the initiatives reached the ballot, the issue was familiar to California voters and had widespread grassroots support. Arizona's campaign was the mirror image of California's. A small cadre of elites—retired Sen. Barry Goldwater among them—organized themselves privately and then pounced with a huge media blitz that introduced voters to the issue as it sought to sway them.
>
> In both campaigns, out-of-state billionaires provided unprecedented bottomless pockets that may not be offered again. The drug-policy reform movement has a long history of shooting itself in the foot. And the initiatives galvanized powerful prohibition interests—parent's groups, treatment corporations, law enforcement—who will resist future reforms. Inauguration day passed, the 105th Congress was sworn in, and the laws changed in California and Arizona, but it was by no means clear whether what happened in two states could ever be repeated elsewhere. As always, the lessons of the movement were available on all sides of the question, to profit from as they may.
> (*Smoke and Mirrors*, p. 339)

On the other hand, the 1990s saw a lot of experimentation with different techniques of harm reduction, especially in Europe. While groups like ACT UP in New York City had to break the law to supply clean needles, some cities in the Netherlands and England have gone as far as heroin maintenance programs. As overdose deaths from hard drugs increased throughout North America, the violent crime associated with the illegal drug market steadily followed the path of cocaine and heroin into small towns across the continent. It became impossible to keep heroin out of the jails, and stories are told about people who were totally clean getting thrown into jail, becoming addicts and dying of overdose deaths because they cannot get methadone treatment and cannot kick the habit alone. As the livelihoods of drug companies and police officers are in part economically dependant upon the continuation of the War On Drugs, they defend their work with vigour, much like an evangelical minister at times. However, the facts speak for themselves, and as places like East Vancouver digress because of prohibition, the public becomes more aware of the problems and ready to seek real solutions. People who had never even seen illegal drugs began seriously questioning the intelligence behind the policy of prohibition.

> Prominent among those currently calling for legislative reform - and going further by making constructive proposals—are police chiefs and city medical officers, people who know only too well that the existing policies in most countries are ineffective and unworkable. When the occasional politician raises her head above the parapet—as the British opposition MP Clare Short did recently in calling for a fresh debate on decriminalisation of cannabis—the response is tediously predictable: widespread condemnation from political colleagues and overwhelming support from those who have to cope with the end result of political inertia. In the case of Ms Short, not only was she speedily reprimanded by the party leader, but also party officials claimed that their non-legalisation stance was entirely logical since legalisation of cannabis would "increase the supply, reduce the price, and increase the usage". According to a Home Office report earlier this year, the number of people taking cannabis has doubled in a decade—without any help from "liberal" measures. Perhaps the politicians' real fear was that freedom to use soft drugs would automatically progress to increased use of substances such as cocaine and heroin. If so, they must have overlooked the recent Dutch government review which

pointed out that decriminalisation of possession of soft drugs has not led to a rise in the use of hard drugs. If the Dutch approach is so successful, why are changes afoot in The Hague to tighten up that country's drug policy? First Amsterdam's mayor proposed closing down half the city's coffee shops that sell cannabis, and in doing so he rejected a report by his health department in favour of legalisation of soft drugs. Then the Dutch government, which had made an election promise to legalise cannabis, last month issued a discussion paper which mirrored the Amsterdam plan. If, as expected, the Dutch parliament agrees the latest proposals, half the country's 4000 cannabis-selling coffee shops will close and the amount that can be sold to an individual will be cut to 5 g. Since the government's own review provides no ammunition for such a change in policy, the real reason behind the new measures must lie elsewhere. One need look no further than the Netherlands' neighbours and co-signatories of the Schengen agreement[...] When France, in particular, threatened to end the agreement, claiming that the Netherlands was the major supplier of Europe's drugs, some action had to be taken and the coffee shops became the scapegoat.

(Editorial, *Lancet*, Nov. 1995)

Many medical cannabis activists in Canada have been working since the mid-1990s to use the Charter of Rights and Freedoms to establish the use, cultivation, and distribution of the herb for those in serious medical need. Starting in Jan. 1996, with the Victoria Cannabis Buyers' Club (now called the Cannabis Buyers' Club of Canada), medical "compassion" clubs began forming in major cities across the country. In June of 1999, Health Canada was forced by the Ontario Court of Appeal in Regina vs. Wakeford to grant individuals who qualified to use cannabis as medicine an Exemption 56 from the Controlled Drugs and Substances Act (CDSA). Health Canada began to study some of the medical benefits of cannabis and started the search for a Canadian source of medical marijuana after the July 31, 2000 Parker decision. That decision by the Ontario Court of Appeal forced the government to create laws regulating the medical use and production of cannabis.

> {10} I have concluded that the trial judge was right in finding that Parker needs marijuana to control the symptoms of his epilepsy. I have also concluded that the prohibition on the cultivation and possession of marijuana in unconstitutional. Based on principles established by the Supreme Court of Canada, particularly in R. v. Morgen-

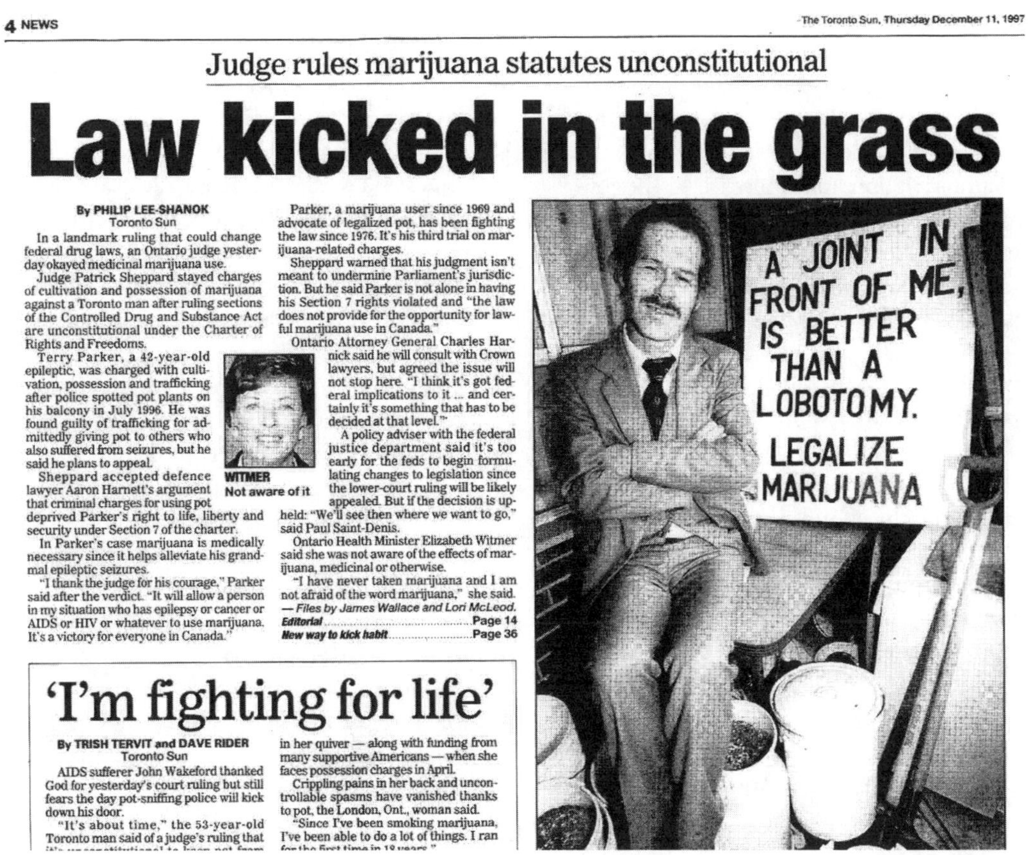

4 NEWS — The Toronto Sun, Thursday December 11, 1997

Judge rules marijuana statutes unconstitutional

Law kicked in the grass

By PHILIP LEE-SHANOK
Toronto Sun

In a landmark ruling that could change federal drug laws, an Ontario judge yesterday okayed medicinal marijuana use.

Judge Patrick Sheppard stayed charges of cultivation and possession of marijuana against a Toronto man after ruling sections of the Controlled Drug and Substance Act are unconstitutional under the Charter of Rights and Freedoms.

Terry Parker, a 42-year-old epileptic, was charged with cultivation, possession and trafficking after police spotted pot plants on his balcony in July 1996. He was found guilty of trafficking for admittedly giving pot to others who also suffered from seizures, but he said he plans to appeal.

Sheppard accepted defence lawyer Aaron Harnett's argument that criminal charges for using pot deprived Parker's right to life, liberty and security under Section 7 of the charter.

In Parker's case marijuana is medically necessary since it helps alleviate his grand-mal epileptic seizures.

"I thank the judge for his courage," Parker said after the verdict. "It will allow a person in my situation who has epilepsy or cancer or AIDS or HIV or whatever to use marijuana. It's a victory for everyone in Canada."

Parker, a marijuana user since 1969 and advocate of legalized pot, has been fighting the law since 1976. It's his third trial on marijuana-related charges.

Sheppard warned that his judgment isn't meant to undermine Parliament's jurisdiction. But he said Parker is not alone in having his Section 7 rights violated and "the law does not provide for the opportunity for lawful marijuana use in Canada."

Ontario Attorney General Charles Harnick said he will consult with Crown lawyers, but agreed the issue will not stop here. "I think it's got federal implications to it ... and certainly it's something that has to be decided at that level."

A policy adviser with the federal justice department said it's too early for the feds to begin formulating changes to legislation since the lower-court ruling will be likely appealed. But if the decision is upheld: "We'll see then where we want to go," said Paul Saint-Denis.

Ontario Health Minister Elizabeth Witmer said she was not aware of the effects of marijuana, medicinal or otherwise.

"I have never taken marijuana and I am not afraid of the word marijuana," she said.

— *Files by James Wallace and Lori McLeod.*

WITMER
Not aware of it

Editorial .... Page 14
New way to kick habit .... Page 36

'I'm fighting for life'

By TRISH TERVIT and DAVE RIDER
Toronto Sun

AIDS sufferer John Wakeford thanked God for yesterday's court ruling but still fears the day pot-sniffing police will kick down his door.

"It's about time," the 53-year-old Toronto man said of a judge's ruling that

in her quiver — along with funding from many supportive Americans — when she faces possession charges in April.

Crippling pains in her back and uncontrollable spasms have vanished thanks to pot, the London, Ont., woman said.

"Since I've been smoking marijuana, I've been able to do a lot of things. I ran

Terry Parker won right to use cannabis as medicine in Canada

> taler, [1998] 1 S.C.R. 30, where the court struck down the abortion provisions of the Criminal Code, and Rodriguez v. British Columbia (Attorney General), [1993] 3 S.C.R. 519, where the court upheld the assisted suicide offence in the Criminal Code, I have concluded that forcing Parker to choose between his health and imprisonment violates his right to liberty and security of the person. I have concluded that the possibility of an exemption under s. 56 dependant upon the unfettered and unstructured discretion of the Minister of Health is not consistent with the principles of fundamental justice.
>
> {124} For reasons that will become apparent, the Crown does not now support the marijuana prohibition on the basis of its historical roots. In the Clay trial and appeal, the Crown expressly renounced any reliance on the theories that marijuana is a "gateway" drug to harder drugs; that it provokes criminal activity; that marijuana use leads to lack of motivation; or causes psychosis. The Crown argues that the objectives of the prohibition are first to prevent the harms associated with smoking marijuana, including harm to human health. In addition, it claims the prohibition is necessary to control the domestic and international trade in illicit drugs and to satisfy Canada's international treaty obligations.
>
> {163} Parliament has created a defence to the possession and cultivation offences if the person can comply with the regulations. Those regulations, for example, permitted a person to legally possess the drug under prescription from a physician. The government's own witness established that this defence or exemption is illusory. This is not consistent with the principles of fundamental justice.
>
> (R. V. Parker {2000}, 146 C.C.C. (3d) 193)

A contract was signed with Prairie Plant Systems to grow cannabis for research and distribution in a mine in Flin Flon, Manitoba. There have been many problems with the Medical Marijuana Access Regulations that have been brought up in court since the introduction of these policies in July 31, 2001. For example, while the MMAR gives legal authority to possess and grow cannabis, the original regulations did not have any means for the applicant to obtain either cannabis or seeds. Meanwhile, several medical clubs have been busted by police for various reasons, including the Montreal Compassion Club, the Toronto Compassion Center, the Sunshine Coast Compassion Club, the Vancouver Island Compassion Society, and the Cannabis Buyers' Club of Canada, who were raided four times by police. Most charges that were laid in any of those arrests or against other dispensaries have been beaten in court, one way or another. The most important decision came from the raid at the TCC.

> {116} The MMAR do not require the state to violate the law. They do, however, create an alliance between the Government and the black market whereby the Government authorizes possession of marijuana for medical purposes and the black market supplies the necessary product. The MMAR provide a viable medical exemption to the prohibition against possession of marijuana only as long as there are individuals who are prepared to commit a crime by supplying the necessary medical marijuana to the individuals that the Government has determined are entitled to use the drug. At the same time, the MMAR force seriously ill individuals who have found to be in need of medical marijuana to consort with criminals to fill that medical need. Forcing sick people to go to the black market to get their medicine can only discourage respect for the law and at the same time signal that the medical needs of these people are somehow not worthy of the same kind of consideration as other medical needs.
>
> {117} A Government scheme that depends on the criminal element to deliver the medically necessary product, and that drives those in need of that product to the black market strikes at the same values that underlie the state's obligation to obey the law. The MMAR, far from placing the Government in the position of a positive role model or on the moral high ground, are calculated to bring the law into disrepute and devalue the worth and dignity of those individuals to whom the MMAR are applied. The Government's obligation to obey law must include an obligation to promote compliance with and respect for the law.
>
> {118} The inevitable consequences of the absence of a legal source of marijuana for those who have been determined to be in medical need of the drug are inconsistent with the fundamental principle that the state must obey and promote compliance with the law. In our view, the absence of a legal source of supply renders the MMAR inconsistent with the principles of fundamental justice.
>
> (Hitzig et al., Oct 7, 2003, Court of Appeal of Ontario, Justices Doherty, Goudge and Simmons JJ.A.)

Though the R. v. Hitzig decision of Oct. 7, 2003 corrected some of the problems in the MMAR, the federal government has still not created a system that adequately meets the needs of the sick. In fact, shortly after the decision was made, Health Canada announced that they would not comply with several parts of the court decision, in particular limiting the number of individuals that a caregiver can grow for. Shortly after this ruling the Supreme Court of Canada ruled, in a 6-3 decision, that the personal use of cannabis does not attract protection under the Charter of Rights and Freedoms.

{86} While we accept Malmo-Levine's statement that smoking marijuana is central to his lifestyle, the Constitution cannot be stretched to afford protection to whatever activity an individual chooses to define as central to his or her lifestyle. One individual chooses to smoke marijuana; another has an obsessive interest in golf; a third is addicted to gambling. The appellant Caine invokes a taste for fatty foods. A society that extended constitutional protection to any and all such activities would be ungovernable. Lifestyle choices of this order are not, we think, "basic choices going to the core of what it means to enjoy individual dignity and independence" (Godbout, supra, at para. 66).

Judges decide how regulations affect plants illustrated by Greta Negrave

> {87} In our view, with respect, Malmo-Levine's desire to build a lifestyle around the recreational use of marijuana does not attract Charter protection. There is no free-standing constitutional right to smoke "pot" for recreational purposes.

After the Hitzig and Malmo-Levine decisions of 2003, the Liberal government put any plans to decriminalize cannabis on the bottom of the agenda, as the laws appeared stable. While it was politically advantageous to talk about changing the laws to minimize life long consequences of a possession charge, it was never a priority for the government to pass new lenient legislation or speak out directly against constant increases in resources used in the enforcement of the law. Every time it was made public that the Canadian government was considering changes to the possession laws, the U.S. government would counter by announcing that they would slow the border down with extensive searches.

It is ironic that LSD, a drug introduced into America by the military as a possible method of mind control, would be so important in the revival of the cannabis plant. Nor would one suspect that soldiers returning from the Vietnam War would bring seeds home and that veterans would turn around to fight the very government they fought for so they could use this medicine. Despite desperate attempts by prohibitionists to destroy the cannabis culture, the many uses of this plant and its powerful impacts have drawn people towards it like moths to a candle. Though the course has not been straight, there can be no doubt now that both hemp and marijuana are making a comeback.

Chapter 7 Cannabis Today

Cannabis Around the World

Every country has a different cannabis culture, with citizens growing in at least 172 countries. In countries like Canada, the use of the herb and enforcement of the law can vary between areas in the same province. With improvements in indoor growing techniques and seeds available on-line, there is no major city in the world where cannabis or hashish is not available.

In a report released by the UN in 2007, the countries with the highest rates of cannabis consumption are Papua New Guinea (29.5%), Micronesia (29.1%), Ghana (21.5%), Zambia (17.7%), Canada (16.8%), Sierre Leone (16.1%), Cyprus (14.1%), and New Zealand (13.4%), with the U.S. at 12.6% and the Netherlands at 6.4%. Lowest rates include Brazil (1.0%), China (0.7%), Japan (0.1%), Singapore (0.004%), and Korea (0.002%). About 3.8% of the adults in the world, or 160 million people, consume cannabis at least once a year.

> Based on information collected from Member States, UNODC estimates global cannabis herb production at 42,000 metric mt in 2005, dwarfing global heroin production (472 mt in 2005) or global cocaine production (980 mt in 2005). This represents a decline of almost 3,000 mt (-7%) over 2004. While these data must be interpreted with caution, they seem to signal, that the upward trend in herb production observed since the early 1990s, may be coming to a halt. The cannabis herb estimate suggests that 10.6 per cent of cannabis herb production was seized in 2005.
>
> (*World Drug Report*, United Nations Office on Drugs and Crime, 2007)

In Japan, the use of cannabis is strictly prohibited, though it is available at a very high cost. Other countries, like Malaysia and Indonesia, are also very tough on drug users, in general. Though China has a large hemp industry, producing hemp fibre board and massive amounts of hemp cloth and twine, the Chinese enforce prohibition laws aggressively. While very little cannabis is imported into China, it is grown for local use in some provinces. India hasn't prohibited its citizens from using cannabis, though tourists can still expect to be harassed by authorities if caught using in public. Most Asian countries do not have large cannabis cultures because of tight military control. There are some exceptions, though.

> Although cannabis is now illegal one would not know it from it's presence. While at Koh Kong at a guesthouse referred to us by our travel booker on Koh Chang, Thailand, no more than 5 minutes had passed when a young guide named Bawn offered me a bag of cannabis. The vacuum-sealed bag, containing about 10 grams was offered to me for $10. I haggled with Bawn and ended up paying about $6 for it. The bag, containing mostly dark brown airy buds of a Sativa variety had a fresh clean aroma to it. I asked him where I could find a larger amount because I wanted to make some photographs of growing fields or plants or at least the bags of cannabis. He looked up at me proudly and said, "my father grew it." Bawn was explaining that cannabis has a stigma of being an old-fashioned, old man's drug and with concern that Cambodians looking for a high are much more likely to drink alcohol or get involved in imported hard drugs like Ecstasy or amphetamines is why the government has made some crackdowns. Bawn quickly put the smile back on his face about his father's cannabis farm and said that the harvest was finished but that there was many kilos still at the house that I could see.
>
> ("Cambodia: A Travel Guide")

In many parts of Asia cannabis is used primarily in bhang, a tradition likely older than smoking. Bhang is used in many Asian agricultural communities where it is recognized as a valuable medicine, and is occasionally used for recreational purposes.

Hashish is commonly used throughout the Middle East, though most religious groups frown upon the use of any intoxicant. However, there is an ancient history of the use of hashish in the lower and middle classes of many of these peoples that continues in countries like Afghanistan, Pakistan, Morocco and Egypt.

> In 2003, the Government of Morocco and the United Nations Office on Drugs and Crime undertook the first survey of cannabis cultivation in Morocco. While confirming the general extent of cannabis production in the Rif region, the 2004 Survey reveals a 10% decline in cultivation to 120,500 hectares—an encouraging step in the right direction.
>
> This year's survey builds on the work of the 2003 Survey by shedding new light on the motivations for cannabis cultivation and highlighting possible motives for change—all of which could eventually contribute to the elaboration of a national strategy to fight cannabis cultivation. The socio-economic findings presented here indicate that cannabis prices have been declining between 1999-2004. This has put pressure on the 800,000 people involved in cannabis production, whose income has dropped 26% as compared to 2003.
>
> Income from cannabis production remains low relative to overall GDP per capita. Unfortunately, although the disparity between incomes in the legitimate sector (US$1,478) and incomes in the illicit sector (US$400) is striking, there are very few alternatives to cannabis production in these isolated and service-deprived regions. In localities heavily devoted to cannabis monoculture, traditional agricultural skills and practices have been lost as a result of the over-dependence on cannabis as a livelihood strategy. This is particularly the case amongst the youth, who have experienced no other livelihood strategy and who view cannabis cultivation as the sole means to independence and prosperity.
>
> (Antonio Maria Costa, Executive Director, United Nations Office on Drugs and Crime, *Morocco: Cannabis Survey 2004*)

There are pygmies in Africa who believe they have smoked cannabis since the beginning of time. Most countries in Africa have been growing cannabis for local consumption since the 1500s. Most of Africa has been forced to put resources into the prohibition of cannabis by international laws and trade. European countries have a range of positions, though there is a general movement towards less enforcement of the laws.

> There are many reasons why a study on cannabis in a Southern African country like Lesotho is relevant (and further research a necessity). Cannabis cultivation and use as a drug are deeply entrenched in the region. Indeed, they are part of the culture of many southern African ethnic groups, and archaeological evidence suggests that cannabis has been grown and used since before the 15th century. It would seem that this tradition is now used in the setting up of a modern commercial "agri-business" of cannabis production and sale on regional, mostly urban, mass markets.
>
> (*Cannabis in Lesotho: A Preliminary Survey*)

In France, hemp has been grown for rolling and cigarette papers for years while the laws are tightly enforced. In Britain, there has been a slight loosening of the enforcement of the cannabis laws in some areas, and while the medical uses seems to be widely accepted, there are no public compassion clubs and few hemp stores. In fact, there are very few medical clubs in Europe. Amsterdam stands out in the world as the most open cannabis city, followed by San Francisco, and Nimbin, Australia, which has an annual festival in which cannabis plays a central part. Portugal has now successfully decriminalized the simple possession of cannabis.

The Hempfest in Seattle had about 250,000 people at its peak in 2009 and deserves some mention, too. In 2006, San Francisco created a moratorium on the creation of new medical clubs, as with 37 in operation already, city officials thought no more were needed. Recently, DEA officers have raided dozens of medical clubs in California, though hundreds still operate. With over 829,000 arrested for simple possession in 2006, the U.S. is the world's largest consumer and producer of cannabis.

> Marijuana is the most widely used and readily available drug in the United States. It is the only major drug of abuse grown within United States borders. The DEA is aggressively striving to halt the spread of marijuana cultivation in the United States. In 2004, the DCE/SP was responsible for the eradication of 3,200,121cultivated outdoor marijuana plants, and 206,896 indoor plants. In

> addition, the DCE/SP has attributed for 8,043 arrests and the seizure in excess of 31.1 million dollars of cultivator assets.
> (DEA Homepage)

The size of the demand from the U.S., and the lack of domestic growers, has meant that the demand for cannabis products has had a dramatic impact upon each of its neighbours. Jamaica seems to be reconsidering the cannabis laws. Several countries in Central and South America, lead by Bolivia, are telling the U.S. to stop exporting the drug war, though the Columbian government is still working close with Washington. In 2006, Mexico almost legalized the possession of small amounts of all drugs until the U.S. administration pressured them into dropping the proposed changes in law. In 2009, the Mexican government did pass these laws.

Cannabis in Politics

There are three ways to politically change cannabis laws in democratic countries: court decisions, ballot initiatives, and legislation. Many countries, like Canada, do not have ballot initiatives and any changes in law must come from elected officials and the political party mechanisms that control policy. The fear of appearing to favour the use of cannabis by discussing any other approach than a punitive model often scares politicians into avoiding the subject because their political enemies will likely suggest they are indifferent to youth drug use. This makes legislation much more difficult, though not impossible.

> For a Food and Drug Administration (FDA) increasingly mired in controversies over the politicization of scientific and regulatory decisions, the agency's April 20, 2006 statement regarding medical use of marijuana may represent an all-time low point.[1] Politics, it appears, has now completely trumped science at this once proudly independent agency. The FDA has announced that "no sound scientific studies" support the medical use of marijuana, contradicting an increasingly large body of scientific literature. To those of us who do research in this area, this is a personal affront. Even the federal Drug Enforcement Agency's (DEA) own Administrative Law Judge, the Honorable Francis Young, stated in 1988, "Marijuana is the safest therapeutically active substance known to man..." He went on to say, "The evidence clearly shows that marijuana is capable of relieving the distress of great numbers of very ill people, and doing so with safety under medical supervision. . .it would be unreasonable, arbitrary and capricious for the DEA to continue to stand between those sufferers and the benefits of this substance." The FDA's announcement is puzzling at many levels. It makes no mention of any recent FDA analysis or investigation, regulatory filing, or any other activity within the normal scope of the agency's work that led to this policy change. Rational, apolitical minds need to take over the debate on marijuana, separating myth from fact, right from wrong, and responsible, medicinal use from other, less compelling usages.
> (*Medical Marijuana: Politics Trumps Science at the FDA*)

Finding the existing parties unwilling or unable to change the cannabis laws, political parties specifically focused upon legalizing the herb sprouted up across the planet. The first political pot party in the world was the Australian Marijuana Party, formed in 1970. The next political cannabis party was in New Zealand, where the Aotearoa Legalise Cannabis Party formed in 1996. The Bloc Pot formed in Quebec, in 1998, before becoming the foundation for the Marijuana Party of Canada. In 1999, the Legalise Cannabis Alliance formed in the UK. Other countries with political pot parties include Israel, with Green Leaf aka Ale Yarok; Spain, with Partido Cannabis; and Ireland, with the Cannabis Legalise Party. The Marijuana Party has chapters in 29 U.S. states and most Canadian provinces. Many in the movement believe the creation of political pot parties is a useful way to educate the public and other politicians about the futility of the drug war. However, others believe that by informing and working with all political parties we can achieve our goals.

Leader of the Green Party of Canada

The political parties in Canada cover the full spectrum of drug policy ideologies, though the cannabis laws are rarely directly debated unless the Marijuana Party is involved, which is itself rare. In November 2006, Saskatckewan delegates at the ruling NDP convention voted for non-punitive approach to cannabis, but the vote was not binding upon the provincial government and had no real effect on enforcement of the federal laws. While the late leader of the federal NDP, Jack Layton, and several senior NDP politicians have supported legalization, the party has not endorsed this as a policy. The Green Party has supported legalization but has traditionally been afraid of being known as a pot party and has not aggressively pursued the issue. Though the Liberal party has proposed decriminalization in the past, the changes were barely an improvement upon the current punitive system and were never considered a priority. The Consevatives' law-and-order mandate supports the war on drugs, and they cut funding for medical cannabis research within the first year of holding office. Even after introducing a "tough new drug policy" in October 2007, the Conservatives do not seem to have a public party policy on the medical cannabis issue.

In the U.S., the Republicans have consistently promoted prohibition, while the Democrats seem open to the medical uses of cannabis. However, ballot initiatives in the U.S. have decriminalized cannabis starting in 1972 with Oregon and then Alaska, Maine, California, New York, Nebraska, Minnesota, Mississippi, and Ohio. Medical marijuana has been legalized or decriminalized in 16 states, including California, Alaska, Arizona, Colorado, Delaware, Hawaii, Maine, Michigan, Montana, Nevada, New Jersey, New Mexico, Oregon, Vermont, Washington, and Rhode Island. Washington, DC has also passed medical marijuana laws. Every state but Hawaii passed these laws with ballot initiatives.

> At least 33 members of the clergy have endorsed ballot Question 7 on the November election ballot, which if approved would make Nevada the first state in the nation to allow people 21 and older to legally possess small amounts of marijuana and purchase it at government regulated and state-taxed pot shops.
>
> The clergy argued the move would cut down on minors' access to marijuana, reduce gang-related violence and generate money for the state to help finance treatment programs instead of making drug dealers rich. "On its face, our current marijuana laws appear to be moral, but it is a cosmetic morality," said the Rev. Paul Hansen, senior pastor at Holy Spirit Lutheran Church in Las Vegas.
>
> ("Nevada Religious Leaders Make Case to Legalize Pot")

These ballot initiatives are very expensive, with billionaire philanthropist George Soros giving millions to the cause along with small donations from working class families. As the population continues to mature, tolerance for cannabis use is growing and the ballot initiatives that fail only lose by a close margin. With the religious right controlling U.S. government policy, it is difficult to imagine real changes in cannabis laws. Given that everyone charged with a serious offence in the U.S. is stripped of their right to vote, activists in that country have a huge challenge in convincing the law-abiding public and politicians to make drug policy reform a major election issue.

Cannabis in the Media

The media has, by distorting viewpoints of cannabis, been very influential in prohibition. Starting in 1916, the newspaper industry, lead by the Hearst Paper Manufacturing Division, began the "Reefer Madness" campaign. The word "Marijuana" was invented by the media to portray the "new drug menace from Mexico" as a threat to youth. Emily Murphy, the first female judge in the British Empire, wrote a series of articles for *Maclean's* magazine, that were eventually published as "The Black Candle," which were instrumental in generating public opinion against cannabis. In 1936, the U.S. government produced a film called *Reefer Madness* that depicts cannabis users in various states of delusional behaviour quite unlike the common experiences of cannabis consumers. Many other films appeared during the time using that theme. Ironically, just a few years later, in 1942, the U.S. government produced another film about cannabis, but this one was titled *Hemp For Victory*, and glorified the benefits of growing hemp for the farmer and the economy.

Hollywood replaced the violent addict with the stoned hippy in the 1960s and 70s with movies like *Easy Rider*, and eventually the *Cheech and Chong* movies. Ron Mann produced the Genie award-winning documentary Grass in 1999, which is the best anti-prohibition film yet, undermining many of the stereotypes suppressing the culture. Meanwhile, the U.S. government has launched several attempts to control the images of cannabis users portrayed in movies and on television. As a result, few positive drug experiences by relatively normal people have been seen on screen since its invention.

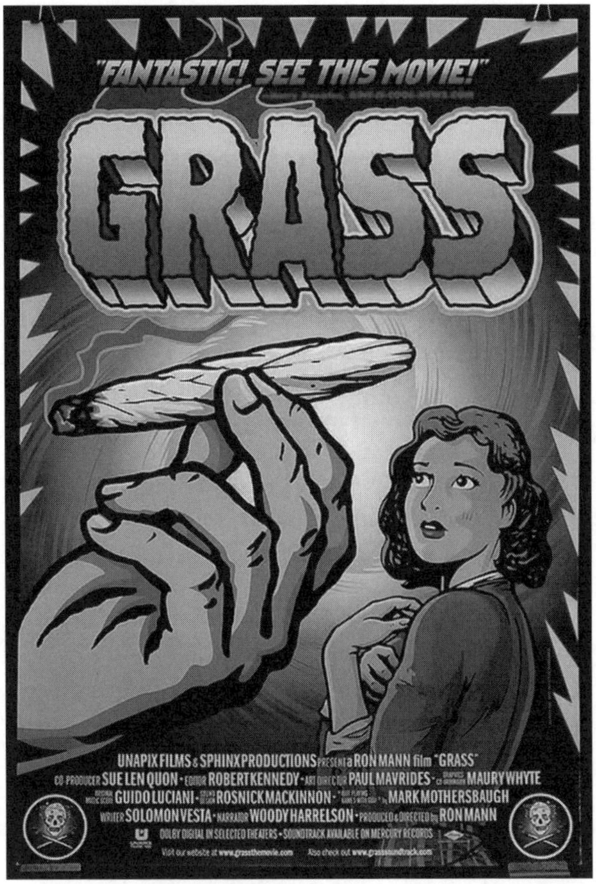

Excellent cannabis documentaries are now available

The portrayal of cannabis users as degenerates and trouble-makers on the screen has not been an accident. Television shows such as *ER*, *Beverly Hills 90120*, *Chicago Hope*, *The Drew Cary Show*, and *7th Heaven* are examples of shows that accepted government money to include anti-drug messages in their stories. Working for President Clinton, drug czar Gen. Barry McCaffrey spent millions on script writers and high-profile magazines to shoehorn anti-drug themes into movies, television shows and celebrity tabloids.

Cannabis is now included as a regular social activity on many TV shows and movies. Unfortunately, much of the cannabis use on TV does not depict pot smokers in a positive light. While the *Trailer Park Boys* are funny, they do not give people who have not been exposed to normal cannabis use a good impression. There is even a TV show called *WEEDS* that gives viewers an often exaggerated look into the life of a suburban mother turned pot dealer.

> To those who believe as I do that the present marijuana laws are unjust and divisive and that the pot debate is more dangerous to the society than pot itself, the current disposition on many questions to treat the whole subject as a joke suggests that basic change may be nearer than we think. As Goode effectively demonstrates, mere evidence, logical arguments, and the other standard devices that are used to persuade and produce consensus among reasonable men do not seem to work in this case—perhaps because the debate is not a real one but only an expression of underlying and unstated motivations, resentments, or political considerations. Perhaps the case for reform can best be made by jokes and laughter.
>
> At any rate, it is evident that a great deal of public joking is being done and that the user of marijuana is not seriously regarded as a genuine criminal. Recent movies, for example, portray the use of pot as a gag, and at least one movie director has stated that real marijuana was smoked during the filming. Pot parties, involving the commission of what the statutes define as heinous crimes, have been presented on the television screen to entertain the viewing public. Various popular television programs regularly include pot jokes. In private conversations such jokes are even more common, and little or no stigma attaches in many circles to admitting in private that one has smoked or would like to smoke. Numerous stories float around about policemen, even narcotic agents, who smoke the weed or have at least tried it. The experiment with alcohol prohibition, it will be remembered, was also to some extent laughed out of court.
>
> (*The Marijuana Smokers*)

For over 30 years, *High Times* magazine has been the largest and most productive anti-prohibition publication. Many magazines have attempted to provide better coverage of the movement, but few have lasted long. While there have been few examples of mainstream comics portraying cannabis in a positive light, the *Fabulous Furry Freak Brothers* have provided laughs and information to the cannabis community for years. Some believe that the spinach that *Popeye* ate to gain superhuman strength was a parody of cannabis use by sailors.

> Last year, in a scandal that rocked the Office of National Drug Control Policy (ONDCP), the press revealed that the ONDCP's advertising campaign included paying television networks to infiltrate regular sitcoms with anti-drug story lines. Cannabis Culture has discovered that they were doing the same thing with comics. What

> the ONDCP was supposed to do with their five-year, billion-dollar advertising budget, was find networks, magazines and other media that were willing to give advertisements at half price, or who would donate an equal amount of advertising free. What the ONDCP did instead was let networks fulfill their requirements by hiding anti-drug messages in television programs. The mainstream press missed the fact that the ONDCP also paid—and continues to pay—comic book manufacturers DC and Marvel for anti-drug ads.
> (*Cannabis Culture* #32, pg 63)

In the last 10 or 15 years, large media companies have begun to provide some balanced reporting on cannabis, though most of the coverage on TV and in print continues to be about police raids and trials. Most reporting done on the subject is superficial and it seems as though the police rarely have to answer any difficult questions from the media regarding the effectiveness of the drug laws. Some major media sources are writing strong editorials supporting legalization.

New forms of communication are proving instrumental in changing cannabis laws by networking activists while providing free instant updates and in-depth reporting to the public. Communicating through email and chat-rooms has made interaction between activists more efficient and cost effective. New webpages are constantly appearing with more information, products and cannabis activities. Though it was the media that lead the prohibition of cannabis, it will be the media that leads the fight for legalization.

Medical Distribution Of Cannabis

Before the last century of prohibition, cannabis was used in a variety of ways, for many different medical problems, by healers around the world. When prohibition laws became enforced, the medical community was one of the last to stop using the plant, with several U.S. doctors continuing to prescribe cannabis for glaucoma into the 1950s. Certainly, through the 1960s and 1970s, many people re-discovered the medical benefits of cannabis by accident or through word-of-mouth, and eventually some of them became brave enough to speak publicly and fight for their right to use the herb.

> In 1976, Robert Randall, a glaucoma patient, succeeded in persuading the federal government to supply him with marijuana under a new FDA "Compassionate Use" protocol. With the support of his physician, Randall, arguing that marijuana was the only drug that would prevent him from going blind, won a lawsuit against the federal government. The government grudgingly agreed to supply Randall with free marijuana from its own research farm in Mississippi. In later years, a dozen more patients managed to enrol in the Compassionate Use program, which required elaborate, time-consuming paperwork from their physicians. Pressed by a flood of new applicants who had been struck by the AIDS virus, the government closed the program to new applicants in 1991. Today, just eight patients receive marijuana legally in the U.S., for conditions including glaucoma, multiple sclerosis, epilepsy, and rare bone diseases.
>
> In 1988, following extensive testimony, DEA Administrative Judge Francis Young ruled that marijuana's medical benefits were "clear beyond question" and that it should be reclassified as a Schedule 2 drug. Judge Young's recommendation was promptly overruled by DEA chief John Lawn, who, despite the fact that morphine and cocaine had earned a Schedule 2 classification, expressed concern that it would send the "wrong message" about marijuana's supposed harmfulness. After further legal twists and turns, the DEA ban was upheld by a federal appeals court in 1993. Hence, marijuana remains a Schedule 1 drug to this day.
> (*Marijuana Medical Handbook*, p.8)

Many sick people without the resources to legally defend themselves from cultivation charges have suffered greatly in the past few decades. After learning about the benefits of cannabis, many people were almost forced into growing their own herb because they could not afford the street prices that they had to pay for their medicine and needed a daily supply for any quality of life. Those who were caught received little sympathy from the courts.

> Will Foster was a productive citizen who paid his taxes, served in the US army and had his own computer programmer/analyst business for 5 years. He, his wife, Megan, and their 3 children were leading ordinary lives in Oklahoma[...]Will has crippling rheumatoid arthritis in his feet, hips, lower back and hands. He did not like the side effects of the drugs his doctors prescribed, which were mostly codeine-based and highly addictive. These drugs left him moody, tired and edgy, making it difficult to enjoy his family and perform his work. On Dec. 28, 1995, based on a

> secret tip from a 'confidential informant', police entered the Foster's home with a 'John Doe' search warrant for methamphetamine. They found no methamphetamine[...]What they did find was his basement garden—66 cannabis plants—and $28. Will refused to take a deal and asked for a jury trial instead[...]He was sentenced to a total of 93 years—70 years for marijuana cultivation, 20 years for possession of marijuana in the presence of a minor child (his own), 2 years for possession with intent to distribute and 1 year for not having a tax stamp. His sentence was reduced to 20 years on appeal.
> (*Shattered Lives*, p. 84)

For many compassionate, intelligent, healthy friends, watching their loved ones and friends suffer without cannabis was intolerable. Many growers give small portions of their crops to their friends and family that truly need the herb and cannot afford to pay for as much as they need, if any at all. Others began to grow specifically for their sick friends. After Denis Peron started the San Francisco Cannabis Buyers' Club in 1993, more people began to recognize the enormous potential of cannabis as a medicine for people with AIDS.

Around the same time, on Bainbridge Island in Washington State, Joanna McKee and her partner "Stitch" were arrested and charged for giving cannabis to other seriously ill individuals. The charges were eventually beaten in court and the Green Cross they founded was instrumental in helping pass a ballot initiative in that state. Many people in the 1990s were dying quickly and horribly from the wasting problems associated with AIDS, so allowing these people to use cannabis was accepted by the general population and the doctors that looked after them.

Lead by Hillary Black with the B.C. Compassion Club Society, and the author of this textbook, organizations across Canada in the mid-1990s began to help supply cannabis products to people with medical problems. In Victoria, we have helped people suffering from permanent, physical disabilities and diseases at the Cannabis Buyers' Club of Canada since January 1996. Other clubs have decided to require members to obtain a recommendation to use cannabis from a doctor. Since there are no regulations, each person or group that begins distributing cannabis products for medical reasons creates a different system to manage product quality control and purchasing, sign-up procedures, organizational structure, public relations, and operational guidelines. The B.C.C.C.S. attempted to address this lack of government-approved regulations by publishing a booklet titled "Operational Standards For The Distribution Of Medicinal Cannabis," in 2003, explaining how compassion clubs should operate. However, the majority of clubs currently operating in Canada existed before this document was published and few have the opportunity to maintain the strict controls for purchasing cannabis that are advised in the report. There are currently about 35 medical clubs in Canada servicing about 50-60,000 members.

> A cannabis buyer's club operates somewhat like a pharmacy, except it is technically illegal. However, despite their illegal status, most CBCs operate openly and inform the local authorities of their existence. In many places, police and local officials have become convinced of the sincerity of the people involved and have decided to look the other way, not formally sanctioning the club's activities but not making any arrests either. Where clubs have made such arrangements, they have generally instituted strict procedures governing who can obtain marijuana.
>
> In these clubs, patients must provide some evidence, such as a written diagnosis from a physician, of a medical condition for which marijuana is reasonably believed to be of benefit. The CBC will often try to verify that information by contacting the patient's physician. The club will also try to determine whether the patient has a physician's approval for using marijuana. Once patients are approved for membership, they are generally issued some sort of identification card that allows them access to the club later. Marijuana is purchased on the premises. The prices are usually the same as what patients can expect to pay in transactions outside of the club.
> (*Is Marijuana The Right Medicine For You?*, p. 182)

We firmly believe that individuals suffering from permanent physical disabilities and diseases have the legal right to determine what medications they use to treat their symptoms. This constitutional right has been guaranteed by the Charter of Rights and Freedoms in Canada, allowing the courts to force the government into accepting the medical use of cannabis. Unfortunately, compassion clubs that force patients to obtain a doctor's recommendation do not recognize the right to choose, and hold people hostage to the whims of their physicians. While the clubs that maintain these policies insist that it is done to protect the organization from prosecution, the clubs that have been raided by police that only require a diagnosis of a serious medical problem have been just as successful in court as those that require a doctor's recommendation. Several of the clubs that have been raided by the police required doctor's recommendations, and paid employee taxes, so while doing those things may sound good to some, in reality they create unnecessary barriers to sick people while providing no real added protection to the group.

Author selling medicine at Cannabis Buyers Club of Canada

The situation in the U.S. is complex because each state has passed a different ballot initiative or law protecting the medical use of cannabis. There is a constant struggle between activists pushing for changes to state law and state officials pushing the federal government to change their laws. Some states like Oregon and Colorado have passed laws granting people permission to grow their own cannabis, but no storefront medical clubs operate. On the extreme end of the spectrum is California, where thousands of clubs operate in municipalities that either tolerate or actually license the facilities. The DEA shut down several dozen of these clubs in 2009, and sent letters to many landlords stating that their property could be seized if it was proven that illegal activities were occurring on the premises with the knowledge of the owner in the last year. The DEA is still active in shutting down clubs that seem to have been randomly selected and threatening their landlords. Most clubs have ignored the threats of the DEA and continued operating, though some cities are becoming much more cautious when allowing the creation of more clubs.

In Europe, there are very few med pot clubs, with some small networks in the UK being the only semi-public, non-government medical distributors on the entire continent. There has been a great deal of debate about the cannabis laws in general in Britain, with several people suffering from medical problems receiving a good deal of positive media attention when going through trial. People with MS have been particularly successful in generating public support for the medical use of cannabis. In the Netherlands, the Dutch government has had a medical program for several years but has had difficulty competing with the coffeeshops, who provide a superior product at a lower price. Efforts are being made to make the program more appealing to medical users. Other countries like Switzerland are creating or considering medical cannabis programs, but few citizens have been brave enough to start public clubs in defiance of the laws in their country.

While not everyone who is in need has a club nearby yet, there is little doubt that with the changing laws, medical marijuana organizations will appear in every large community. However, it is the opinion of many of us that the government should be supplying or subsidizing the cost of cannabis for those who need it as medicine, and that clubs such as ours should not exist. This is a situation we at CBC of C would very much like to see, as we envision large greenhouses at every hospital and a wide variety of medical products made from cannabis. However, until this happens, we will continue providing the services that our membership depends upon.

The distribution and use of cannabis for medical purposes has caused much controversy and division, in and out of the cannabis movement. While some see all use of cannabis as medicinal, others argue that only medical users should be allowed to use the herb and everyone else treated like a criminal. Prohibitionists point out the obvious fact that regulating the medical use of cannabis will eventually lead to the full-scale legalization of cannabis and try to deny that there are any medical benefits to the herb at all. Most medical distributors do little to advocate for the legalization of cannabis, even though it should be clear that until it is legal for everyone to use the herb, those who use it for medical purposes will always face discrimination, ignorance and legal barriers that have no place in a civil society.

Overgrowing the Government

Co-ordinated acts of passive, civil disobedience create opportunities for dialogue on sensitive issues between opposing parties that would otherwise not occur. By carefully planning actions that get the attention of one's intellectual foe, while drawing media attention and public interest, civil rights activists can effectively channel tension and confrontation into positive, concrete action. One simple act of civil disobedience that many enjoy is growing marijuana.

The 10,000 year co-evolution of cannabis and humanity has had a profound impact on both plant and humans. Cannabis has affected our cultural history; we have affected the plant's biological evolution. From small populations of ancient progenitors, hundreds of varities or strains of cannabis have evolved.

(*Marijuana Grower's Guide*)

Cannabis plants are pretty and smell great

If you want to grow indoors, buy a good book. An excellent grower/writer is Jorge Cevantes. His book, *Indoor Marijuana Horticulture* is considered to be a akin to the bible for many. Please do not spend time and money on growing cannabis until after you have spent money on a useful book and taken the time to read the entire thing. Though there is a lot of good information and several excellent chat rooms on the net, it is important to learn from one source before starting to grow, and then you can start to experiment with other techniques. Growing indoors is not easy to do well, given that extraordinary measures need to be taken to avoid detection. Bugs, mould, heat, and power losses cause many problems for people trying to grow indoors. Of course, the biggest problem to avoid is the law, which is a difficult task given the new technology and techniques the police are constantly coming up with.

By revealing unusual heat patterns, thermal infrared imaging gives police the ability to scan homes for cannabis grow lights and vents. They are quite expensive, which makes them rare in police departments and almost impossible to get on the black market. This system can not see into homes but it can sense energy emissions through walls or the roof. It is almost impossible to keep these devices from picking up on a grow-op if the lights are on. Usually police only use these if they are already investigating someone or a location, and they are not used by police driving around on fishing trips for growers.

The most difficult part of growing herb indoors is being stealth so the neighbours and your visitors cannot tell what is going on. Aside from the visual appearance of the house, the biggest source of problems for growers is often their own behaviour or the friends they choose. For most people it is best to keep very quiet, be very careful with whom you trust and make it look like you do something else for a living.

While there are many ways to grow pot outdoors, this is my favourite: find a low wetland area that gets plenty of sunlight and has tall weeds or small trees. Find a spot where the water table is just below the surface and clear a round area three to five feet in diameter of any rocks or branches. After turning the soil over in the middle of the clearing, dig a trench around the outside perimeter deep enough to create a water-filled channel surrounding the mound of dirt. This water barrier stops worms from leaving your garden and prevents slugs from eating your plants. You should mix some organic fertilizer into the earth, old barn manure is perfect, but if you cannot pack plant food into the bush, use moss, leaves or other nearby plant materials, anything but pine needles. To increase the PH level, you can use ashes from a fire, in place of purchasing and carrying lime from a store.

After you have evenly mixed the soil and nutrients, you can put your seedlings in the garden. If you need to clean out the trench, you can scoop out the mud from the bottom and spread it around the base of the plants. This feeds the plants with good organic material while covering the ground to combat weeds. It makes sense to tie the plants down as they grow, as you can spread out your garden, increasing your yield while reducing the plant's visibility. These small gardens are perfect for part-time pot growers who enjoy the outdoors.

Plants make sugar using light, water and carbon dioxide in a process called photosynthesis. The sugar molecules are twisted to form carbohydrates which are used to create tissue. Amino acids are formed when nitrogen atoms are integrated into the molecules, eventually forming proteins. That is why light, water and CO2 are so important for growing good herb.

After being cut down, the best way to cure cannabis is by hanging the plant upside down for a week in a dry, cool room, only cutting off a few of the larger leaves to begin with. After a couple of days you should take a few more leaves off, but if you can leave the plant hanging upside down for a week it gives the resins a chance to mature. The cannabinoids are still forming for about 18 days after the plant is harvested. While applying heat speeds the drying process, it does not maximize the THC content of the herb and may in fact speed the breakdown of cannabinoids. After a week, you can take down the plant, trim some more leaves, and place the buds on a screen. After a few days on the screen when the buds are quite dry, put them in a glass jar (preferably) or a plastic bag. This will help draw the moisture from the stalk without over-drying the herb. Be very careful, though, because if you put the herb in a jar or plastic bag when it is still too wet it will form mould very quickly. You should leave the container open some days to allow more water to evaporate.

Cannabis can be made into food and skin products using a variety of methods. Historically, cannabis has been cooked into different foods, milk, and vegetable oils, distilled into alcohol to make a tincture, or made into a powder or pill. We will explain how the products at the CBC of C are made in an attempt to helps others maximize their potential medical benefits from using cannabis. This is distinctly different from making hashish or honey-oil, which is a concentration of the resins.

At the CBC of C we infuse the cannabinoids directly into the oil we are using, which is usually extra virgin olive oil because of its own benefits. Massage oils are half the strength of cookies. The herb should first be ground up and placed upon a cookie sheet. Bake the cannabis at 300°F for about 30 minutes. This changes the THC-acid into THC. For every ounce of good leaf (1/2 oz for massage oil, or 1/4 oz buds for Cannoil) add 1 cup of olive oil or 1/2 lb of butter and put everything into a cooking pot. Cook on the stove at a low temperature for 4 to 6 hours. Too high a temperature and you could start to destroy the active chemicals. Cannabis should get cooked at a low temperature that activates inactive cannabinoids, thereby increasing its potency. Take the top pot off and set aside to cool. Strain the cannabis/ oil mix through one or two layers of cheesecloth into a clean measuring cup and squeeze as much oil out as possible.

Don't worry about getting all of the oil out with the cheesecloth because now you are ready to make a Cannapatch! We usually divide the oil into two containers ready for use. We make 50 cookies or 100 lozenges from 1/3 cup of cannoil. You can also bottle it at this point to add to whatever food you like in the quantity you need at the time. The next thing you need to remember is that low heat applies to baking as well. Cookies are baked at 250°F for 1/2 an hour. Cakes need to bake at the least 300°F, so brownies and things like that are usually preferred.

It's time to reveal the secret ingredient—lecithin! It comes from soybeans, eggs, corn, wheat, and nuts. You can get it in liquid or powder for baking (also great for greasing your muffin tins with), or in capsules as a supplement. Lecithin is found in all living cells of the human body. It aids the body's use of fats and oil-soluble vitamins by emulsifying them to a form we can use. This is why we add it to our cannabis baking, to help our bodies use more of the cannabinoids. Lecithin breaks up cholesterol to help prevent Arteriosclerosis. Lecithin is essential to a healthy nervous system as it is found in higher concentrations in the Myelin sheath, (the fatty protective coating of the nerves) so it will help problems like Multiple Sclerosis.

Cannapatches are a poultice made of recycled plant materials produced in the making of Cannoil, wrapped in fresh cheesecloth. They are applied directly to varicose veins, sore joints and muscles and insect stings. They relieve arthritic inflammation and rheumatic pains and help with broken bones, sprains and bursitis. Cannapatches may also be used to help sore or inflamed eyes, pull sties and alleviate pinkeye. Placed upon the back of the neck, Cannapatches also help people suffering from migraine headaches. They can be warmed and placed upon upset stomachs, irritable bowels or used for menstrual cramps. Cannapatches work best if you apply some cannabis massage oil first. Some herbs like arnica, St. John's Wort, and wild yam oil work very well with cannabis massage oil. You can make medicine from virtually every part of the noble cannabis plant, be it male or female, kola, seed, or root.

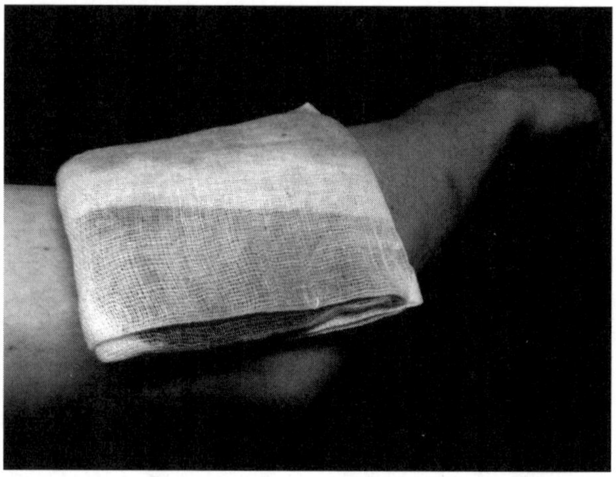

A Cannapatch is a poultice made with butter-soaked cannabis

There are several ways to extract THC from buds and leaves to produce hash or oil. Some of these methods are dangerous and some preparations that people make are harmful to smoke because they use unhealthy products.

Always be very careful if using heat to extract THC into oil, as many have been burned and even killed while trying to do this. Producing hash is a much safer way of collecting the resin glands from cannabis. There are now several easy ways to make hash, including simply breaking the resin glands off the leaf material by shifting the leaves over a fine screen, or soaking the leaf in ice-cold water before screening it through a specially made bag. Hash can also be collected directly from the fingers after handling the plant. Other methods of extraction can involve alcohol and vegetable-based oils, which can be used to produce a number of edible and skin products.

> The philosophy behind tincture is to capture the spiritual and physical essence of the plant. This is done by using the power of ethyl alcohol to dissolve and preserve the herb in question, in our case cannabis. Produced biologically by the fermentation of either sugar or starch, ethanol may be used as a solvent for organic chemicals, or as a starting compound for manufacturing dyes, drugs, perfumes, and explosives. Different plant species demand different strengths of solvent or alcohol. For example, opium requires 70% pure grain for effective alkaloid leaching. Resinous plants such as cannabis, along with countless other alkaloid-rich botanicals, are ideally suited for extraction in high-proof spirits such as 90% pure grain alcohol (such as Everclear). The cannabis used for soaking must be dry. When fresh bud is used, the end result is disappointing. Scissoring up the plant material effectively facilitates extracting all psychoactive constituents. Cannabis should soak anywhere from one to 10 days. Some folks soak it for up to four weeks, following that up with a secondary five day soak in fresh ethanol just to ensure all cannabinoids have been leached. However, some others insist that the buds remain in the solvent no longer than six hours. They claim that solvents instantly grab onto THC molecules, and anything after this time frame benefits only terpene, oils, and chlorophylls, contaminating the final product. From my personal experience seven days is adequate, but you should experiment with different time frames to see what works for you and your buds. The recommended minimum cannabis to alcohol ratio is one gram of bud per 35ml (one fluid ounce). Some prefer up to seven grams per 35ml but others might find this too strong. Individual needs vary. Cautious experimentation is the key. Throughout the soaking period use only enough ethanol to cover the plant material and occasionally agitate. After you've soaked the bud for the desired time, shake and strain the plant material. After filtering the cannabis solution, it is ready to be stored. This is done best within a blue apothecary medicine bottle. This will protect the precious mixture from degradation by light, while also imbuing mystery to the potion. For further protection, the tincture should be kept in a cool, dark place. Yet cannabis preserved in ethanol has a long shelf life. Tincture medicines do not come with an expiry date.
>
> ("Timeless Tinctures")

With so much happening with cannabis today, many consumers, human rights activists, and entrepreneurs have no trouble finding one way or another to include cannabis and the fight to legalize it into their daily lives. There is almost nowhere on the planet that cannabis has not appeared, in one form or another, and with more people dedicating themselves to the plant's revival, it is sure to stay rooted in our history forever.

Chapter 8 Cannabis in the Future

Legalization or Bust

It is impossible to calculate the cost of prohibition today, or in the past, because there are so many affected areas within our society and individual consciousness. Of course, on the other side of the coin, it is impossible to accurately calculate the benefits derived from our connections to cannabis and all the potential rewards that legalization would bring with it.

> [...]in a free and democratic society, which recognizes fundamentally but not exclusively the rule of law as the source of normative rules and in which government must promote autonomy insofar as possible and therefore make only sparing use of the instruments of constraint, public policy on psychoactive substances must be structured around guiding principles respecting the life, health, security and rights and freedoms of individuals, who, naturally and legitimately, seek their own well-being and development and can recognize the presence, difference and equivalence of others.
>
> (*Report of the Senate Special Committee on Illegal Drugs, 2002*, p. 7)

While there are many legal, social, medical, and religious reasons to legalize cannabis, the economic arguments for regulation are the most persuasive and easiest to explain. Prohibition gives an unregulated, untaxed market to semi-organized criminals, while legalization adds a new industry to the economy and eliminates costs associated with law enforcement and court. The exact dollar figures can be estimated and debated, but the core economic argument for legalization is simple and makes sense to anyone in the business community.

> If only it were legitimate, there would be much to admire about the drug industry. It is, to start with, highly profitable. It produces goods for a small fraction of the price its customers are willing to pay. It has skillfully taken advantage of globalization, deftly responding to changing markets and transport routes. It is global but dispersed, built upon a high level of trust, and markets its wares to the young with no spending on conventional advertising. It brings rewards to some of the world's poorer countries, and employs many of the rich world's minorities and unskilled.
>
> Taken at retail prices, it is almost certainly the world's largest illicit market, although probably smaller than the widely quoted estimate by the United Nations Office of Drug Control and Crime Prevention of $400 billion, which would put it ahead of the global petroleum industry.
>
> (*The Economist*, July 28, 2001)

In fact, the Fraser Institute published an article called "The Costs Of The War On Drugs," by Richard Stevenson, in the June 1998 edition of the *Fraser Forum*, which claims that eight percent of world trade is in illegal psychoactive drugs. While the UN Office of Drug Control and Crime Prevention estimates the international illegal drug trade to be worth $400 billion, *The Economist* gives a more conservative guess of $150 billion. There is no doubt that a great deal of the profits made selling illegal drugs have been used to set up and maintain countless businesses around the world. Many financial institutions and businesses in many countries have turned a blind eye to suspicious transactions to protect customers from government agencies. There are many people making piles of money in various industries that oppose legalization, primarily because it would seriously affect their profit margin.

> World governments have handed profits worth billions of dollars annually to criminals, but there is a catch. Criminal firms are denied the use of normal corporate strategies. One would not wish to express strong sympathy for drug dealers, but

> consider their predicament. In illegal trades, contracts do not have the backing of the law. Disputes cannot be settled, and debts cannot be recovered by appeal to the courts. Firms cannot compete by normal means. Drug dealers cannot use the media to advertise new products, special offers or 'spring sales'. Illegal drug firms are not quoted on stock exchanges so the 'dawn raid' takes on special meaning. In the absence of normal competitive processes, firms protect and expand their markets by the use of violence, or the threat of violence.
> (*Fraser Forum*, June 1998, p. 15)

Many people oppose prohibition and the War on Drugs, not because they believe people should use drugs, but because of the serious documented problems that result from the illegal drug trade. Cocaine and heroin overdoses would be reduced significantly if they were available over the counter, by doctor's prescription only, because the drug's purity and potency could be regulated. Infectious diseases would obviously be easier to control if clean needles were made available. The high costs of these powerful drugs causes addicts to take extreme risks to pay for their habit. Prices for black market heroin, for example, are at least five thousand times the hospital costs. A study done in 1992 suggests that the annual cost of drug abuse born by society, in Ontario, Canada alone, was $500 million dollars. This figure could not possibly include all of the real costs felt by citizens from the War On Drugs. Crimes happen all of the time because of prohibition. It is apparent every night on the six o'clock news with reports of robberies and violence. At the same time, prohibition has not stopped many people from using illegal drugs, though it has forced some from "soft" drugs to "hard" drugs because of lack of availability. The failure of the War On Drugs is also evident by how accepted cannabis use is within the general public.

> The S.A.M.H.S.A. today announced that current illicit drug use among youth ages 12-17 continues to decline. The rate has been moving downward from 11.6 percent using drugs in the past month in 2002 to 11.2 percent in 2003, 10.6 percent in 2004 and 9.9 percent in 2005. The baby boomer generation presents a different story. Among adults aged 50 to 59, the rate of current illicit drug use increased from 2.7 percent to 4.4 percent between 2002 and 2005.
> (U.S. Substance Abuse & Mental Health Services Administration, Press Release, Sept. 7, 2006)

Decriminalization has been discussed as an alternative to prohibition by those who are reluctant to support legalization but aware that the drug war is a failure. They want to discourage cannabis use with some penalties, but not life-long criminal records. The argument is that by arresting the producers, smugglers, and dealers of illegal drugs, we can stop the flow of drugs to the street, which combined with proper education, will eradicate the use of drugs considered by the State to be dangerous. Harsh penalties for supplying people with illicit substances will deter anyone from dealing drugs, according to the decriminalization argument. It serves many other beneficial purposes for others employed in the criminal justice system that want to retain, if not expand, their investment in the drug war. In reality, decriminalization would give organized crime the perfect opportunity to consolidate and control many illegal drug markets.

In my opinion, decriminalization is a lawyer's term for job protection, as the production, transport, and sale of these illegal substances would still provide jobs for the legal teams, police officers, customs agents, and jail guards, while allowing organized crime to control the large scale production and distribution of illegal drugs. Decriminalization actually forces the prices of illegal drugs higher because those taking the risk to supply the substance demand more cash. This causes the exact opposite effect to those promoting decriminalization claim to be striving towards because all of the crimes associated with the illegal drug market become magnified when the price goes up.

With decriminalization the stigma that is directed towards those who choose to consume what are currently illegal substances will still be engrained in public policy, school curriculums and sermons from the pulpit. Under decriminalization, the state could still force citizens to take urine analysis if they wish to go to school, get a driver's licence, travel, or get a job. Instead of being treated like criminals, pot smokers would be treated like addicts, being forced into detox programs, taking cleansing drugs, and potentially living under constant surveillance. The other major problem with this policy is that it ignores the enormous profits that are being made by the illegal drug trade.

> There are about one million people employed in the commercial marijuana industry, including growers, retail dealers, wholesale distributors and importers. Some of these are part-time or occasional. With sales at about $25 billion, we estimate net income for people involved in the U.S. marijuana industry at about $15 billion.

> Domestic farmers supply a large percentage of the marijuana market; so much so that certain analysts estimate that marijuana is the largest domestic agricultural crop. The estimated value of the U.S. marijuana crop is $15 billion to $20 billion a year; however, much of that is grown for personal use rather than commercial use. That is more than 8% of the total gross revenue of legal agricultural crops ($240 billion in 2000). As a percentage of net farm income, marijuana revenues are even higher. With estimated profits of $15 billion, marijuana farming is 20% of total farm income ($46.4 billion in 2000).
>
> (*Why Marijuana Should Be Legal*, p. 26)

That is a huge amount of money being filtered through the banking systems every day. Many smaller countries throughout the world have created loose banking laws to attract people with cash that cannot be easily invested in countries like the UK, the U.S., and Canada. For example, the Cayman Islands has one bank for every 49 people, a statistic which clearly points to the fact that thousands of bank accounts which store drug profits exist in many small countries.

> The estimated value of Canada's marijuana production—up to $7 billion—exceeds its farm receipts of both cattle ($5.63 billion) and wheat ($1.73 billion), or the $4.3 billion taken in by forestry and logging. Only oil and gas extraction, worth $15.8 billion, is worth more.
>
> Canada's legal farm operators have net margins of 5.5%. An economist in Vancouver's Simon Fraser University figures pot growers have a 72% annual rate of return, after discounting for costs, labour, thefts and arrests.
>
> (*Forbes*, Nov. 10, 2003)

The most efficient way for recreational drug profit to benefit humanity would be the gradual legalization of all psychoactive plants and substances, starting with cannabis. Different models of legalizing cannabis have been proposed, each with obvious strengths and weaknesses. One model has strict corporate control over the production and distribution of cannabis, similar to the regulation of the tobacco industry. Many in government see this system as an easy means of tax collection and quality control. The business community sees massive profits in a new market. Another model proposes a system that encourages the development of small to mid-sized producers and distributors, similar to the way the wine industry works. This would essentially allow the current producers to obtain licenses to grow cannabis for sale at local retail facilities. By encouraging the development of small producers for local markets, this model maximizes the economic benefits of legalizing cannabis.

Many individuals currently earning a living producing and distributing cannabis would greatly benefit if their livelihood were to become legal. These benefits would range from health care benefits to Workers Compensation to pensions. Insurance companies would provide valuable services to producers who currently cannot hire licensed electricians or security companies to control potential problems like theft and fires. Other industries would benefit from legalization, as the entire economy will grow. Some benefits, like increased availability of rentals because homes will not be needed for cultivation any more, would be hard to calculate though the various intangible socio-economic benefits of thoughtful regulations would become obvious very quickly.

> This report examines the budgetary implications of legalizing marijuana—taxing and regulating it like other goods—in all fifty states and at the federal level. The report estimates that legalizing marijuana would save $7.7 billion per year in government expenditure on enforcement of prohibition. $5.3 billion of this savings would accrue to state and local governments, while $2.4 billion would accrue to the federal government. The report also estimates that marijuana legalization would yield tax revenue of $2.4 billion annually if marijuana were taxed like all other goods and $6.2 billion annually if marijuana were taxed at rates comparable to those on alcohol and tobacco.
>
> ("The Budgetary Implications of Marijuana Prohibition")

Legalization would force the creation of a Cannabis Control Board, or similar organization, which would monitor the sale and production of cannabis products to ensure quality control. This body would regulate the industry to protect the consumers from unhealthy cannabis products and help collect taxes. Taxes applied to cannabis should not be so great as to increase the current prices paid by consumers in the current mature market. If the price of legal cannabis were significantly more than black market prices, then neither consumers nor producers would have incentive to move to a legal system. Any system of legalization should let people get a personal license to grow or allow everyone to grow personal amounts of cannabis at home. People have a right to grow their own.

The production and sale of cannabis products for people with medical issues should be separate from that grown for recreational use. Many medical cannabis products developed by drug companies will appear on the market under any system of legalization. It would be possible for drug companies and local compassion clubs to operate simultaneously, providing a full range of choices to the ill. Prices for medical cannabis should be less than for recreational users, and many believe the best system would have casual smokers directly subsidize medical use in taxes.

Not everyone, though, believes that legalization is the best solution to the situation.

> Consider this: government approved legalization is GOVERNMENT CONTROL!! They will not bring the price down! When was the last time they gave a free prize to anyone? All the money they used to make off tobacco has to come from somewhere.
>
> Alcohol is now controlled by guys in various parliaments & can only be obtained through their sterile government outlets at their price. If they get a hold of cannabis, it will be instantly, irreversibly, PROCESSED, PACKAGED, ADVERTISED, SOLD, HEAVILY TAXED AND GOVERNMENT CONTROLLED.
>
> It will be a snap for them to put a stable, controlled minimum THC level in a joint, so you'll always expect the same standard stoned reaction every time you smoke the same standard ration of marijuana. The thrill of "hey! What a good batch" will no longer exist.
>
> The whole dope scene may shift from a folksy down home stone, to a calculated, sophisticated social intoxicant, if cannabis is made readily available. We must therefore only change the law so that society allows us to keep it, not so that they give it to us. If cannabis is controlled and legalized then there is no turning back! It will become a concrete social custom, as fucked up as it is!
>
> (*Grow Yer Own Stone*, p.11)

While most people will admit that the War on Drugs is wrong, there is a fear that the alternative—the legal use and distribution of mind-altering substances—will give youth access to harmful substances, which they will make poor choices of consumption and behaviour with. This is the crux of the issue for many people. Parents need to realize that the War on Drugs gives people addicted to cocaine and heroin the incentive to give youth free or cheap drugs so they will become hooked, life-long customers. The legal distribution of all substances will reduce crime dramatically, nurture the development of positive patterns of substance use and allow our society to interact based upon practised ideals of tolerance, respect, and freedom.

While many will admit the War on Drugs is a failure, the idea of legalizing, especially drugs like cocaine, is very intimidating. This uncertainty that many people share today about the future can only be calmed by continuous rational action by those who make decisions regarding health programs, consumer spending, public policy, and educational reform. The legalization of cannabis will be the first step in a gradual, global retreat from the drug war. The end of the War on Drugs is a goal worth struggling towards in this drive to create a better future.

Future vision of a cannabis dispensary illustrated by Sean Newton

Put Your Money Where Your Mouth Is

Money is power. The majority spend a great deal of time thinking about what they could do with money, then they spend the few spare dollars they earn as quickly as possible, only to think more about what they will do the next time they have cash. Most people do not actually sit down and reflect upon their spending patterns. They do not write up a list of expenses to see the real cost of an expenditure, in economic, environmental, or social terms, nor do they prepare a budget for reference in the future. Corporations stream out tons of advertising and propaganda about the "high-life" of the rich and famous, forcing the average person to ingest huge loads of conscious and subliminal messages which are contrary to their personal beliefs, health, financial capabilities, and even contrary to Mother Nature. Every dollar that you spend is effectively a vote for that company's environmental standards, their treatment of employees, political lobbying efforts, and charitable activities, and the tax collected by the country of origin is also a vote for the ruling party that they can count in their war chest.

> Before the advent of modern advertising, there were few national brands for common household items such as candles, clothing, or cleaning products. Most goods were made from plant-based materials that often were grown and processed in the same region where they were sold.
>
> Today, the world's best-selling non-food brands are made primarily from petrochemicals and/or rely on petrochemical additives. Manufacturing and distribution systems (shipping, for example) depend upon fossil fuels, often transported over great distances. Modern products typically are packaged in brightly coloured, resource-intensive materials—paper and plastic—and sold by means of expensive marketing campaigns designed to build brand recognition and loyalty. Additional corporate overhead accrues through high executive salaries and bonuses.
>
> Because the industrial processes that yield many major brand-name products rely upon deforestation and the use of toxic petroleum byproducts, significant environmental liabilities and public-relations nightmares occur. This risk requires corporations to retain expensive law firms for defensive purposes and liability insurance policies; to hire entire departments to create prefabricated media sound-bites; and to give large donations to politicians in order to maintain corporate subsidies and/or weaken environmental regulations. Thus, the price we pay at the retail level for the actual product—be it a bar of soap or a finished garment—accounts for a very small percentage of its true cost.
>
> (*Hemp Horizons*, p.108)

The introduction of cannabis into the marketplace will only have a limited environmental, economic, and social impact if other changes in human behaviour do not happen at the same time. If everyone who believed in the environment, fair wages, and social justice only spent their money on goods produced by organizations and individuals who practised those polices, then the world would improve dramatically. We need to support groups and individuals with genuine motivations, and be wary of opportunists who are ready to take advantage of ignorant, well-intentioned people with false advertising and superficial promises.

> In today's consumer society, with its instant coffee, frozen dinners, and fast foods, even psychological and religious transformations are simplified and shortened to render them suitable for mass marketing. As Vine Deloria laments, learning shamanistic techniques in a few short seminars typifies many quasi-religious activities which have acquired legitimacy. New Age seekers are vulnerable "to every kind of mercenary hustler imaginable. It's all very pathetic, really (Deloria quoted in Churchill 1990:94). [...]
>
> Many who participated in the development of the 1960's counter-culture now support New Age events sold over-the-counter by entrepreneurs. What New Age seekers must learn from Timothy Leary, Carlos Castaneda and other gurus from the psychedelic sixties is that it is not enough to be a non-conformist, to be out of the formation, to belong to a counter-culture. We must get our culture back on course again. To do so, requires, among other things, retaining what is viable and valued in our culture, such as critical thinking and high ethnographic standards. Scholars who have studied authentic shamans should join Indian activists taking action to prevent trivialization, if not desecration, of native spirituality. We must also work diligently to protect the inalienable right of Huichols and other Native Americans to freely exercise their religions. The best way to show our appreciation for those Native Americans who are still able to perform rituals which stimulate heartfelt reverence for the earth and its web of life is to help defend their traditional way of life.
>
> (*Carlos Castaneda, Adademic Opportunism and the Psychedelic Sixties*, p. 20)

Respect for the earth and its people can be shown in a variety of ways. By reducing our environmental footprint, we can improve our own health while ensuring the world will be a good place to live for future generations. As people are becoming more aware of the impact their purchasing habits have upon the environment, alternatives like hemp are gaining interest. Unfortunately, most people are not willing to consider changing their purchasing habits until after negative consequences from using unhealthy products become apparent in the environment or their physical health. Many are looking for alternatives to chemical-based products, and the cannabis community is striving to replace these products.

> After the passage of Vermont's 1996 hemp bill (see chapter 3), a study conducted by the University of Vermont assessed citizen interest in purchasing hemp products. A random sample of 770 Vermonters (average age forty-seven) was conducted by telephone. The survey results clearly showed that citizens of Vermont are ready and willing to purchase hemp products:
> -if hemp jeans were priced competitively with cotton jeans, 54% would substitute hemp for cotton in all current purchases;
> -37% would pay more for hemp jeans than for cotton ones;
> -69% would buy hemp-based computer paper, if it were price-competitive;
> -67% would pay between 2.5 and 10% more for hemp-based writing paper.
> Regional manufacturers of hemp products from soaps to jeans may capture market share from entrenched corporate brands by using guerrilla-style marketing tactics. In progressive communities, the catchphrase "Grown, manufactured, and marketed in Hometown, U.S.A." will attract sales, even if such products are priced a bit higher than national brands.
> (*Hemp Horizons*, p.112)

Though there are groups and individuals constantly struggling to reintroduce hemp to American farmers, the U.S. government has successfully squashed any attempts to do so. In the UK, construction began in January 2008 on a hemp processing plant in Suffolk by Hemcore, to produce various building materials. The plant will process 50,000 tonnes of hemp and employ 35 people. Hemptown plans to open a facility in Craik, Saskatchewan to produce hemp cloth. Hemptown is working with the National Research Council to produce a new hemp enzyme that would help process the fibre faster.

Despite the ban on growing hemp, there is a sizeable industry in the U.S. Hemp food sales in 2005 were approximately $12 million, up 50% from the previous year and increased to $20 million in 2006. With Body Shop products leading the way, sales in hemp cosmetics were up 15% to about $40 million in 2005, and increased to $50 million in 2006. There is no reliable information about cloth sales, but a substantial amount of hemp clothing is sold in the U.S.

China is the world's largest producer of hemp clothing and products, with some farms starting to treat their workers respectfully in "fair-trade" arrangements. Many in the hemp industry have difficulty dealing with these products because they do not want to support the military rulers of that country.

> By far the largest source of hemp textile material in the world is China. For 10,000 years the Chinese have used this plant for food and clothing, and two thousand years ago, they invented paper using hemp fibres. There are some Eastern European hemp textiles, but to make comfortable soft clothing my company sources hemp, hemp/cotton and hemp/silk blends of fabrics from China.
> So, my dilemma: Do I join the Canada Tibet Committee in boycotting all Chinese made products? Or do I retain my environmental agenda of introducing hemp as a better choice to the more degrading cotton and petrochemical nylon type fabrics and continue to use Chinese hemp?
> (Bill Finley – owner of H&C and Shift Natural Fashion, Hemp & Company web-page)

Until the facilities are built to produce paper and clothing from hemp in North America, we will be dependant upon China for these products. Regardless of the

Bill Finley in his store Hemp & Co.

problems faced by the industry, new hemp products are constantly appearing on the market around the world. Hemp milk from two companies in three flavours is now available in North America. Several German companies are developing hemp-based plastics.

The concept of using environmentally friendly building materials like hemp is not only fashionable but is starting to make economic sense in countries where the lumber supply is limited and agricultural land is available. As demand for biodiesel grows, hemp will become a vital agricultural crop. With the technology available today, a farmer could grow hemp to easily produce all the seed they need to fuel their tractors and trucks, provide heat and power to their facilities, and feed their livestock and family, while still having fibre left for sale.

Many communities are finding it possible to create locally controlled businesses that promote healthy environmental and labour practices. The term Community Economic Development (CED) has become the expression used to generally describe the formation of locally owned and controlled economic entities that generate public and private benefits. Organizations based upon CED principles focus upon employee rights, environmental protection, and skill development. These groups can take the form of worker, consumer, producer, housing or financial coops, land-share developments, nonprofit businesses, credit unions, micro-loan centres, community-owned natural resources, business incubators, professional educators and consultants, craft fairs, or simple, unstructured community activities. As these organizations are by definition owned and controlled by local people, the external effects of these activities upon the environment, community, customers, and employees are very important to the management. Community economic development projects using hemp will help small towns rediscover their neighbour's skills, getting people working together for the benefit of the planet and each other.

By using alternative forms of trade, by having little to do with money or banks, by helping out in community programs, by doing work for yourself and your loved ones without even asking for anything in return, and by buying locally made, environmentally-friendly products in locally owned stores, you can use your money, time, and energy to fight the corporate agenda and limit your impact upon the planet. It is time to stop complaining about the problems in the world due to the tightening up of government funds, pollution from factories, human rights abuses, government cutbacks, and loss of job opportunities in the marketplace. In many ways cannabis has the potential to play an important role in the restoration of the environment, redistribution of wealth, and health of the world, but we need to take advantage of it for that to happen.

Hempology 101

The first public meeting called Hemp 101 occurred at Simon Fraser University in July 1993. Dana Larsen, Ian Hunter, and others organized it, with the headline speaker being criminology professor Neil Boyd. Danna Rosek, manager of Hemp BC at the time, began hosting weekly Tuesday night Hempology 101 meetings in her studio/apartment, Terrapin Station, in November 1994. The general mandate of the groups has been "Legalization by Education" since the beginning. Events were planned by the group, and the group decided upon the name *Cannabis Canada* for the magazine, which became *Cannabis Culture*, and has since evolved into an online format. After Danna left for Nelson, B.C., the meetings continued in a café on Commercial Drive until sometime in 1997 when they came to an end.

Hempology 101 marches to BC Legislature every September

A grassroots organization is able to communicate directly with members of the community and, at the same time, influence decisions made by local, federal, and international governments. By focusing upon education, Hempology 101 is empowering individuals with important knowledge. This increases the ability of individuals to communicate regarding these issues with an intelligent, informed platform. Second, by gathering people together to network their ideas and creations, as well as organizing larger events, educational forums, and fundraisers, we can install a sense of freedom and trust within the cannabis culture. Not everyone has to work in the hemp industry or the illegal marijuana trade to be included within the movement. You do not even have to smoke marijuana to be involved. Participatory education in constant, passive, civil disobedience is very empowering.

This author attended his first Hempology 101 meeting in January 1995. Inspired by the idea that my family in Ontario could be growing hemp, and with a love of the herb, I soon decided to expand Hempology 101 to Victoria and write a textbook for the organization. The first Hempology 101 meeting in Victoria was held the first Wednesday night of September 1995, at a park by the Johnson Street bridge known as the Whale Wall. The meetings occurred every Wednesday night, in various locations throughout downtown Victoria, until November 2007 when they were cancelled due to too much drinking within the large crowds of young people that gathered at the event. Some of the annual, traditional events are still being organized. The Victoria (now International) Hempology 101 Society was incorporated in February 1996, soon after the formation of the Victoria Cannabis Buyers' Club.

> Ladies and gentlemen, the time has come for change. The time has come for Canada to end the war on drugs—the longest, most expensive, deadliest, and inhumane international conflict ever fought in known history. This savage battle has turned child against parent; parent against kid; while neighbours and employees spy on each other; addicts overdose and die forgotten, sick with AIDS and Hepatitis C, while their dealers kill each other in the streets. Countless millions stare into space numbed by prescription drugs or alcohol while sick and dying people are denied access to an easily grown herb. Young men waste their lives in jail for taking a chance working in a field that provides more money than other options paying minimum wage while retired generals and bankers trade weapons for drugs with desperate people all over the planet… In the meantime, many of us refuse to sit writing letters to politicians hoping for change to come from the source of the problem. We have resorted to continual passive resistance, putting up our lives, property and reputations at risk to both authorities and criminals[...]
>
> (Ted Smith presenting to the Special Senate Committee On Illegal Drugs, Chair Sen. Pierre Claude Nolin, Nov. 7, 2001)

Hempology 101 also started a club at the University of Victoria in September of 1995. The University of Victoria Student Society Hempology 101 Club organized an information booth a couple of times a year until the 1st Annual Cannabis Convention was held in 1999, the same year that weekly 420 meetings were held at the fountain near the library.

> November 15, in Victoria, BC, activist Ted Smith was arrested and charged for trying to distribute cannabis cookies at an annual Medical Marijuana Day event. Smith had prepared 420 cookies, intending to hand them out for free. In court, the prosecution argued that Smith should be held until trial, as he was likely to re-offend, and because some of the pot-cookies could have ended up in the hands of children. Smith explained that he wasn't remanded to jail because the judge recognized his record in the community. "I've done a lot of volunteer work with street youth and non-profit organizations," commented Smith. "I have an established record as an outstanding citizen in Victoria." Smith wonders where some of the cookies went, as police listed only 383 cookies as being seized. "I think 37 cookies were eaten as unofficial evidence," he conjectured.
>
> Smith had been charged a few weeks earlier for trafficking, because during a weekly meeting of "Hempology 101" at the University of Victoria campus, Smith had passed joints out to the crowd. One was pocketed by an undercover officer, and Smith was later arrested in the parking lot. Although he's now banned from the campus, Hempology 101's weekly 4:20 meetings continue. "They put a cell phone up to the microphone so I can still speak to the crowd," chuckles Smith.
>
> Smith is also founder of a medical cannabis buyers' club, which has over 300 members. The club is celebrating their 5-year anniversary by expanding into a second location.

Hempology 101 is one of the largest clubs at the University of Victoria

> (*Cannabis Culture* #30, Mar. 2001)

Delays for constitutional reasons meant the trials did not occur until January and October, 2005. I was found guilty of trafficking at the University of Victoria and given a $500 fine, and guilty of trafficking THC by a jury a given and one day jail sentence. I represented myself before the BC Court of Appeal to challenge the first conviction, though I failed, and ran out of money to pay for transcripts in the second appeal. While I was banned from the University of Victoria, I organized a Hempology 101 Club at Camosun College and held four conventions there until I was allowed back at the University. The club has now become one of the largest at the University of Victoria, with over 420 members every year now.

> Although smoking marijuana is illegal, Campus Security and the Saanich Police turn a blind eye when the Hempology 101 Club meets at 4:20 p.m. every Wednesday and clouds of smoke rise over Petch Fountain. "It is not on our radar. We have much bigger problems to deal with: sexual assaults, violence and rapes," said Hunter McDonald, Director of Campus Security. "If you look at the problems we have, they don't involve kids smoking dope at the fountain." Chris Horsley, media relations officer for the Saanich Police, said, "The police department is still very concerned with drug use on campus." Nevertheless, marijuana use on and off campus is something Horsley believes has not had a lot of police attention in the last few years. "The police have to look at the bigger issues of public safety and public harm," said Horsley. "Just because the police aren't showing up every week doesn't mean we are agreeing to what is happening," Horsley added.
> ("Pot Smoking 101")

I started teaching a free lecture series in September 2006, with 22 classes featuring many guest speakers each semester. Most classes are shown live on the net and have been recorded and are becoming available on YouTube. Over the years many attempts to raise public awareness about the medical benefits of cannabis, the follies of the drug war, and the struggles of the Cannabis Buyers' Clubs of Canada have generated media attention and community support.

> Just in time for RRSP season—$25 CANNABONDS. No, they are not tax deductible, but they are redeemable for a ¼ ounce of high grade pot once—or is that if—marijuana is made legal. The Victoria based International Hempology 101 Society began selling the certificates Friday, hoping to raise $25,000 in it's fight against Canada's cannabis laws. That is, if anybody can figure out what the laws are anymore. Ottawa's approval of medical marijuana, a couple of recent court decisions, and the federal Justice Minister's musings about decriminalization have wrapped police, users, judges and politicians in a smoky cloud[...]
> ('Legal-Pot Crusaders Bond Financially')

Even though Hempology 101 has not yet expanded into every community and not everyone is able to live in or travel to Victoria—though two more university clubs have started at Vancouver Island University, in Nanaimo, and the University of British Columbia, in Vancouver—there are still many things people can do to support the movement without directly interacting with us. Of course, the internet is making it possible for many to work together on various issues, and there is no doubt it shall play an increasingly important role in our cause to educate the public. The next list is only a general description of possible ways one can help

Speakers at 13th Cannabis Convention at the University of Victoria

WHAT CAN YOU DO TO HELP

There are lots of things you can do to get involved and help effect positive change. Following are some basic suggestions:

1. Educate yourself and be vocal. Talk to others about what you have learned.

2. Write letters to editors of newspapers and magazines. Call into talk shows and express your views.

3. Contact your local officials at all levels of government. Call or write them and tell them you want to work for legislation that respects human rights and is against unjust laws. Educate them on the issues. Hold them accountable.

4. Work with local government, schools, community and professional groups and organizations to effect changes in policy and priorities.

5. Get involved with your school curriculum. Demand honest drug education.

6. Use your skills. Students can write papers, essays, speeches, and do research on this topic. Writers, musicians, artists, and actors can be especially creative in spreading the message of tolerance and reform through various media. Business owners can enforce a "no drug testing" policy in their business. Attorneys can challenge the laws in court and help defend victims of the Drug War, pro-bono.

7. Use the power of the ballot box to vote for change. Run for office on a reform platform or help sympathetic politicians get elected. Work on voter initiatives or petitions.

8. Join or donate to a local or national group that supports reforms. Volunteer to help out or organize events that bring attention to these issues.

9. Become an Internet activist. Do more research, network with people who have the same interest, and blast your opinions to a wide audience. Link your websites.

Whatever you do, start doing it now, before it's too late.

(*Shattered Lives*, p. 112)

One of the main benefits of legalization will be that youth will be told the facts about different drugs—using medical information—and not be taught about drug use based upon political, moral, or legal influences. The classroom should become the place where teachers have an open, honest discussion about the effects of different substances upon an individual's health, social orientation, and spiritual development. As long as the conversation is focused upon moral and immoral choice of substances, instead of being centred on healthy patterns of substance use, we will continue to experience problems with substance abuse—especially with legal drugs like alcohol and prescription pills. By teaching youth to respect their bodies by waiting until they are physically and mentally mature before experiencing non-ordinary reality, we will be reinforcing behaviours which are responsible, healthy, and respectful of one's ability to make intelligent choices.

Honesty is the best policy. In order for children to grow up and make responsible decisions, adults must give them accurate information and guidance. Propaganda-type programs based on scare tactics and indoctrination are less effective in preventing drug problems than are public health curricula that emphasize personal safety and responsibility. Children are smarter than that, and they can be taught that certain rights and privileges come with adulthood, and some things are not for kids. As part of a health and life skills curriculum, effective drug education strengthens their ability to make good choices regarding various aspects of their lives and understand the consequences of their actions and the decisions they make.

Drug education begins at home. Parents who talk to their children and show by example how to responsibly manage their lives impart invaluable lessons to their children. If parents drink alcohol or have experimented with drugs (as a good many have), they must pass on their knowledge and best advice to their children. Hiding from and lying to them leads to a breakdown of communication and a breakdown in family relationships.

Studies show that most young people who get into trouble with drugs do so in the hours between 4:00 and 8:00 in the afternoon. Left unsupervised with nothing to do, kids often look for excitement. After-school programs that provide interesting activities with adult supervision or parental involvement have been shown to deter drug use better than anti-drug programs do.

Opening the discussion on how to best serve our young people is an area that deserves exploration. Zero tolerance policies that go beyond drug education and expel troubled children from schools, randomly search lockers and drug test students have serious consequences that also need to be considered. What will happen to children who are cast out from schools? What lessons do children learn about trust when they are treated with distrust? How can we better help children attain success in their lives?

(*Shattered Lives*, p.106)

Today, the classroom has become a battlefield upon which the War on Drugs is fought every day. Children in schools are being encouraged to turn their parents in for smoking marijuana, not realizing that they could be taken away from their families by the state if their parents are suspected of having a drug problem. Drug search teams force students out of classrooms while dogs sniff lockers and desks for illegal substances. Lies about the negative effects of drug use are constantly driven into the heads of youth who will quite often find out later in life that smoking pot isn't nearly as bad as they were told. The conversation about drugs is being brought to our youth at younger and younger ages, stimulating thought about subjects that ideally should not be considered until a later age when their body is mature enough to absorb these substances without chance of hampering emotional, social, or physical development. When youth are exposed to topics regarding intoxication they are naturally curious about the experience. After a young person smokes some pot they realize that they have been mislead by their elders and begin to question authority and everything they have been told about other drugs. This leads to experimentation and irresponsible patterns of substance use, while creating a wall of mistrust between generations.

Change Comes From Within

The myth that pot makes people dopey and lazy is a story that circulates among those unfamiliar with the drug, or those who only see and perceive superficial characteristics of the plant's powers. Some weak people can become slow and unmotivated from smoking pot all day long. These people are also likely to become addicted to other patterns of behaviour that are unproductive, and for some of these people marijuana can become a crutch. Others, however, can lead full, productive lives while smoking moderate amounts of cannabis every day. There are two ways, though, that smoking pot does affect a person's desire to work. First, a puff is sure to cause a person to relax immediately, lowering the blood pressure and slowing down reaction time. While at times, with some people, productivity is drastically reduced, for other people on certain occasions, smoking a joint can be inspirational or can at least make a boring job pass by faster. The other factor which leads directly to resistance towards work is much more powerful and influential, though rarely discussed by the media. When many people smoke cannabis they tend to become more critical of the economic and political forces behind prohibition. Instead of rushing off to the next experience, cannabis smokers will relax and reflect upon their lives and the world around them. If pot made people lazy, this book would not be here.

> Because of its subliminally psychedelic effect, cannabis when pursued as a lifestyle, places a person in intuitive contact with less competitive behaviour patterns. For these reasons marijuana is unwelcome in the modern office environment, while a drug such as coffee, which reinforces the values of industrial culture, is both welcome and encouraged. Cannabis use is correctly sensed as heretical and deeply disloyal to the values of male domination and stratified hierarchy.
>
> (*Food of the Gods*)

Corporations that do not help people working within their organization achieve higher states of learning and free, healthy lifestyles are doomed. As consumer awareness grows, economic support will become channelled towards those corporations that show genuine concern for their employees, customers, and the environment. Money is power, and if the cannabis community can learn to use their resources effectively, many consumers will turn to cannabis-based products, as the benefits touch so many issues.

The Internet has incredible potential as a learning instrument and organizational tool. People and non-profit organizations can seize the opportunity to print and publish news, and tell the public exactly what is going on. This powerful tool provides special interest groups around the globe with the ability to network, educate, and activate each other without huge financial costs or other physical restraints imposed upon local activities or telephones. This new technology is proving to be a very influential, practical tool in the global cleansing of the economic system that created it. However, the Internet could also turn into the ultimate propaganda tool for the elite, if the information available upon it becomes censured. We must be wary of everything we read, including this book!

Cannabis is ready to rise-up to claim its rightful position in society. The cultural umbrella of the Western world that has suppressed this plant, periodically to the most brutal, severe degree, is ready to crack and crumble. The cycle of production, consumption, and waste that has almost destroyed every ecosystem on the planet, must be slowed down considerably. We must learn to adapt to life on Earth as a global community, with a limited population, living in sustainable, healthy work and living environments. If we do not dramatically change the current patterns of consumption in the Western world, then we shall perish as the environment falls into ruin. If we do not stop wasting our government resources on the War on Drugs, we will never see an end to organized crime, violence, overdose deaths, and corrupt legal authorities. Cannabis can help save the planet, but only if we help it along the way.

> Since the most highly saturated fatty acids are located in the brain and nervous system, there we find the highest density of pi-electron cloud flux, and in the cloud flux, the brain generates mind. Mysteriously, mind, which cannot be measured directly by any scientific measures to date, acts upon the nervous system moving the living body

to work against entropy towards its own goals. Those goals are manifest as ideas and images in the mind. And what are ideas and images but meaningful light revealing possibilities erupting from the super-unknown. The revelation of ideas erupting from the super-unknown into the mind of one can be conveyed to other minds. Each mind awakened to the revelation of ideas can convey revelation and ideas to still others. And each mind acting and reacting to revelation and ideas is itself part of a neural net of minds collectively and individually manifesting the super-conscious Mind of God. In the New Golden Age the youniverse of mind in the body of Man will unite with the youniversal Mind of God in the body of the universe.

The development of scientific and technical knowledge has been essential to the greater understanding of the phenomenal universe. This advancement of knowledge about the operations of the universe has lead to reformations of previous religious ideas as humanity evolves towards the golden age when union with the godhead becomes an every day event in the lives of forward looking humanity. Revelation of ideas within the "cloud of knowing" in a mind rich in pi-electron cloud flux connects that individual with divine gnosis in the transcendent youniversal Mind.

If the revelation of ideas is not happening from within because the "cloud of knowing" is vapid from an inadequate flux of pi-electron cloud energy, then the revelation of ideas has to be conveyed by those in the cloud of knowing. The dim ones must accept revelation on faith or some other justification employing reason or logic. Still, it is easier for the dim ones to repeat in comfort the rhetoric of the past as orthodox tradition—until their own mind clouds are invigorated by nutritional therapy with Essential Fatty Acids obtained from seed oils, especially marijuana-hemp seed oils.

(*Green Gold*, p. 419)

For all of you who are sitting at home smoking a joint, waiting for someone to legalize pot so that the world might become a better place, I have a couple of things to say to you. One, get the fuck up off your ass and do something about this crazy shit—though I must at least congratulate you for reading this book to this point, for that proves that you do some things of your own accord. Two, search for the truth about drugs and prohibition at every opportunity, and do not be afraid to debate the issues as much as possible. Three, if you thought it was going to be easy, then you read too much fantasy. Finally, for those who have just joined this quest for knowledge, prosperity, health, peace, and love, welcome aboard. The journey has just begun!

We can change our current patterns of consumption, production, and waste by carefully inspecting our personal habits, professional activities, and public policies. Improvements within these areas of human activity will only occur when individuals decide to take responsibility for ensuring that positive changes unfold. We will not create a better world with wishful thinking alone. The cannabis plant could be an invaluable part of the world's healing and development, but we have to make it happen.

Abel, Earnest. *Marijuana, the First Twelve Thousand Years*. New York: Phenum Press, 1980.

Adams, R., and B.R. Baker. "The Structure of Cannabinol VII. A Method of Synthesis of a Tetrahydrocannabinol Which Possesses Marijuana Activity". *Journal of the American Chemistry Society* 62 (1940): 2405-2408.

Aldrich, Micheal. "Cannabis and its Derivatives." *High Times Encyclopedia of Recreational Drugs*. New York: Trans High Corp., 1978.

Alexander, B.K. *Peaceful Measures: Canada's Way out of the 'War on Drugs'*. Toronto: University of Toronto Press, 1990.

Alexander, Tom, and Trisha Coene, eds. *Sinsemilia Tips: the Best from 10 Years of Sinsemilia Tips Magaizine and More*. Corvalis, OR: New Moon, 1996.

Allegro, John. *The Sacred Mushroom and the Cross*. London: Hodder & Stoughton, 1970.

Allen, J.R., and L.J. West. "Flight from Violence: Hippies and the Green Rebellion." *American Journal of Psychiatry* 125 (1968): 364-370.

Allentuck, S., and K.M. Bowman. "The Psychiatric Aspects of Marijuana Intoxication." *American Journal of Psychiatry*. (1942): 248-251.

Ames, F. "A Clinical and Metabolic Study of Cannabis (Marijuana) and Narcotics." *Bulletin of Narcotics* 16 (1964): 23-28.

Anderson, William. *Green Man : The Archetype of Our Oneness with the Earth*. San Francisco: Harper Collins, 1990.

Andrews, G., and S. Vinkenoog, eds. *The Book of Grass: an Anthology of Indian Hemp*. New York: Gross Press, 1967.

Anslinger, H.J., and C.R. Cooper. "Marijuana: Assassin of Youth." *American Magazine* 24 Jul. 1937: 19-20, 150-153.

Anslinger, H.J., and W.F. Tompkins. *The Traffic in Narcotics*. New York: Funk and Wagnalls, 1953.

Baigent, Michael, and Richard Leigh. *The Dead Sea Scrolls Deception*. New York: Touchstone, 1991.
---. *The Temple and the Lodge*. New York: Arcade, 1989.

Baigent, Michael, et al. *The Holy Blood and the Holy Grail*. New York: Dell, 1982.

Barrett, Francis. *The Magus: A Complete System of Occult Philosophy*. New York: Citadel, 1967.

Barrett, Leonard E. *The Rastafarians*. Boston: Beacon Press, 1977.

Becker, H.S. "History, Culture, and Subjective Experience: an Elaboration of the Social Bases of Drug-Indused Experiences." *Journal of Health and Social Behavior* 8 (1967): 163-176.

Benet, Sula. *Early Diffusion and Folk Uses of Hemp: Cannabis and Culture*. Ed. V. Rubin. The Hague: Moutan, 1975.

Bennett, Chris. *Green Gold the Tree of Life; Marijuana in Magic and Religion*. Alahambra, CA: Access Unlimited, 1995.

Bennett, Chris and Neil McQueen. *Sex, Drugs, Violence and the Bible*. Gibsons, BC: Forbidden Fruit Publishing Company, 2001.

Berridge, V., and G. Edwards. *Opium and the People: Opiate Use in Nineteenth Century England*. London: Allan Lane, 1981.

Bible: Authorized King James Version with Apocrypha. Cary, NC: Oxford UP, 1998.

Birch, E.A. "The Use of Indian Hemp in the Treatment of Chronic Chloral and Chronic Opium Poisoning." *Lancet* 1 (1889): 625.

Blackwell, J.S., and P.G. Erickson, eds. *Illicit Drugs in Canada: a Risky Business.* Scarborough, ON: Nelson Canada, 1988.

Boire, Richard Glen. *Marijuana Law.* Berkeley: Ronin, 1993.

Bocsa, Ivan, and Micheal Karas. *The Cultivation of Hemp: Botany, Varieties, Cultivation, and Harvesting.* Sebastopol, CA: Hemptech, 1998.

Boling, Rick. "Dark Age Drug Farmers." *Omni* May1989: 34.

Boyd, N. *High Society.* Toronto: Key Porter, 1991.

Breecher, E.M. *Licit and Illicit Drugs.* Boston: Little Brown and Co., 1972.

Budge, E.A. Wallis. *Egyptian Magic.* Mineola, NY: Dover, 1971.
---. Osiris and the Egyptian Resurrection. 2 vols. Mineola, NY: Dover, 1973
---. The Divine Origin of the Craft of the Herbalist. Mineola, NY: Dover, 1971

Budwig, Johanna. *Flax Oils as a True Aid Against Arthritis, Heart Infraction, Cancer and Other Diseases.* Vancouver: Apple, 1992.

Burke. "Pot and Presidents." *Green Egg.* June 1975.

Burman, Edward. *The Assassins: Holy Killers of Islam.* Wellingborough: Crucible, 1987.

Burroughs, W. "Points of Distinction Between Sedative and Consciousness-Expanding Drugs." *Evergreen Report* Dec. 1964.

Caldwell, D.F. et al. "Auditory and Visual Threshold Effects of Marijuana in Man." *Perceptive Motor Skills* 29 (1969), 755-759.

Campbell, J.M. *Myths to Live By.* New York: Bantam, 1988.
---. *Occidental Mythology: the Masks of God.* New York: Penguin, 1982.
---. "On the Religion of Hemp." *Excerpts from the Indian Hemp Drugs Commission Report with Centennial Thoughts on Indian Hemp and the Dope Fiends of Old England.* Ed. Tod H. Mikuriya.

San Francisco: Last Gap, 1994.
---. *Oriental Mythology: the Masks of God.* New York: Arcana, 1991.
---. *Primitive Mythology: the Masks of God.* Arkana, 1991.

Campbell, Joseph, with Bill Moyers. *The Power of Myth.* New York: Doubleday, 1988.

Carver, Joseph. *How to Grow the Finest Marijuana Indoors Under Lights.* Seattle: Homestead, 1996.

Cervantes, Jorge. *Marijuana Horticulture: the Indoor/Outdoor Medical Grower's Bible.* Vancouver, WA: Van Patten, 2006.

Chopra, G.S. "Man and Marijuana." *International Journal of the Addictions* 4 (1969): 215-247.

Chopra, R.N. and G.S. Chopra. "The Present Position of Hemp Drug addiction in India." *Indian Medical Research Memoirs* 31 (1939): 1-119.

Christison, A. "On the Natural History, Action and Uses of Indian Hemp." *Monthly Journal of Medical Science* 13 (1851): 26-45, 117-121.

City of New York. *La Guardia Report: The Marijuana Problem in The City of New York*. New York: 1944.

Clarke, Robert Connell. *Marijuana Botany*. Berkeley: Ronin, 1981.

Clorfene, Richard, and Jack S. Margolis. *A Child's Garden of Grass*. North Hollywood: Contact, 1969.

Cohen, Sidney, and Richard Stillman, eds. *The Therapeutic Potential of Marijuana*. New York: Plenum, 1975.

Conrad, Chris. *Hemp: Lifeline to the Future*. Los Angeles: Creative Xpressions, 1992.

Coomaraswamy, Ananda K. and Sister Nivedita. *Myths of the Hindus and Buddhists*. New York: Dover, 1967.

Crancer, A., et al. "Comparison of the Effects of Marijuana and Alcohol on Simulated Driving Performance." *Science* 164 (1969): 851-854.

Creighton, C. "On Indications of the Hasheesh Vice in the Old Testament." *Janus* (Amsterdam) 8 (1903): 241-246, 297-303.

Crowley, Aleister. *777 & Other Qabalistic Writings*. Boston: Weiser, 1977.
---. *Book of Lies*. Boston: Weiser, 1986.
---. *Book of the Law*. London: Ordo Templi Orientis, 1938.
---. *Book of Wisdom and Folly*. Boston: Weiser, 1962.
---. *Magick in Theory and Practice*. Paris: Lecram, 1929.
---. *Magick Without Tears*. Tempe, AZ: New Falcon, 1986.
---. "The Psychology of Hashish." *Roll Away the Stone: an Introduction to Alestair Crowley's*

Writings on the Psychology of Hashish. ed. Israel Regardie. Van Nuys, CA: Newcastle, 1994.

Cunningham, Scott. *Cunningham's Encyclopedia of Magical Herbs*. Woodbury, MN: Llewellyn, 1990.

Dalley, Stephanie, trans. *Myths from Mesopotamia*. London: Oxford UP, 1989.

Davis, J.P., and H.H. Ramsey. "Antiepileptic Action of Marijuana-Active Substances." *Federation Proceedings* 8 (1949): 284-285.

Diodorus. *Histories*. Cambridge, MA: Harvard UP, 1935.

Doane, T.W. *Bible Myths and their Parallels in Other Religions*. New York: Commonwealth Co., 1882.

Domestic Council Drug Abuse Task Force. *White Paper on Drug Abuse*. Washington: USGPO, 1975.

Drake, Bill. *The Connoisseur's Handbook of Marijuana*. San Francisco: Straight Arrow, 1971.

Dupius, Charles-Francois. *The Origins of Religious Worship*. Trans. New Orleans: C. W. Muller, 1872.

Eliade, Mircea. *History of Religious Ideas.* 3 vols. Chicago: University of Chicago Press, 1983.

Elaide, Mircea. *Shamanism*. New York: Pantheon, 1964.

Emboden, William A. "The Genus Cannabis and the Correct Use of Taxonomic Categories." *Journal of Psychoactive Drugs* 13:1 (1981): 15-22.

---. "Ritual Use of Cannabis Sativa *L.*: A Historical-Ethnographic Survey." *Flesh Of The Gods*. Ed. P. T. Furst. New York: Praeger, 1974. pp. 214-236.

Ethiopian Zion Coptic Church. *Marijuana and The Bible.* 1986.

Evans, Arthur. *Witchcraft and The Gay Counter-Culture.* San Francisco: Bookpeople, 1981.

First, Peter J. *Hallucinogens and Culture.* Novalto, CA: Chandler and Sharp, 1976.

Fortune, Dion. *The Mystical Qabala.* London: Williams and Norgate, 1935.

Fox, Steve, et al. *Marijuana is Safer: So Why are We Driving People to Drink?*. White River Junction, VT: Chelsea Green, 2009.

Frank, Mel, and Ed Rosenthal. *Marijuana Growers Guide*. San Francisco: Level, 1979.

Frazier, Jack. *The Great American Hemp Industry*. Peterstown, WV: Solar Age, 1973.

Garraty, John A., and Peter Gay, eds. *Columbia History of the World*. New York: Dorset, 1981.

Geber. *The Alchemical Works of Geber*. Trans. Richard Russel. New York: Samuel Weiser, 1994.

Gieringer, Dale H. *Review of the Human Studies on Medical Use of Marijuana*. San Francisco: NORML, 1996.

Gimbutas, Marija. *The Goddesses and Gods of Old Europe, Myths and Cult Images*. Berkeley: University of California Press, 1992.

Glowa, John R. *The Encyclopedia of Psychoactive Drugs: the Inhalants.* New York: Chelsea House, 1986.

Godwin, Joescelyn. *Mystery Religions and The Ancient World.* London: Thames and Hudson, 1981. Gold, D. *Cannabis Alchemy*. Berkeley: And/Or, 1973

Goodspeed, Edgar, trans. *The Apocrypha, an American Translation*. New York: Modern Library, 1959.

Gordon, Cyrus. *Before Columbus, Links Between the Old World and Ancient America*. New York: Crown, 1971.

Graves, Kersey. *The World's Sixteen Crucified Saviours; Christianity Before Christ.* Boston: Colby and Rich, 1875.

Grierson, G.A. "On References to the Hemp Plant Occurring in Sanskrit and Hindu Literature." *Excerpts from the Indian Hemp Drugs Commission Report with Centennial Thoughts on Indian Hemp and the Dope Fiends of Old England*. Ed. Tod H. Mikuriya. San Francisco: Last Gap, 1994.

Grinspoon, Lester. *Marijuana Reconsidered.* Boston: Harvard UP, 1971.

Grinspoon, L., and Bakalar, J. *Marijuana: the Forbidden Medicine*. New Haven, CT: Yale UP, 1997.

Haining, Peter. *The Hashish Club: an Anthology of Drug Literature.* 2 vols. London: Peter Owen, 1975.

Harding, Esther M. *Psychic Energy, Its Source and its Transformation.* Princeton: Princeton UP, 1973.

Hartsuiker, Dolf. *Sandus: India's Mystic Holy Men.* Rochester, VT: Inner Traditions International, 1993.

Hastings, James et al, eds. *Encyclopedia of Religion and Ethics*. New York: Charles Scrinber's Sons, 1921.

Herer, Jack. *The Emperor Wears No Clothes*. Van Nuys, CA: Ah Ha, 1985.

High Times Editors. *High Times Encyclopedia of Recreational Drugs*. New York: Stonehill, 1978.

Holland, Julie. *The Pot Book: a Complete Guide to Cannabis*. Rochester, VA: Park Street, 2010.

Hopkins, J.F. *A History of the Hemp Industry in Kentucky*. Lexington, KY: University of Kentucky Press, 1951.

Howarth, Stephen. *The Knights Templar*. New York: Dorset, 1982.

Hoye, David. *Cannabis Alchemy: the Art of Modern Hash Making*. New York: High Times/Level Press, 1976.

Huxley, Aldous. *The Doors of Perception and Heaven and Hell*. New York: Harper, 1963. Idries, Shaw. *The Sufis*. New York: Anchor, 1971.

Jacob, Joseph W. *Medical Uses of Marijuana*. Vancouver: Liberty, 1995.

Jaynes, Julian. *The Origin of Consciousness in the Breakdown of the Bicameral Mind*. Boston: Houghton Mifflin, 1976.

Joy, Janet E. et al, eds. *Marijuana and Medicine: Assessing the Science Base*. Washington: National Academy Press,1999.

Jung, Carl G. *Alchemical Studies*. Princeton: Princeton UP, 1983.
---. *Mysterium Cununctionis*. Princeton, Princeton UP, 1977.
---. *Psychology and Alchemy*. Princeton: Princeton UP, 1980.
---. *Symbols of Transformation*. Princeton: Princeton UP, 1976.

Kaufman, J., J.R. Allen, and L.J. West. "Runaways, Hippies and Marijuana." *American Journal of Psychiatry* 126 (1969): 717-720.

Kersten, Holger. *Jesus Lived in India: His Unknown Life Before and After the Crucifixion*. Dorset: Element, 1994.

Kimmens, Andrew, ed. *Tales of Hashish*. New York: Morrow, 1977.

King, A.B., and D.R. Corven. "Effect of Intravenous Injection of Marijuana." *Journal of the American Medical Association* 215 (1969): 724-725.

King, F. "Marijuana and LSD Usage Among Male College Students: Prevalence Rate, Frequency and Self-Estimates of Future Use." *Psychiatry* 32 (1969): 265-276.

King, Francis. "Tantra: The Way of Action." *The Origins of Tantra, Drugs and Western Occultism*. Rochester, VA: Destiny Books, 1986.

Kingman, R. "The Green Goddess: A Study in Dreams, Drugs and Dementia." *Medical Journal and Record* 126 (1927): 470-475.

Knight, R.P. *The Symbolic Language of Ancient Art and Mythology*. Whitefish, MT: Kessenger, 1982.

La Barre, Weston. "Shamanic Origins of Religion and and Medicine." *Journal of Psychoactive Drugs* 11:1-2 (1979): 7-12.

Lamb, Barbara. *High Cuisine: The Cannabis Cookbook.* Toronto: Mount Olivet Press, 1996. Lapidus, and Stephen Skinner. *In Pursuit of Gold: Alchemy Today in Theory and Practice.* New York: Samuel Weiser, 1976.

Lexchin, J. *The Real Pushers: A Critical Analysis of The Canadian Drug Industry.* Vancouver: New Star Books, 1984.

Li Shih-Chen, F. Porter Smith, eds. *Chinese Medicinal Herbs*. Trans. F. Porter Smith and G.A. Stuart. San Francisco: Georgetown, 1973.

Loye, David. *The Sphinx and The Rainbow: Brain, Mind and Future Vision.* Boston: Shambala, 1983.

Ludlow, F.H. *The Hasheesh Eater: Being Passages From The Life of a Pythagorean.* New York: Harper and Bros., 1857.

Malarek, V. *Merchants of Misery: Inside Canada's Illegal Drug Scene.* Toronto: Macmillan, 1989.

Mandel, J. "Hashish, Assassins and The Love of God." *Issues In Criminology* 2 (1966): 149-156.

Manning, P.K. *The Narc's Game: Organization and Information Limits on Drug Enforcement.* Cambridge, MA: MIT Press, 1980.

Masters, R.E.L. *Eros and Evil.* New York: AMSP, 1962.

Matthews, Patrick. *Cannabis Culture*. Edinburgh: Bloomsbury, 2000.

McKenna, Terence. *Food of The Gods.* New York: Bantam, 1992.
---. *True Hallucinations*. San Francico: Harper, 1993.

McKenna, Terence, and Dennis McKenna. *The Invisible Landscape: Mind, Hallucinations and The I Ching.* San Francisco: Harper, 1975.

Mead, G.R.S. *Fragments of a Faith Forgotten: Some Short Sketches Among The Gnostics Mainly of The First Two Centuries - A Contribution to The Study of Christian Origins Based on The Most Recently Recovered Materials*. London: Theosophical Publishing Society, 1900.

Mechoulam, Raphael, ed. *Cannabinoids as Therapeutic Agents.* Boca Raton, FL: CRC Press, 1986.
---. "Marijuana Chemistry." *Science* 168 (1970): 1159-1166.

Mercer, John. *The Spinners Handbook.* Dorset: Prism, 1978.

Merrill, F.T. *Marijuana, The New Dangerous Drug.* Washington: Opium Research Committee, Foreign Policy Association, Inc., 1938.

Mikuriya, Tod H. "Historical Aspects of Cannabis Sativa in Western Medicine." *The New Physician* Nov. 1969: 902-908.
---. ed. *Marijuana: Medical Papers*. Oakland: Medi Comp Press, 1973.

Mikuriya, Tod H. M.D., Dale Gieringer and Ed Rosenthal, *Marijuana Medical Handbook, A Guide To Therapeutic Use.* Oakland: Quick American Archives, 1997.

Miller, Richard Allen, *The Magical and Ritual Use of Herbs.* Rochester VA: Desitny, 1983.

Mitchell, C.N. "A Justice-Based Argument For The Uniform Regulation of Psychoactive Drugs." *McGill Law Journal* 31 (1986): 221-63.

Mookerjee, Ajit. *Kundalini, The Arousal of The Inner Energy*. New York: Destiny Books, 1982.

Mukerji, Babu Abhilas Chandra. "On The Origins and History of Trinath Worship in Eastern Bengal." *Excerpts from the Indian Hemp Drugs Commission Report with Centennial Thoughts on Indian Hemp and the Dope Fiends of Old England*. Ed. Tod H. Mikuriya. San Francisco: Last Gap, 1994.

Murphy, Emily. *The Black Candle.* Toronto: Thomas Allen, 1920.

Muses, Charles. *Gateways to Inner Space: Sacred Plants, Mysticism, and Psychotherapy*. Ed. Christian Ratsch. Dorset: Prism, 1990.

National Academy of Sciences. *Marijuana and Health, Report of The Institute of Medicine*. Washington: National Academies Press, 1982

Novak, W. *High Culture: Marijuana and the Lives of Americans.* New York: Knopf, 1980.

Ohio Medical Society. *Transactions of the 15th annual meeting of the Ohio Medical Society at White Sulphur Springs, June 12th through 14th*. White Sulphur Springs, OH: 1860. 75-100.

O'Shaughnessy, W.B. "On the Preparation of The Indian Hemp of Gunjah (Cannabis Indica): The effects on the Animal System in Health and Their Utility in the Treatment of Tetanus and Other Convulsive Diseases." *Transactions of the Medical and Physical Society of Bombay* 8 (1842): 421- 461.

Oursler, Will. *Marijuana: The Facts, The Truth.* New York: Paul S. Eriksson, 1968.

Owens, Joseph. *Dread, The Rastafarians of Jamaica.* Kingston: Sangster, 1976.

Pagels, Elaine. *The Gnostic Gospels.* New York: Random House, 1979.

Parliament of Canada. *Ledain Commission of Inquiry Into the Non-Medical Use Of Drugs.* Ottawa: Information Canada, 1972.

Peet, T.E., and Wooley, C.L. *City of Ahkenaten.* London: Egypt Exploration Society, 1923.

Piggot, Stuart. *The Druids.* London: Thames and Hudson, 1968.

Potter, Beverly, and Dan Joy. *The Healing Magic of Cannabis*. Berkeley: Ronin, 1998.

Rabelais, Francois, *Gargantua and Pantagruel.* Trans. Sir Thomas Urquhart of Cromarty and Peter Antony Motteux. Derby: Moray, 1894.

Rachleff, Owen S. *The Occult in Art.* London: Cromwell Editions, 1990.

Randall, R. C. *Cancer Treatment and Marijuana Therapy.* Washington: Galen, 1990.
---. *Marijuana and Aids: Pot, Politics and PWAS in America.* Washington: Galen, 1991.
---. *Marijuana, Medicine and The Law.* Washington: Galen, 1988.
---. *Marijuana, Medicine and The Law II.* Washington: Galen, 1989.
---. *Muscle Spasm, Pain, & Marijuana Therapy*. Washington: Galen, 1991.

Rawlinson, George. *Five Great Monarchies of The Ancient Eastern World.* 3 vols. London: John Murray, 1865.

Reynolds, J.R. "Therapeutic Uses and Toxic Effects of Cannabis Indica." *Lancet* 1 (1890): 637-638.

Robertson, Diane. *Live Longer, Look Younger, With Herbs*. Kingston: Stationary and School Supplies, 1990.

Robicsek, Francis. *The Smoking Gods: Tobacco in Mayan Art, History and Religion*. Norman, OK: University of Oklahoma Press, 1979.

Robinson, James M. ed. *The Nag Hamadi Library in English.* New York: Harper Collins, 1990.

Robinson, Rowan, *The Great Book of Hemp*. Rochester, VA: Park Street, 1996.

Rosenthal, Franz. *The Herb: Hashish vs. Medieval Muslim Society*. Leiden, NL: Brill, 1971.

Rosevear, J. *Pot: a Handbook of Marijuana*. New York: University Books, 1967.

Roulac, John W. *Hemp Horizons: the Comeback of the World's Most Promising Plant*. White River Junction, VA: Chelsea Green, 1997.

Rubin, Vera D. *Ganja in Jamaica*. Hague: Mouton De Gruyter, 1975.

Rudenko, S.I. *Frozen Tombs of Siberia*. London: Littlehampton Book Services, 1970.

Russo, Ethan, ed. *Cannabis: From Pariah to Prescription*. New York: Hawthorn Integrative Healing, 2003.

Sandars, N. K. ed. *The Epic of Gilgamesh*. Harmondsworth: Penguin Books, 1960.

Schultes, Richard E. and Hofman, Albert. *Plants of the Gods: Origins of Hallucinogenic Use*. Maidenhead: McGraw-Hill, 1979.

---. *Plants of the Gods: Their Sacred, Healing, and Hallucinogenic Powers*. Rochester, VT: Healing Arts Press, 1992.

Schure, Edouard. *The Ancient Mysteries of Delphi: Pythagoras*. Blauvelt, NY: Rudolf Steiner, 1971.

Seligman, Kurt. *Magic, Supernaturalism, and Religion: a History of Magic and its Influence Upon Western Civilization*. New York: Grosset & Dunlap, 1968.

Sheldrake, Rupert. *A New Science of Life: the Hypothesis of Formative Causation*. London: Blonde and Brigs Ltd., 1981.

Siegel, Ronald K. *Intoxication: Life in Pursuit of Artificial Paradise*. New York: Dutton, 1990.

Silver, Gary, and Michael Aldrich, eds. *The Dope Chronicles, 1850-1950*. San Francisco: Harper and Row, 1979.

Soloman, D. *The Marijuana Papers*. Indianapolis: Bobbs-Merrill, 1966.

Souief, M.I. "Hashish Consumption in Egypt, With Special References to Psychological Aspects." *Bulletin of Narcotics* 19 (1967): 1-12.

Southern, Terry. *Red Dirt Marijuana and Other Tastes*. New York: Signet, 1968.

Storm, Daniel. *Marijuana Hydroponics: High-Tech Water Culture*. Berkeley: Ronin, 1987.

Sumach, A. *A Treasury of Hashish*. Toronto: Stoneworks, 1976.

Taylor, B. *The Land of the Saracens; or, Pictures of Palestine, Asia Minor, Sicily and Spain*. New York: Putnam Sons, 1855.

Thornton, Mark. *The Economics of Prohibition*. Salt Lake City: University of Utah Press, 1991.

Touw, Mia. "The Religious and Medicinal Uses of Cannabis in China, India, and Tibet." *Journal of Psychoactive Drugs*]13.1 (1981): 23-34.

United Nations. *United Nations Single Convention on Narcotic Drugs*. New York: 1961.

United States. Cong. House. Ways and Means Committee. *Taxation of Marijuana*. 75th Cong., 1st sess. House Report 6385. Washington, 1937.

Von Bibra, Baron Ernst. *Plant Intoxicants; a Classic Text on the Use of Mind-Altering Plants*. Rochester, VT:, Healing Arts Press, 1995.

Wainwright, Geoffrey. *Eucharist and Eschatology*. London: Epworth, 1971.

Wakefield, Walter. *Heresy, Crusade, and Inquisition in Southern France*.Berkeley: University of California Press, 1974.

Walker, Barbara G. *The Woman's Encyclopedia of Myths and Secrets*. New York: HarperOne, 1986.

Walker, Benjamin. *Tantrism: Its Secret Principles and Practices*. London: Aquarian, 1982.

Watts, A.W. *The Joyous Cosmology: Adventures in the Chemistry of Consciousness*. New York: Random House, 1965.

Wasserman, James. *Art and Symbols of the Occult*. Randolph, VT: Destiny, 1993.

Weil, Andrew W. *The Marriage of the Sun and Moon: a Quest for Unity in Consciousness*. Boston: Houghton Mifflin Co., 1980.

Weil, A., and W. Rosen. *Chocolate to Morphine: Understanding Mind-Active Drugs*. Boston: Houghton Mifflin, 1972.

White, Tim. *Catch a Fire: the Life of Bob Marley*. New York: Holt & Co., 1983.

Wilhelm, Richard, trans. *The Secret of the Golden Flower, a Chinese Book of Life. With Commentary by C.G. Jung*. London : Kegan, Paul, Trench, Trubner, 1931.

Williams, Gertrude. *Madame Blavatsky, Priestess of the Occult*. New York: A. A. Knopf, 1946.

Wilson, Robert Anton. Cosmic Trigger. Tempe, AZ: New Falcon, 1977.
---.Sex and Drugs: A Journey Beyond Limits. Tempe, AZ: New Falcon, 1988.

Winick, C. "The Use of Drugs by Jazz Musicians." *Social Problems* 7 (1960): 240-253.

Wolkstein, Diane, et al. *Innana Queen of Heaven and Earth: Her Stories and Hymns from Sumer*. New York: Harper and Roe, 1983.

Wolstenholme, G.E.W., and Julie Knight, eds. *Hashish: Its Chemistry and Pharmacology. Ciba Foundation Study Group, No. 21*. London: J. and A Churchhill, 1965.

Wood, T.B., W.T.N. Spivey and T.H. Easterfield. "Charas: the Resin of Indian Hemp." *Journal of the Chemical Society* 69 (1896): 539-546.

Wooley, Leonard C.W.W. The Sumerians. London: Norton & Co., 1965.

Zinberg, N. E. "On Cannabis and Health." *Journal of Psychoactive Drugs* 11:1-2 (1979): 135-44.

Zinberg, N. E. and A.T. Weil. "A Comparison of Marijuana Users and Non-Users." *Nature* 26 (1970): 119-123.